I0042057

The American History Series

SERIES EDITORS
John Hope Franklin, *Duke University*
A. S. Eisenstadt, *Brooklyn College*

To All My Teachers

Peter Iverson
ARIZONA STATE UNIVERSITY

"We Are Still Here"

American Indians in the Twentieth Century

HARLAN DAVIDSON, INC.
WHEELING, ILLINOIS 60090-6000

Library of Congress Cataloging-in-Publication Data

Iverson, Peter
    We are still here: American Indians in the twentieth century / Peter
    Iverson
    p. cm. — (The American history series)
    Includes bibliographical references and index.

    ISBN 0-88295-940-9
    1. Indians of North America—History—20th century. I. Title.
II . Series: American history series (Wheeling, Ill.)
E77.I94   1998
973´.0497—dc21   97-38321
                                                           CIP

Cover photograph: Iroquois drummers at Onondaga Nation Festival ©
Mike Greenlar, 1994.

Manufactured in the United States of America
03 02 01 00 99 2 3 4 5 6 VP

FOREWORD

Every generation writes its own history for the reason that it sees the past in the foreshortened perspective of its own experience. This has surely been true of the writing of American history. The practical aim of our historiography is to give us a more informed sense of where we are going by helping us understand the road we took in getting where we are. As the nature and dimensions of American life are changing, so too are the themes of our historical writing. Today's scholars are hard at work reconsidering every major aspect of the nation's past: its politics, diplomacy, economy, society, recreation, mores and values, as well as status, ethnic, race, sexual, and family relations. The lists of series titles that appear on the inside covers of this book will show at once that our historians are ever broadening the range of their studies.

The aim of this series is to offer our readers a survey of what today's historians are saying about the central themes and aspects of the American past. To do this, we have invited to write for the series only scholars who have made notable contributions to the respective fields in which they are working. Drawing on primary and secondary materials, each volume presents a factual and narrative account of its particular subject, one that affords readers a basis for perceiving its larger dimensions and importance. Conscious that readers respond to the closeness and immediacy of a subject, each of our authors seeks to restore the past as an actual present, to revive it as a living reality. The individuals and groups who figure in the pages of our books appear as real people who once were looking for survival and fulfillment. Aware that historical subjects are often matters of controversy, our authors present their own findings and conclusions. Each volume closes with an extensive critical essay on the writings of the major authorities on its particular theme.

The books in this series are primarily designed for use in both basic and advanced courses in American history, on the undergraduate and graduate levels. Such a series has a particular value these days, when the format of American history courses is being altered to accommodate a greater diversity of reading materials. The series offers a number of distinct advantages. It extends the dimensions of regular course work. It makes clear that the study of our past is, more than the student might otherwise understand, at once complex, profound, and absorbing. It presents that past as a subject of continuing interest and fresh investigation.

For these reasons the series strongly invites an interest that far exceeds the walls of academe. The work of experts in their respective fields, it puts at the disposal of all readers the rich findings of historical inquiry, an invitation to join, in major fields of research, those who are pondering anew the central themes and aspects of our past.

And, going beyond the confines of the classroom, it reminds the general reader no less than the university student that in each successive generation of the ever-changing American adventure, from its very start until our own day, men and women and children were facing their daily problems and attempting, as we are now, to live their lives and to make their way.

John Hope Franklin
A. S. Eisenstadt

CONTENTS

ACKNOWLEDGMENTS

When John Hope Franklin and A. S. Eisenstadt asked me to contribute to this series, I wondered whether I should accept their flat-
tering invitation. It surely constituted an impossible assignment.
How could I, how could any person, tell in one concise volume a
story that involved so many communities and so many people over
so long a period of time? After I agreed to give this project a try, I
had second and even third thoughts. I have been able to write this
book because of all the help I have received. The long list below
gives some idea of my indebtedness. Although I completed this
book in 1997, in some ways I began it in 1969, when I was privileged to join the faculty of the first tribal college. At that time,
most American Indian histories focused almost exclusively upon
loss and victimization. Those accounts were and are important, but
I have chosen here to tell a different story, one consistent with my
previous writings. I do not deny difficulty nor do I ignore racism,
but I emphasize the determination and the ability of Native peoples to
adapt, to create, and, above all, to continue.

Five years ago, during the quincentenary observance of the
Columbus landing, Native peoples emphasized the related subjects
of survival and continuation. A major exhibit of Native art in New
York City in 1992 was entitled "We're Still Here." After I had fin-
ished what I hoped would be the final version of this manuscript, I
started to read the new anthology edited by Joy Harjo and Gloria

Bird, *Reinventing The Enemy's Language: Contemporary Native Women's Writings of North America* (New York, 1997). In the introduction to this extraordinary volume, Harjo said: "We are still here, still telling stories, still singing whether it be in our native languages or in the 'enemy' tongue." "We are still here" expressed precisely what I hoped to convey in these pages. After some considerable hesitation, I decided to include these words, in quotation marks, as part of the title. Although I am not part of that "We," I employ "We are still here" to convey a major theme and to honor a writer whose words have been important to me.

I want to voice my thanks to all those who helped shape *"We Are Still Here": American Indians in the Twentieth Century*, including those Native colleagues who reassured me about the title. This is a work of synthesis. It is based in part on the written work of countless colleagues; the bibliographical essay near the end of the volume gives a partial sense of this literature. I offer my deep appreciation to all those whose writings have informed and enriched what follows. I also have been informed and enriched by what many individuals have told me or have demonstrated to me through their anecdotes, jokes, stories, memories, and written and oral histories. I have been honored to write this book, and I am pleased to dedicate it, with respect and gratitude, to all who have taught me. My mother's parents, Paul and Veronica Schmitt, and my parents, William and Adelaide Iverson, first instructed me about the power of memory, the meaning of place, the value of listening, and the potential of storytelling. Bob Berkhofer, Al Bogue, and Catharine McClellan were important mentors in my final stages of graduate study. When I came to teach at Navajo Community College, Francis Becenti, Clifford Beck, Kenneth Begay, Bahe Billy, Larry Emerson, Priscilla Goggles, Ned Hatathli, Bob Hilgendorf, Dean Jackson, Jack Jackson, Richard Mike, Lucy Moore, William Morgan, Mabel Myers, Bob Roessel, Ruth Roessel, William Morgan, and Bea Yazzie were among those who introduced me to different dimensions of the Navajo Nation. Through the years at various gatherings, usually sponsored by the Newberry Library's D'Arcy McNickle Center for American Indian History, Colin Calloway, Jack Campisi, Dave Edmunds, Don

Fixico, Ray Fogelson, Larry Hauptman, Charlotte Heth, Fred Hoxie, Craig Howe, Alvin Josephy, Clara Sue Kidwell, Brenda Kay Manuelito, Harvey Markowitz, D'Arcy McNickle, Alfonso Ortiz, Paul Prucha, Bill Swagerty, Helen Tanner, and Dave Warren broadened and deepened my understanding of Native peoples and their histories. When I taught at the University of Wyoming and in my continuing study of the Plains country, Leonard Bruguier, Vine Deloria, Jr., Ray DeMallie, Karen Easton, Loretta Fowler, Tom Hagan, Herb Hoover, George Horse Capture, Wes Martel, Bea Medicine, Joe Medicine Crow, Pius Moss, Dan Old Elk, Barbara Sage, Steve Schulte, Anne Slater, Deborah Welch, and John Wunder helped me become more acquainted with major issues and concerns. Since I returned to Arizona to teach at Arizona State University, I have learned from Gretchen Harvey, Paivi Hoikkala, Rex Lee Jim, Jennie Joe, Ron Lewis, Tsianina Lomawaima, John Martin, Devon Mihesuah, Josiah Moore, Roger Nichols, Nancy Parezo, James Riding In, Scott Riney, Kay Sands, Cal Seciwa, Martin Sullivan, Karen Swisher, Bob Thomas, Glojean Todacheene, Bob Trennert, Harry Walters, and Peterson Zah. I have also learned a great deal from students at Arizona State University. In particular, I thank graduate students Richard Adkins, AnCita Benally, Myla Carpio, Wade Davies, Melissa Dyea, Andrew Fisher, Shawn Kline, Michael Lawson, Tracy Leavelle, Mara Rutten, Victoria Smith, and Scott White, who all read this manuscript. They contributed many significant ideas and examples that I have incorporated here. I thank research assistants Shawn Kline and Victoria Smith for their help in locating various materials. Brenda Child, Phil Deloria, Al Hurtado, Patty Loew, George Moses, Jean O'Brien, Margaret Connell Szasz, and Mark Trahant have contributed to my understanding of this subject. I have tested their friendship with my initial version of this book, and I am grateful to them for furnishing many perceptive suggestions. Adelaide Iverson and Erika Iverson are also still willing to read my first drafts. I appreciate their seasoned counsel. John Hope Franklin and A. S. Eisenstadt, those who reviewed the manuscript for Harlan Davidson, Inc., and publisher Andrew Davidson asked necessary questions, forced me to rethink assumptions, and improved the final result. To Erika, Jens, Scott, Tim, and Laurie; to my mother, my brothers, and all my relatives: thank you for all you have given me. Although this book must honor many people through a more general dedication, it is also, as always, for Kaaren.

Peter Iverson
Tempe, Arizona

INTRODUCTION

This book begins with the tragedy of Wounded Knee. In another volume of the American History Series, *Farewell My Nation, The American Indian and the United States, 1820–1890* (1990), Philip Weeks employs the same event to start his analysis. Books such as *Farewell My Nation,* Robert Utley's *The Last Days of the Sioux Nation,* and Dee Brown's *Bury My Heart at Wounded Knee,* use Wounded Knee to mark the end of a long story. Until recently, for most students of American Indian history, Wounded Knee sounded the death knell of Native life within the United States. In the deaths of Lakota men, women, and children on the Pine Ridge reservation in December 1890, the final chapter of the so-called "Indian wars" had been written, and Indians as identifiable peoples appeared destined for disappearance.

Indian communities endured great hardships and suffered enormous losses in the nineteenth century. And yet, as we near the end of the twentieth century, we can perceive more clearly that the final years of the 1800s comprised a more complicated scenario than usually has been presented. The end of the nineteenth century witnessed the conclusion of warfare and the assignment of Indian nations to various reservations within the western portion of the lower forty-eight states. But for the Native peoples of the East, the Midwest, the South, and of Alaska, this era did not necessarily have the same meaning. Moreover, within the West the status of Indian peoples varied considerably. Some Indian communities had been removed far from their homelands. Some had been moved in order to share reservation lands with other Native groups, sometimes with those whom had been their rivals. Other Indians were denied any land. Still others saw the size of their land base increase. This variety of experience and this range of outcomes form one of the important themes of this book and show that Indian history must be presented as a national and as a regional and as a local story.

At the same time, regardless of location or land status, Indians faced common questions. One was the presence and the influence of the federal government. "The Great Father" continued to cast a long shadow over Native individuals and communities. Federal court decisions, federal laws, and the actions of commissioners of Indian affairs all had a major impact on Indian lives. Thus, although this book is an account centered on the Indians themselves, it cannot ignore the actions of the U.S. government. Especially in the first six decades of this century, the successive commissioners of Indian affairs played a major role in Indian country, and their actions merit detailed attention. However, historians often have ascribed too much power to the federal government and its overall effect on the daily lives of Indians. Most standard studies of relations between Indians and other Americans or of federal policy toward the Indians portray Washington in particular and non-Indians in general as the actors and Indians as the acted upon. In such analyses, Indians emerge too exclusively as powerless, as victims with little or no ability to shape their day-to-day lives or chart their own futures. I fully acknowledge the failure of most federal policies and the pervasive presence of racism in American life, but I believe that any historian who wishes to present a more complete picture must account for the efforts of Native men and women who have succeeded, often against great odds, in achieving meaningful lives on their own terms and in insuring the survival of their own communities.

As we anticipate the dawn of the twenty-first century, Indians are still here. They have contradicted the assumptions of 100 years ago that they were vanishing Americans. There are many more American Indians in 1997 than there were in 1897. Although there has been loss of land and loss of language for some groups, there also has been the acquisition and retention of territory and cultural revitalization by others. All Native peoples have allowed for some degree of change in regard to the construction of their identity. As Robert F. Berkhofer, Jr., once observed, we don't consider ourselves "less American" than Abraham Lincoln because we drive automobiles and watch television and Lincoln did not. Somehow non-Indians are inclined to classify Native peoples as "less Indian" if they incorporate comparable changes in their lives, even though Indian identity has never depended upon isolation. Rather, increased contact with other Americans frequently caused Native peoples to recast and strengthen their different senses of who they are. Federal policies designed to hasten assimilation often have caused quite contrary results. In the same sense, students of Indian history should realize that periods that have been presented in almost entirely negative terms, such as the "Americanization" era from the 1880s through the 1920s or the "termination" era from the mid-1940s through the 1960s, yielded mixed, instead of entirely unhappy, consequences.

Even in the limited number of pages afforded to this synthesis, it is not enough to declare that Indians have defied the conventional wisdom of the late nineteenth century. It is necessary to try to explain why they have succeeded in doing so. Indian history is an extremely complex subject, and the tremendous range of Indian experiences makes any generalization suspect. The land itself, with its secular and sacred significance, is one element that has encouraged and inspired Native persistence. Choices about how the land would be used reflected not only economic but cultural and social priorities. Control of and the meaning given to territory mattered. Reservations represented an imposed form of land holding, but imposition did not ultimately dictate that reservation lands could never have meaning for their residents. The twentieth century did not see the end of challenges to Indian communities to hold on to their remaining estate. The story of resistance to the erosion of that control encompassed failure and success. And success has been as striking as failure. The degree to which Indian land bases have been maintained has rested upon the largely unsung and uncelebrated men and women who worked not only to keep acreage from being wrested away but also to nurture and to sustain socially and culturally what those acres represented. In addition, one should also note both the growth of towns on reservations and the building of new Indian communities in off-reservation towns and cities. This migration dates back to well before World War II. The urban experience, both on and off reservation, has been a more central dimension than usually is recognized.

The history of American Indians in this century, then, should include the story of tribal governments and tribal leaders. It should also ponder how Indian communities have carried on and redefined "tradition." It should encompass large and small Native nations, and it should give attention to groups in all parts of the United States. It should address education and economics. It should present the stories of individual men and women. It should consider architecture, art, and athletics; it should say something about dance, literature, and music. It should analyze both rural and urban experiences—within the boundaries of reservations and in the off-reservation towns and cities of this country. Migration, new forms of transportation, and urbanization have affected the lives of most Indian families in the United States, with significant consequences in terms of economic, political, social, and cultural change.

No one term can be used for all Native peoples. Although "Indians" share many common historical experiences, including being dealt with or seen as a monolithic entity, they are members of different groups. In the United States, "Indian" and "Native American" have been commonly employed during the past several decades, while in Canada, the term of "First Nations" has often been utilized. This alternative has yet to find widespread use south of the forty-ninth parallel. "Indian" and "Native American" both have their limitations. I still prefer "American Indian" because most "Indian" people I know prefer it. For the purposes of linguistic variation and out of deference to others who do not like the term "Indian," I also use "Native" or, less frequently, "Native American," in these pages. "Native" is always spelled here with a capital "n" so as to distinguish it from "native American," an identity shared by many other residents of the United States.

There are hundreds of groups that are often termed "tribes" or "nations," and there remain hundreds of aboriginal languages. Within Indian tribes or nation, one generally belongs to a particular clan and has defined ties to various relatives. So any Native individual is likely to be a member of several different entities that coexist. In addition, as the twentieth century has progressed, it has become increasingly likely that an individual will be linked by family to more than one "tribe." Defining membership in a particular community and defining the nature of that community both have been important questions throughout this century. There have been accompanying misconceptions about the degree of self-sufficiency or independence necessarily possessed by an Indian "nation." Vine Deloria, Jr. (Standing Rock Sioux), noted a generation ago that all nations are not self-sufficient; moreover, a group does not need to be a certain size or have an army to merit use of the term. Perhaps it is still useful to recall that the Navajo Nation is larger than Switzerland, that the Jicarilla Apaches possess more land than is included in Luxembourg, or that Duck Valley is nearly twice the size of Bahrain.

Nonetheless, "tribe" is certainly a problematic construction. As Jack Campisi demonstrates in his history of the Mashpees, the term can be subjected to endless scrutiny and debate. This matter has been an issue throughout this century, starting with the landmark U.S. Supreme Court decision of *Montoya* v. *United States* in 1901. The Court then defined a tribe as "a body of Indians of the same or a similar race, united in a community under one leadership or government, and inhabiting a particular, though sometimes ill-defined, territory." *Montoya,* of course, sparked additional debate about the meaning of each noun, adjective, and verb in this definition. Decades later, in *Mashpee Tribe* v. *New Seabury, et al.,* Campisi was asked for his definition of tribe. He replied that it is "a group of Indian people whose membership is by ascription, who share or claim a common territory, have a 'consciousness of kind,' and represent a community with a recognized leadership." During the same case, Vine Deloria, Jr., said that a tribe is a group of Indian people "living pretty much in the same place who know who their relatives are." When you try to make the definition more elaborate, he contended, you start adding or subtracting all kinds of footnotes.

I do use "tribe" in the unfootnoted pages that follow, but I will also employ "community" or "group" or "nation." Another related matter is the names by which these communities or confederations of different communities have become or are now known. These names often have been changed, formally or informally, as the century has progressed. Many groups have formally discarded terms inflicted upon them by outsiders and substituted the term by which they call themselves in their own language. But there are inconsistencies and differences of opinion in this area, too. Labels such as "Sioux" or "Chippewa," for example, have been in place for so long that they are difficult to erase, and some tribal communities still officially call themselves "Sioux" or "Chippewa." The Navajo Nation remains that, although its institution of higher learning is now Diné College instead of Navajo Community College. I regret any unintended errors or misunderstandings in this regard. If a group has been known by more than one name, I try to introduce them both at the group's first mention. An appendix provides a listing of these names.

This book is divided into six chapters. The first two cover the years from the late nineteenth century through the end of the 1920s. During this period we see attempts to assimilate Indians into the mainstream of American society through enforced changes in land ownership and land use, schooling, and religious belief. We also observe the initiatives of Native individuals and communities to establish places in the new day of the twentieth century. The Native American Church, the *Winters* doctrine of Indian water rights, the Society of American Indians, the creation of new Indian land bases and the attempts to develop land resources, the participation of Indians in World War I, and transitions in Indian cultural and social life are all part of this era. In the 1920s Indians and their allies mounted an increasingly influential attempt to call attention to the failure of prevailing federal policies; they also finally achieved the goal of citizenship for all Native Americans. The second two chapters extend from the beginning of the 1930s through the start of the 1960s. Here the narrative moves from the mixed results of the "Indian New Deal" and the experiences of World War II to urban relocation, political revitalization, and the attempted termination of federal trust status. The last two chapters consider the final decades of the twentieth century. This period witnessed new forms of activism and persistent campaigns to gain greater self-determination and sovereignty. At century's end, inevitably, many questions remained unresolved about the present and future status of American Indians. Yet one could not question the resoluteness with which Indians continued to work to build better futures for themselves and their communities.

The story of American Indians in the twentieth century is an ongoing one. It remains a narrative too little known to most Americans, who too often persist in caricaturing Native peoples and in presenting their place in national history only in the distant past and as a foil to the chronicle of non-Indian advancement. But modern Native American history is far more intricate and revealing than most Americans realize. It continues to encompass great disappointment and difficulty, aspiration and achievement. It is certainly a different story than most people would have anticipated a century ago. It is a story that we begin and end at Wounded Knee.

State and Federally Recognized U.S. Indian Reservations*

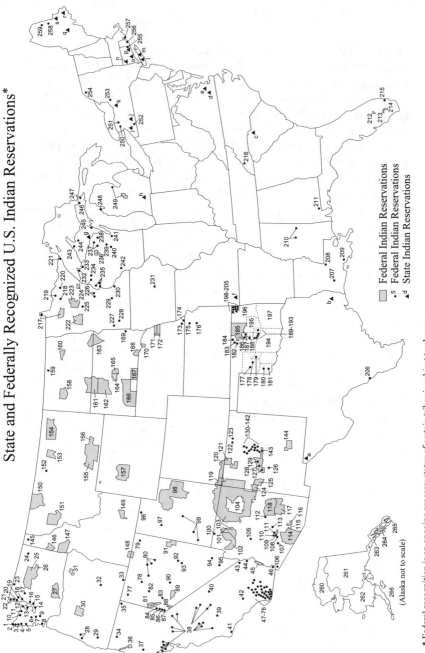

Federal Indian Reservations

•5 Federal Indian Reservations

▲ State Indian Reservations

(Alaska not to scale)

* Federal recognition is an ongoing process; status of certain tribes is subject to change.

CHAPTER ONE

"We Indians Will Be Indians All Our Lives," 1890–1920

On the day after the massacre the blizzard came. Two days later the weather cleared and the young Dakota physician assumed charge of the 100 people, most of them Indians, who ventured forth to seek the living and the dead. He never forgot that scene:

Fully three miles from the scene of the massacre, we found the body of a woman completely covered with a blanket of snow, and from this point on we found them scattered along as they had been relentlessly hunted down and slaughtered while fleeing for their lives. Some of our people discovered relatives or friends among the dead, and there was much wailing and mourning. When we reached the spot where the Indian camp had stood, among the fragments of burned tents and other belongings we saw the frozen bodies lying close together or piled upon one another. I counted eighty bodies of men who had been in the council and who were almost as helpless as the women and babies when the deadly fire began, for nearly all their guns had been taken from them.

The doctor was Ohiyesa, or, as he was called as a student at Dartmouth College and the Boston University medical school, Charles Eastman. Eastman had departed from New England in

1890 to serve as physician on the Pine Ridge reservation in western South Dakota. He was Wahpeton and Mdewakanton Dakota, rather than Oglala Lakota, who comprised most of the Pine Ridge population. Proud of his Native heritage and eager to serve a Native community, he had arrived in November in a dust storm that obscured what he later described as his "bleak and desolate" surroundings. By year's end, he confronted the harrowing assignment of retrieving the few survivors as well as the dead from the frozen earth near Wounded Knee.

The massacre occurred in the waning days of warfare on the northern Plains. The Lakotas formed the western portion of the peoples who came to be known as the Sioux, while the Dakotas, to the east, included the four bands of the Santee: Mdewakanton, Sisseton, Wahpekute, and Wahpeton. The Yankton and Yanktonai were between the Santee bands and the Lakota bands. The seven bands of western Lakotas (or Teton Sioux)—Hunkpapa, Itazipco (Sans Arc), Mnikowoju (Minniconjou), Oglala, Oohenunpa (Two Kettles), Sicangu (Brulé), and Sihasapa (Blackfeet)—had migrated westward centuries before. They had supplanted other Indian nations, claimed much of the northern Plains country as their own, and made the Black Hills into sacred ground. They thus had become Plains people, then emerged as the most powerful of them. The Lakotas vigorously defended their rights to what had become their homeland. By the mid-nineteenth century they were destined to conflict with the other expanding power in the region, the country called the United States, whose citizens had pushed into the heart of the northern Plains, demanding access to all of its resources.

In order to expedite the settlement by outsiders of Native land, and in the wake of the successful military campaign that Red Cloud (Oglala Lakota) had directed along the Bozeman Trail, the U.S. government in 1868 had negotiated one of the last major treaties with Indian communities. Through the Treaty of Fort Laramie, the Lakotas had obtained what was called the Great Sioux Reservation, a substantial enclave that included the Black Hills. However, the discovery of gold in the Black Hills soon thereafter caused the U.S. government to abandon promises it had just made. Federal officials never received the signatures of three-fourths of the adult Lakota population required to alter the Fort Laramie treaty, but they still approved the "Agreement" of 1876, which robbed the Lakotas of their sacred land.

Anger over federal actions sparked renewed resistance among the Lakotas. During the summer, just before the United States observed its centennial, the Lakotas and their allies had triumphed at the Little Big Horn over George Armstrong Custer and his men. Memories of Lakota military prowess remained vivid among the members of the Seventh Cavalry, Custer's unit. The era since the triumph on the Greasy Grass had been increasingly difficult for the Lakotas. In 1889 further pressure from intruders had prompted the U.S. government to reduce and fracture the Great Sioux Reservation into fragments: Pine Ridge, Rosebud, Cheyenne River, Standing Rock, Lower Brule, and Crow Creek. Restricted in their movements, hungry, and embittered, many Lakotas as well as many Yanktons, Yanktonais, and Santees were receptive to the teachings of a Native prophet in distant Nevada. The Paiute messiah, Wovoka, had promised a new day, when the Whites would disappear, the buffalo would reappear in great numbers, and the Indians would be reunited with their loved ones who had gone before. Lakota representatives traveled to Nevada to meet with Wovoka, and they brought home their own interpretations of the Ghost Dance. They believed that the shirts they wore in observing the ritual would make them invulnerable to bullets.

In 1890 a new federal agent, Daniel Royer, arrived at Pine Ridge. He proved to be ill-suited for this assignment. The Lakotas quickly gave him a name: Young Man Afraid of Indians. Royer panicked at the sight of the Ghost Dancers on Pine Ridge. Within three days after he arrived, he began to appeal to the U.S. army for troops. Such military assistance was hardly necessary, but the army's own designs made a confrontation almost inevitable. The army brass, especially General Nelson Miles, was determined to put on a show of force. Miles believed the army rather than the civilian agency, the Office (later Bureau) of Indian Affairs, should be in charge on the reservations. Taking control would provide a role for the western army in peacetime and would guarantee order in the chaos of the early reservation years. Miles thus acceded to

Royer's request, and soon the bluecoats were in the field. Some of them hailed from the Seventh Cavalry.

In December two terrible confrontations occurred. One took place on Standing Rock on December 15. There, in a violent standoff between some of his followers and Lakotas who had joined the agency police force, the old Hunkpapa leader, Tatanka Iyotanka (Sitting Bull) was killed. The other tragedy transpired two weeks later at Pine Ridge. Mnikowoju Lakotas under the leadership of Big Foot had left their home at Cheyenne River, both terrified by the news about Tatanka Iyotanka and anxious to visit Pine Ridge at the invitation of Red Cloud. However, Big Foot's band, riddled by hunger and illness, never made it to Red Cloud. Intercepted by the Seventh Cavalry, they were taken to Wounded Knee Creek, about twenty miles from the village of Pine Ridge. On the following morning of December 29, the Lakotas were ordered to surrender all their weapons and implements. Members of the cavalry took away nearly all of the Lakotas' weapons before an argument between a Lakota who refused to surrender his rifle and some soldiers almost instantaneously escalated into a hail of fire from the soldiers' rifles and the four Hotchkiss cannons that had been placed on a hill above the encampment. There are different estimates of how many of thc Lakotas were killed, but at least 300, and perhaps 350, Lakotas died in the massacre. Twenty-five Whites also perished, some of them fatally wounded by cross fire from within their ranks. Many of the Lakota dead were women and children who had been killed immediately or who had been shot down as they tried to flee into the countryside. The federal government later awarded the American soldiers present at Wounded Knee seventeen Congressional medals of honor.

Disappearing Peoples?

Wounded Knee in time became a metaphor for the struggle between Whites and Indians in the West. In his poem, "American Names," Stephen Vincent Benet wrote, "bury my heart at Wounded Knee." Writer Dee Brown used the phrase in 1970 as the title for his history of the "Indian wars" in the American West. In

1973 Native protesters who took over the village of Wounded Knee briefly captured the attention of the national media. The year of the first Wounded Knee, 1890, was also used by the Superintendent of the U.S. Census to declare the end of the frontier. The young historian Frederick Jackson Turner soon employed this census report to speak of the end of an era in American life.

The year 1890 thus denoted closure; it declared an ending. However, both the massacre and the census had been given a degree of power that they did not fully possess. Wounded Knee was forever carved in the Lakota memory. But the event did not have exactly the same meaning for all Indians. Many other Native nations had their own wars to remember. For those who resided east of the Mississippi River, South Dakota was distant, unknown land. So other occurrences took precedence in their memories and shaped separate tribal identities. Wounded Knee was ignored or conveniently forgotten by most non-Indians who lived in other parts of the country. If recalled, it became a "battle" rather than a "massacre." And 1890 did not signal the end of the frontier. Prospective farmers, ranchers, miners, and others continued to seek the natural resources of lands new to them, whether or not those lands already were occupied. They still found their way into the interior of the West and ventured north to Alaska.

However, it did appear in 1890 that a transition was well underway. Three years after the United States signed a series of treaties with Indian tribes in 1868, confident that the tide had turned in the wars to gain control of the West, Congress passed a law calling for an end to formal treaty-making. From now on any compact signed would be formally labeled an agreement rather than a treaty. Congressional representatives thus stated that the balance of power had shifted sufficiently that the United States no longer needed to enter into the same kinds of negotiations. Custer's defeat in 1876 suggested Congress had been premature in its declaration, but the completion of the transcontinental railroad, the growth of towns and cities, and the development of new industries to exploit the natural resources of the West all testified to increasing U.S. control over Indian communities. Whether they were labeled or agreements, these documents were taken more seriously by the Indians who signed their names or left their marks upon them. Non-Indians thought they knew better. They saw the pacts as convenient, bloodless means through which Native lands would be opened and their occupants confined. They perceived the treaties and agreements as legal documents that provided legitimate and permanent claims to lands that would hereafter be theirs.

Non-Indian Americans, after all, tended to portray American history as beginning with the arrival of their particular ancestors or with the landing of the first English-speaking immigrants. However, because Indians were here first and had every intention of remaining on their lands, various colonial and then U.S. representatives had to confront the aboriginal nations. In the early years of the United States, the Supreme Court under Chief Justice John Marshall was forced to consider the nature of the Indian presence and the kinds of rights the Indians possessed. Law professor Charles F. Wilkinson has concluded: "Chief Justice Marshall's opinions made it clear that Indian tribes were sovereign before contact with Europeans and that some, but not all, sovereign powers continued in existence after relations with Europeans and the United States were established." In *Worcester* v. *Georgia* (1832), Justice Marshall declared that before contact "America, separated from Europe by a wide ocean, was inhabited by a distinct people, divided into separate nations, independent of each other and of the rest of the world, having institutions of their own, and governing themselves by their own laws." He added: "The Indian nations had always been considered as distinct, independent political communities retaining their original natural rights, as the undisputed possessors of the soil, from time immemorial, with the single exception of that imposed by irresistible power."

Here were the roots of the "tribal sovereignty" that became the rallying cry of Indian peoples in the twentieth century. Marshall's Court considered specifically the situation faced by the Cherokees of the southeastern United States. The state of Georgia, with the full support of President Andrew Jackson, was trying to justify its attempts to deny the Cherokees their rights to remain within Georgia's borders. Georgia, in essence, denied that the

Cherokees had any right to exist as any kind of separate entity. Marshall's decision in *Worcester* did not prevent the removal of thousands of Cherokees from their home country. It did establish the legal foundation for the movement for modern Indian sovereignty through which tribes, as Wilkinson has written, attempt to achieve or maintain a form of self-rule that sustains self-determination and self-identity. Thus, sovereignty entails a governmental structure and a way of life "premised on a unity with the natural world, a stable existence, and a deep connection to place and family." These ideals, present one hundred, two hundred, five hundred, and more years ago, continue to inform the Native American presence on this continent. They provided a kind of anchor in the late nineteenth and early twentieth centuries, when nearly all non-Indians concluded that Indians were destined for disappearance.

Such a disappearance, non-Indians generally determined, was in everyone's best interest, including the Indians themselves. Non-Indians saw the reservations as little more than temporary enclaves. The Indians, said newcomers who wished to grow wheat and graze cattle on these lands, were not even using their remaining acreage to full advantage. The Indians, said Christian missionaries who wished to convert them to different, often competing, versions of a new faith, were not worshipping the proper God. The Indians, said federal officials who observed the onrush of immigrants past Ellis Island, were not speaking the correct language or adjusting to the ways of modern America. The Indians, they all determined, needed less land and more of everything else: more Christianity, more English, more private ownership. They needed "real" houses, "real" marriages, and "real" names.

The interested parties predicted such a transition should not take too long. The wills of the Indian people seemingly had been broken. One could see defeat and submission in the images of the day. One heard of Geronimo (Goyathlay) of the Chiricahua Apaches and Joseph (Heinmot Tooyalakeet) of the Nez Perces living in exile. The federal official in charge of the government bureau responsible for Indian policy, Commissioner of Indian Affairs Thomas Jefferson Morgan, predicted that other than the Sioux, the Navajos, and the Pueblo communities, most tribes would disappear. "The great body of Indians," Morgan forecast, "will become merged in the indistinguishable mass of our population." The census takers in 1900 offered evidence in support of Morgan's prediction. When they counted the Indians in Vermont, they came up with a grand total of five. The Mashantucket Pequot population had dwindled to less than twenty. The photographer Edward Curtis believed that a way of life was coming to an end. He thus embarked upon an extended foray to portray on film what he termed "the vanishing race." In 1911, the last survivor of the Yahi people made his way out of the foothills in northeastern California. One by one, members of his tribe had been killed or had died from diseases brought in by newcomers. Anthropologists Alfred Kroeber and Thomas Waterman took this man from the town of Oroville to San Francisco. He became known as "Ishi," the word for man in the Yahi language. In the city, living within the confines of the University of California Museum of Anthropology, this quiet, gracious person offered Kroeber and Waterman the details of his people's history and culture. In 1916 he died from tuberculosis. During the previous year, sculptor James Earle Fraser had fashioned "The End of the Trail." This bronze of a slumped warrior on horseback was created for the Panama-Pacific International Exposition in San Francisco. Fraser's statue demonstrated altered circumstances. He paired it with another of a pioneer confidently gazing into the future.

A group of non-Indian men and women had begun to address the status of American Indians in American life. These "Friends of the Indian," as they called themselves, had started to gather in 1883 for an annual meeting at a new hotel on Lake Mohonk, New York. The hotel's owners, Albert and Alfred Smiley, had a strong interest in the subject under consideration; Albert Smiley had been appointed in 1879 to the Board of Indian Commissioners, a group of wealthy philanthropists who advised the government on its policy toward Indians. Some of the people who came to Lake Mohonk also had joined the Indian Rights Association (IRA), organized in 1882, and already the most significant of the associations lobbying for reform of that policy. The IRA's leader, Herbert Welsh, spoke in 1886 at Lake Mohonk on "The Needs of the

Time." He argued that such reform would "make the Indian a man among men, a citizen among citizens." Welsh knew that Indians could "be safely guided from the night of barbarism into the fair dawn of Christian civilization."

In Welsh's view, Indians were no different from other Americans. They should be treated just like everyone else; they should be expected to meet the same standards society set for others. When given access to schooling, Christianity, private property, and the privileges and responsibilities of citizenship, Indians would compete equally in contemporary America. The reformers thus embarked upon a crusade to reach these objectives. This drive to assimilate the Indians—to make the Indians at home in America, as one proponent phrased it—dominated the federal agenda for decades. This effort and its effects, both intended and unanticipated, form a central theme for the era from 1890 to 1920.

Nevertheless, contrary to the expectations of Edward Curtis, the Indians did not vanish. Their lands and their lives changed, to be sure. The assimilative assault of the period had severe consequences. Indians lost millions of acres of land to sale and cession; still more lands were leased to outsiders. Indian religious ceremonies were prohibited; Native children were compelled to attend school, often in institutions far from home. At the same time, the reservations did not entirely disappear and new ones were even established in the early years of the twentieth century. For those who inhabited them, these reservation lands began to take on new meaning and new significance. Indian religious observances may have been outlawed, but that did not mean they either stopped or were erased from memory. A new Native religion also won thousands of adherents. Even in the matter of education, the results proved more complicated than one might have assumed. These additional developments are also central to our understanding of these decades.

In the late 1970s, an old man looked back upon this time. Olney Runs After remembered the occasion as though it had taken place just the other day. He had traveled to Dupree, South Dakota, a new town constructed on land that had once been part of the Cheyenne River reservation. In 1912 the future of the reservation seemed very much in doubt. Runs After recalled the words of a speaker at the fair, Congressman Henry L. Gandy: ". . . he said forty years from now there won't be no Indians. He come near make it. . . . But we Indians will be Indians all our lives, we will never be white men. We can talk and work and go to school like the white people, but we're still Indians."

Education

An examination of Native American education, religion, ties to the land, and identity helps clarify what Runs After meant. Providing schooling for American Indians represented a challenge, because public education remained out of reach for many Americans, especially those who were poor and who did not speak English as a first language. The states showed little, if any, interest in educating Native students. Indians on reservations lived far away from established schools for non-Indian children, and the reservations lacked a tax base to pay for school construction and operation. Moreover, many Indian parents distrusted the means and ends of non-Indians' kind of education.

The federal government and Christian denominations had a vested interest in the provision of education for Indian children. And during this era most Native children who went to school did so at an institution operated by the government or by a Christian church. Many of these institutions boarded their students, requiring many of their charges to move far away from home. Proponents of these distant boarding schools argued that such isolation was necessary to remove children from the harmful, counterproductive influences of their homes and communities. The students, they contended, should even be encouraged never to return to their former residences. At the time, boarding schools in England and New England offered an exemplary education to the privileged sons and daughters of the wealthy, but the kind of tutelage students received in Indian boarding schools obviously was designed to meet other goals.

The Board of Indian Commissioners in 1880 had not minced words in proclaiming the need for such schooling: "The Indian, though a simple child of nature with mental faculties dwarfed and shriveled, while groping his way for generations in the darkness of barbarism, already sees the importance of education; bewildered by the glare of the civilization above and beyond his comprehension, he is nevertheless seeking to adjust himself to the new conditions by which he is encompassed." Commissioner of Indian Affairs J. D. C. Atkins stated in 1886 that instruction must be in English, "the language of the greatest, most powerful, and enterprising nationalities beneath the sun." Use of a common language would break down tribal distinctions and encourage the common bond of citizenship. Atkins understood the importance of the task. In 1887 he emphasized the government "must remove the stumbling block of hereditary customs and manners, and of these language is one of the most important elements." He had made up his mind: "This language, which is good enough for a white man and a black man, ought to be good enough for the red man."

At Carlisle Indian Industrial School in Pennsylvania, Richard Henry Pratt established a model for Indian education. Pratt had been a captain in the army, fought in the Civil War, and later worked with Indian scouts in the Red River war. At Fort Marion, Alabama, he sought to instruct Indian prisoners in English and generally to prepare them for assimilation into U.S. society. Pratt had been in the Tenth Cavalry and had developed an interest in the African-American men who had served in his unit. He knew of the new school in Virginia, Hampton Institute, that another military man, General Samuel Armstrong, had founded for Black students. Pratt took twenty-two of his Indian students from Fort Marion to Hampton in 1878 and recruited more Indian pupils from the West to the school. By the following year he had decided to found his own school at an abandoned military installation in Pennsylvania. At Carlisle, for a quarter of a century thereafter, Pratt directed what became the most prominent school for Indians in the United States. He was forced out eventually as superintendent in 1904, and Carlisle closed its doors permanently during World War I. In its time, however, the school had a significant influence on how Indians would be educated.

Part of that influence came through the efforts of the tireless Pratt. He appeared at the Lake Mohonk conferences and publicized his labors through endless correspondence and frequent speeches. Non-Indian Americans generally applauded the image of Carlisle. Captain Pratt appeared to be bringing discipline to young people who, it was assumed, previously had not known the commodity. Pratt pledged to "kill the Indian in him and save the man." He ordered before-and-after photographs taken of the pupils, so that even casual observers could see the effect of his program. These images vividly captured the spirit of the transformation Pratt hoped to realize. Long hair was shorn and tribal dress discarded, the after-image revealing students with neat haircuts and dressed in military school uniforms. In addition, new names were bestowed upon those enrolled. One of the first students at Carlisle recalled: "I was told to take a pointer and select a name for myself from the list written on the blackboard. I did, and as I could not distinguish any difference in them, I placed the pointer on the name Luther. I then learned to call myself by that name and got used to others calling me by it, too."

Its athletic program also enhanced Carlisle's profile. Because Carlisle attracted and recruited older students, it fielded teams that especially in football and track-and-field were competitive at the intercollegiate level. Jim Thorpe (Sac and Fox), a future Olympic pentathlon and decathlon champion and Pro Football Hall of Famer, attended Carlisle. So, did two Anishinabe (Chippewa) men from the White Earth reservation in Minnesota: Charles A. "Chief" Bender and Joseph Guyon, who later entered, respectively, the baseball and pro football halls of fame. Another student, Lewis Tewanima (Hopi), represented the United States in track-and-field in two Olympics, winning a silver medal in the 10,000-meter run in 1912. Coached by Glenn "Pop" Warner from 1899 to 1914, Carlisle football teams routinely defeated their college opponents. In the 1907 season, Carlisle won ten of eleven games, defeating Minnesota, and, at a time when it mattered, Chicago.

Principals and superintendents of other schools also recognized that successful athletic programs inspired enrollment and continuation by pupils. Upon occasion, students even became a bit too enthusiastic. James McCarthy, a Tohono O'odham (Papago), extended his education by moving from Santa Fe Indian School to Phoenix Indian School to Albuquerque Indian School, changing his name and running away from one place to the next, primarily so he could keep playing baseball and keep competing against the best teams. Boys and girls often found in sports the one dimension of their educational experience that they could remember with genuine fondness.

At the turn of the century, about 50 percent of the Indian children were enrolled in school. Most attended schools west of the Mississippi that resembled Carlisle. After Carlisle's demise, Haskell, in Lawrence, Kansas, became the most prominent of these institutions. Other large schools such as Chemawa (Oregon), Chilocco (Oklahoma), and Phoenix, attracted students from many different communities. Competition among the schools for students intensified to the point that Commissioner of Indian Affairs William Jones in 1902 banned all but the two most prominent, Carlisle and Haskell, from national recruitment campaigns. These schools at first bore considerable resemblance to each other in their insistence upon military uniforms and drill, their emphasis on vocational-technical training, their dedication to the eradication of Indian languages and cultures, and their separation of curriculum for boys and girls in attendance.

The emphasis on the practical mirrored the approach taken in Tuskegee Institute and other schools for peoples of color during the era. Unfortunately, the Indian schools generally emphasized outmoded skills such as blacksmithing and expropriated student labor not for instructional purposes but simply as a ready and captive workforce. School officials assumed that young women were learning nothing of value in their communities. They had no sense of Indian societies in which young women customarily learned how to plant, tend, and gather useful plants, as well as weave, cook, and assist in the care of children. Girls and young women thus were subjected to heavy-handed attempts to prepare them to become housewives who would transmit appropriate middle-class values and behaviors within their households. Pratt once queried: "Of what avail is it that the man be hard-working and industrious . . . if the wife, unskilled in cookery, unused to the needle, with no habits of order or neatness, makes what might be a cheerful, happy home only a wretched abode of filth and squalor?" The curriculum for female students at the Morris Indian School in Minnesota, for example, stressed sewing, cooking, and doing the laundry. At Sherman Institute in California, by contrast, girls received instruction in the preparation of shrimp cocktails. Polingaysai Qoyawayma, a Hopi, learned at school how to bake cakes and pies and then returned home to discover that these dishes were undesirable additions to the fare of her family.

Many students, parents, and other relatives detested these schools. Family members wept as the children departed. Some of the students were older, but many were little ones for whom the sudden change of worlds was all the more traumatic. Boarding schools comprised an ongoing onslaught against Native families and Native belief systems. Students away from home could not participate in tribal ceremonies, including important rituals that marked puberty or other stages of life. Many boarded students were homesick, despised the particular routine, loathed the food, and resisted the prohibition of the use of Native language. More than a few students, at one time or another, attempted to run away. An Eastern Cherokee boy from North Carolina decided to return home from Haskell. One way or another he reached Knoxville, Tennessee, then walked through the Smoky Mountains. A Jemez Pueblo girl attending the Santa Fe Indian School was always hungry and missed the food of home. It took her and two other girls three days to complete the eighty-mile trip back to Jemez, walking much of the way. Soon after she arrived, her father took her back to Santa Fe. Not all students survived their attempts at escape. Two boys who fled the Rapid City Indian School in South Dakota followed the railroad tracks out of town, fell asleep near the tracks, and were killed by a train. One boy who departed Santa Fe in the winter lost his legs to frostbite; another boy froze to death. Students who returned to school after running away generally faced some form of punishment, from incarceration to extra chores to the wearing of a gunnysack for two days. The disciplinarians often were Indians themselves, frequently graduates of the institution that now employed them. Having made it through the school, they now strictly enforced policies and rules. Schools discouraged students from returning home during the summer, instead often hiring their pupils out to farms and other industries seeking cheap labor. Parents and other relatives, of course, missed their children and agonized over their recurring illnesses. Indeed, a considerable number of students in those early years died and were buried far from home, "through," Luther Standing Bear observed, "with all earthly schools. In the graveyard at Carlisle most of the graves are those of little ones. . . ."

Even under such tragic and traumatic circumstances, however, some parents chose to send their children away to the only schools then available. They believed that the next generation had to obtain the means of coping with American society. Many students who became fluent in English were destined to play leadership roles on future tribal councils. For students who came from extremely poor dysfunctional families or had no family at all, the schools offered food, clothing, and shelter. Friendships and occasional opportunities for extracurricular adventures attracted some students to the schools. Anna Moore (Pima) was hardly the only person to meet a future spouse at a boarding school. She remembered the "first and only romance of my life began in 1912" at Phoenix Indian School when Ross Shaw (Pima) began to pay attention to her. They eventually married and enjoyed a long and happy life together.

In many families the success of one brother or sister at a particular institution encouraged the enrollment of younger siblings. Anna Bender of White Earth enrolled in Hampton Institute in 1902 and graduated in 1906. Four of her siblings followed her to Hampton, with three graduating from the school. A fourth stayed a year before transferring to and graduating from Roe Institute in Wichita, a school established in 1915 by Ho Chunk (Winnebago) educator Henry Roe Cloud. The Boutangs, the Brokers, and other families from White Earth followed the same, if not always equally successful pattern, sending more than one son or daughter to Hampton or to Carlisle. Presence of a sibling at a school also increased one's chances for continuation. Prior educational experience also made a difference. By the time she enrolled at Hampton, Anna Bender had attended other off-reservation schools and had adjusted to life away from home. The attitudes of parents and extended family members also affected the student's perspective. Just as families and their circumstances might change over time, the schools also did not remain exactly the same, but evolved from one decade to the next.

Federal off-reservation schools could not remain the only alternative for Indian students. Many parents exerted pressure for their children, especially the youngest ones, to be able to attend school closer to home. It cost too much to transport students to distant institutions, and Christian missionaries wanted to have students attend schools run by their respective denominations. Sympathetic commissioners of Indian affairs sometimes promoted contract schools. Under this arrangement, a particular denomination agreed to run a school for Indian students subsidized by funds from Washington.

The federal off-reservation schools, however, also failed to deliver what they had pledged to achieve: the assimilation of their students into American society. Too many of their students dropped out. Moreover, upon their return home many of them embraced again the customs and traditions of their communities. By 1900 the transition was well underway from complete reliance on off-reservation schools. As of that date, 7,430 students attended the twenty-five federal off-reservation boarding schools, 9,600 students were enrolled in eighty-one federal reservation boarding schools, and about 5,000 attended reservation day schools.

In assessing the effect of schooling on young Indian people of this period, it is important to recognize that many students were scarred by their experiences, both by what happened to them at school and what they missed at home by being away. On the other hand, it is also necessary to point out that many children did not attend school at all and many others were enrolled only for a short period of time. In addition, attendance at the multitribal schools was as likely to reinforce tribal identity as dissolve it. Students finding themselves in unfamiliar surroundings tended to associate with others who spoke their same Native language and who shared common experiences and memories, thereby proving the general theory that greater contact with another culture can strengthen one's loyalty to one's own, rather than promptly eliminate it. The students had loyalties and bonds that were too deep to be easily or quickly uprooted. The schools thus did not necessarily accomplish at all what Pratt and his colleagues wanted. The boarding schools even proved to be places where students became aware of new Indian institutions. For example, through contact with people of other tribes, it was at Carlisle that many Natives first learned about a new religious movement, the Native American Church. Such assistance, of course, had not been part of Richard Henry Pratt's plan.

Religions

In the late nineteenth century federal officials were determined to eradicate Native religious practices and impose Christianity on Indian peoples. They outlawed the Sun Dance and other Indian ceremonies and empowered local agents to jail those who organized or attended such gatherings. Protestant and Catholic missionaries seemed to be ubiquitous. Looking back on this period, Elizabeth Cook-Lynn of the Crow Creek reservation wrote of "the Dominican priests who roamed the prairies, as much nomads as any Indians had ever been." The 1880s and 1890s immediately followed an era of rapid acceleration in mission activity. During the 1870s the Christian churches had been involved directly in the nomination, selection, and supervision of federal agents to many Indian communities, and individual denominations had been asked by the federal government to take primary responsibility for particular reservations in Indian country. This division of territory had favored "mainstream" Protestant churches. The more conservative pentecostal and evangelical denominations and the Church of Jesus Christ of Latter-day Saints (the Mormons) had been largely shut out by the process, although the Mormons did initiate a highly successful mission to the Catawbas in South Carolina.

In a few instances, Christian churches serving Native parishioners chose to incorporate Native languages or symbols. For example, a Baptist church service on the Eastern Cherokee reservation in North Carolina featured sermons in Cherokee. Although missionaries sometimes attempted to learn the language of the people in Indian communities, they rarely succeeded, and even those who gained some degree of fluency utilized the skill for evangelical rather than pluralistic purposes. The Franciscans at St. Michael's in Navajo country were rare in their degree of their interest in and knowledge of Navajo ceremonialism.

Some Native peoples chose to develop worship services that combined Christian tenets with Native beliefs. Many Native Christians also wanted to be in charge of their own worship rather than have the process directed by outsiders. The Native American Church would eventually emerge as the most significant of these religious movements, but the Indian Shaker Church in the Northwest also evolved into a viable Native religion. A Squaxin from the lower Puget Sound area of Washington, John Slocum, established the Indian Shaker Church in 1883, after surviving two nearly fatal illnesses. He told others that he had, in fact, died, but come back to life in order to save Indians from the evils of gambling, drinking, smoking, and the traditional healers or shamans. Slocum asked relatives to build a church for him, wherein his followers soon became known as "shakers" for the trembling they experienced as they worshipped. Despite this name, they were not related to the Shaker communities founded earlier in eastern America. Although Slocum died in 1897, the church continued and was legally incorporated in 1910. It combined Christian and traditional Puget Sound area Native beliefs and practices. The church's message against the abuse of alcohol, together with the obvious devotion of its adherents and its willingness to permit local communities to establish autonomous congregations, helped it expand beyond the Puget Sound to the Olympic Peninsula and Yakama in Washington, southern British Columbia, Warm Springs, Umatilla, lower Siletz, and Klamath in Oregon, and Smith River and Hoopa Valley in far northern California. The Indian Shaker Church continues today in this area, with approximately twenty congregations and a few thousand members.

The Native American Church appealed to a wider membership. Its rituals employed the buttons or tops of the peyote cactus which grew primarily in northern Mexico and in the lower Rio Grande valley of South Texas. The bitter tasting buttons contain alkaloids that produce psychedelic or hallucinogenic effects upon those who chew them. Peyote had been employed for ceremonial use for hundreds of years by various aboriginal groups in Mexico. A number of the elements in the old Mexican peyote ritual continued in the version of it inaugurated in the United States, including the gourd rattle, cleansing in fire, smoke and incense, an all-night ceremony, cigarettes, and, above all, the supernatural power of peyote. To those who participated in these rites, peyote was sacred.

Bands of the Apaches most likely originated the peyote ritual in the United States, with the Lipan Apaches bringing the ceremony at the beginning of the 1870s to the Comanches, Kiowas, and Apaches in Indian Territory. These tribes resided in the area that later became a part of the state of Oklahoma, but at this time was reserved for Indians indigenous to the regions and those who had been forcibly removed to this location. The railroad, that intruder that had bisected Indian country and contributed to the near extermination of the buffalo, aided in the spread of the new religion. When the railroad came to south Texas, it became possible to ship dried peyote by rail from Laredo north to Indian Territory, and from there all over Indian country. Diffusion of the peyote ritual also was hastened by the network of off-reservation boarding schools and by charismatic practitioners, road men, who spread the word about and the details of the new faith. By the middle years of the 1910s, the use of peyote had spread to Colorado, Iowa, Kansas, Nebraska, Minnesota, Montana, New Mexico, South Dakota, Utah, and Wyoming.

The peyote ritual varied somewhat from one community to another, but everywhere the ceremony contained certain elements that contributed to its acceptance. It incorporated both Christian and tribal symbols, thus representing a syncretic message of accommodation yet persistence of Indianness. It provided an opportunity for the people to congregate; in many instances it offered a substitute for other tribal rituals that had been repressed or abandoned. It employed symbols with common meaning: the earth, moon, and sun. And it took place in a tipi. The Native American Church perpetuated a tradition of seeking visions and finding power. For men on the Plains who had been denied the responsibility and attendant achievement of hunting and making war, practice of the new faith brought new opportunities for leadership. Adherents of the ritual preached abstinence from alcohol. As alcoholism had become a scourge in many Native communities, this dimension of the church proved especially important. In sum, the Native American Church offered a striking example of the ability of Indians to combine continuity and change in order to build a viable Native future.

The use of peyote, however, provoked a severe reaction from individuals and groups who saw it, to state it mildly, as a counterproductive addition to Indian life. Christian missionaries, federal officials, and more conservative Indians united to harass the peyotists. Gertrude Simmons Bonnin, or Zitkala-Sa, a Yankton Sioux writer and activist, lambasted the new faith, labeling peyote a drug. She claimed that it "excites the baser passions and is demoralizing—similar in its abnormal effects to that of opium, morphine, and cocaine." Congressman Henry L. Gandy and other elected representatives led the charge against peyote, introducing bills in Congress calling for its prohibition and for imprisoning those who persisted in using it.

In response, Indians who had found meaning in the new ritual counterattacked. In February 1915, for example, fifty-four Omahas signed a petition to Commissioner of Indian Affairs Cato Sells, calling for religious freedom, including the freedom to conduct peyote ceremonies. Several Omahas also composed statements attesting to the positive impact that the peyote ritual had had on their lives, particularly in regard to helping them turn away from the abuse of alcohol. Francis La Flesche (Omaha) joined with ethnologist James Mooney to testify before Congress in 1916. La Flesche spoke of all the problems brought to his people by bootleggers. Now, he said, "Practically all of those of my people who have adopted the peyote religion do not drink. . . . I have a respect for the peyote religion, because it has saved my people from the degradation which was produced by the use of the fiery drinks white people manufacture. . . ."

The strident opposition against them encouraged some peyotists to formally incorporate the ritual as the Native American Church. In El Reno, Oklahoma, in 1918, Mack Haag and Sidney

White Crane (Southern Cheyenne), Charles W. Daily, George Pipestem, and Charles E. Moore (Otoe), Frank Eagle (Ponca), Wilbur Peawa and Mam Sookwat (Comanche), Kiowa Charley (Kiowa), and Apache Ben (Apache Tribe of Oklahoma) formed "a religious and benevolent association under the laws of the State of Oklahoma." They incorporated, they stated, "to foster and promote the religious belief of the several tribes of Indians in the State of Oklahoma, in the Christian religion with the practice of the Peyote Sacrament as commonly understood and used . . . and to teach the Christian religion with morality, sobriety, industry, kindly charity and right living, and to cultivate a spirit of self-respect and brotherly union. . . ." At the close of the 1910s, the legality of the use of peyote for religious purposes remained in doubt, but the foundation had been established for the Native American Church's growth and prosperity. It became in time the largest and most significant Native association of the twentieth century.

Land

The most powerful part of the assimilationist crusade was directed at Indian land holdings. Reservations consisted of lands set aside by the federal government for the occupation and use by Indian communities. They exemplified two contradictory strains in American thought about "minority" groups: segregation and assimilation. In order to accomplish the goal of assimilation, policy-makers had segregated Indians on separate enclaves. They assumed such arrangements were temporary. As Indians disappeared as separate, identifiable groups, then reservations would vanish as well.

Henry L. Dawes wanted to expedite the process. The senator from Massachusetts sponsored legislation that gained approval in 1887 as the General Allotment (or Dawes) Act. Allotment or division of Indian communal or tribal lands into individually owned parcels was an old idea, dating back to 1633 in New England. Given the importance of private property in the workings of American life, allotment boasted continuing currency. Americans also continued to pay homage to the agrarian ideal, even as small-scale farming became less viable and the national economy expanded through rapid industrialization. Versions of the General Allotment Act had been proposed in Congress for a generation prior to final approval of this particular piece of legislation. Under the Dawes Act, which resembled the Homestead Act of 1862, heads of families received 160 acres of land. Single persons aged eighteen years and over and orphans under eighteen years of age could claim eighty-acre allotments. If land remained after such a division among tribal members, this "surplus" could be sold to non-Indian applicants. The Dawes Act furnished a temporary safeguard for these allotments; for twenty-five years they could not be sold or leased without federal approval. Not all tribes were affected equally by the Allotment Act. The Five Tribes of the Indian Territory—the Cherokees, Chickasaws, Choctaws, Muscogees (Creeks), and Seminoles—avoided allotment for the time being. So, too, did the Osages, Miamis, Peorias, and Sac and Foxes of Indian Territory. The Senecas of New York also were exempted. Other tribes might escape the act's provisions, if the demand did not arise for division of their lands. In other words, the Indian reservations most directly in the path of non-Indian pressure would be the ones most likely to be allotted.

The Five Tribes had been excluded since these nations were perceived as more advanced. The "Five Civilized Tribes" had gained this appellation because so many of their members were well educated, attended Christian churches, and lived in substantial homes. However, they also received different treatment because their representatives had lobbied in Washington against passage of different versions of allotment. "The change to individual title," they argued, "would throw the whole of our domain in a few years into the hands of a few persons." In addition, they contended, "a large portion of our country, and at least two-thirds of the Indian Territory, are only suitable for grazing purposes. No man can afford to live by stockraising and herding who is restricted to 160 or even 320 acres, especially lands away from water."

The proponents of allotment believed that keeping the tribal estate tribal or communal held individual Indians back. Reformers such as Merrill Gates concluded that Indians had to become "more intelligently selfish." Too many Indians, he decided, had not been "touched by the wings of the divine angel of discontent." Gates thus conveyed in 1896 that it was time "to get the Indian out of the blanket and into trousers—and trousers with a pocket in them, and a pocket that aches to be filled with dollars!" Regarding land, most Native Americans persisted in honoring the old values of reciprocity and generosity. They saw the kind of personal acquisition lauded by Gates as hoarding; they generally shared their resources rather than keeping them solely for themselves.

Passage of the Allotment Act did not spell instantaneous disaster for all Indians. In the first eight years after the law went into effect, relatively few reservations were allotted. Leasing rarely occurred. This deliberate speed, however, soon accelerated as more western states joined the Union and gained additional representation in Washington. These men had no patience with patience. Just as they sought to open public lands for private exploitation by state citizens, in a related sense, they wanted to open Indian lands. Thus pressure dramatically escalated to hasten the division and diminution of tribal lands. Congress began to tinker with allotment to make it easier for Indians to lease their lands. It also tried to cede blocks of remaining reservation land.

In the first decade of the new century the map of Indian country started to take on a new look. The Supreme Court decision of *Lone Wolf* v. *Hitchcock* in 1903 had far-reaching implications. It involved, among other plaintiffs, Lone Wolf, a Kiowa man who had appealed the opening of the Kiowa, Apache, and Comanche lands in Oklahoma Territory because appropriate tribal consent had not been obtained, as specifically stipulated in the Treaty of Medicine Lodge Creek of 1868. The Jerome Agreement, which permitted the opening of the lands, had been rejected by the Kiowas, Apaches, and Comanches in 1892 but had been approved by the Congress in 1900. Secretary of the Interior Ethan Allan Hitchcock had concurred with congressional judgment, arguing that such an opening could take place without tribal consent. In *Lone Wolf,* the Court ruled that the power existed for Congress "to abrogate the provisions of an Indian treaty."

Lone Wolf permitted a previously formed congressional commission charged with negotiating land cessions to proceed whether or not the Indians involved wish to make a deal. Reservation communities, in fact, were not necessarily unwilling to negotiate, but they insisted on a fair price for any lands they surrendered. Now they possessed little bargaining power. U.S. Special Agent James McLaughlin was dispatched to carve out the cessions. Armed with the *Lone Wolf* decision, within two years McLaughlin had gained hundreds of thousands of acres to be opened for non-Indian settlement at Crow and Flathead in Montana, Rosebud in South Dakota, Uintah in Utah, and Wind River in Wyoming. McLaughlin argued that such reservations were larger than necessary for their Indian residents. Ironically, following the erosion of the tribal estate during these years, federal officials of the mid-twentieth century would claim that reservations were not large enough and did not contain sufficient resources to sustain Indian communities.

Lone Wolf also undermined the more altruistic intentions of allotment. It pressured the government to speed up the leasing and sale of Indian lands. The Burke Act of 1906 empowered the Secretary of the Interior to grant any "competent" allottee fee-simple title to his or her land, thus permitting the individual to lease or sell the acreage at any time. This designation of competency resembled the later policy of termination. Indians deemed able to fend for themselves were perceived as not needing federal protection; in the same sense, "competent" Indian tribes at mid-century would be subjected to withdrawal of trust status for their lands. The western states and various commercial interests discovered in commissioners of Indian affairs Francis Leupp, Robert Valentine, and Cato Sells men willing to push vigorously for development of Indian lands. The commissioners placed more emphasis on leasing these lands to cattle companies and sugar beet companies than they did on promoting the evolution of sustaining, independent tribal economies. Indians often were caught in the vise of demand for their lands and the inadequacy of making a living on the relatively meager acreage granted to them. They frequently took the easy way out and leased their holdings. Leasing yielded small cash payments but it did not inspire people to work hard and become independent. Inheritance also complicated leasing. Parcels over time were subdivided into smaller entities, making it even more likely for leasing to occur.

By 1920 those reservations containing the most promising deposits of natural resources had become checkerboarded by non-Indian intrusions. The population of the United States grew from 63 million in 1890 to 106 million in 1920. Both immigrants and migrants sought to generate their fortunes on lands previously owned and occupied by Indians. The federal government clearly bowed to public pressure and relinquished its trust responsibility in its acquiescence to non-Indian demands. The northern Plains were particularly hard hit by allotment and subsequent sale, but other parts of Indian country were also affected. Timber and mineral leases as well as farming and ranching leases subdivided more and more Native land.

Oklahoma furnishes a good example of non-Indian goals taking precedence. Following removal to Indian Territory, the Five Tribes had rebuilt. They had developed their own schools, constructed capital cities, and made noteworthy progress in farming and ranching. Their very success in demonstrating the potential of their lands ultimately worked against them, for a horde of prospective settlers and speculators lobbied to open up this region to the rest of the American population. By 1893 these "Boomers" had convinced Congress to revoke the initial exemption the Five Tribes had received under the terms of the Allotment Act. A commission headed by the retired Senator Dawes then established tribal rolls despite tribal objections. The rolls provided specific lists of who officially was included as a member of a specific Indian community. The rolls were established as a prelude to dividing tribal lands among these individuals. The Curtis Act of 1898 denied the authority and legitimacy of existing tribal governments in Indian Territory and approved allotment of Native lands. Many of the original occupants of Indian Territory spoke of establishing a separate Indian state, which they proposed to name Sequoyah, after the man who developed the system for writing the Cherokee language. However, when allotment was carried out among the Five Tribes, hopes for Sequoyah evaporated. Instead Oklahoma became the 46th state, gaining admission to the Union in 1907.

Allotment had targeted primarily the tribal lands of the West, but Indian communities outside of the region did not escape unscathed. The Choctaws of Mississippi and the White Earth Anishinabeg of Minnesota supply two examples. In 1898 the Dawes Commission concluded that Choctaws who had managed to remain in Mississippi and avoid removal earlier in the century now could participate in the allotment process if they agreed to migrate to Indian Territory and claim parcels of land following a three-year residence there. Two attorneys, Robert Owen and Charles F. Winton, spied a situation too lucrative to ignore. A thousand Choctaws signed contracts with them to serve as their claims lawyers, with Owen and Winton to obtain 50 percent of any awards. Other attorneys then vied for the attention of the Choctaws, while Protestant and Catholic missionaries took sides on the matters of migration and the claims process. In the segregated South, Christianity did not usually stand for assimilation; ministers often preached segregation and the Choctaw churches, with their prayers and hymns in the tribal language, evolved into central symbols of a persisting Choctaw identity. The Dawes Commission enrolled 2,240 Mississippi Choctaws, but others, especially in more remote communities, boycotted the procedure or simply were not included in the count.

By the first few years of the twentieth century hundreds of Mississippi Choctaws had been moved to Oklahoma. They did not all find happiness in this new location. Some of the lawyers did represent them well and the Oklahoma Choctaws fought against any addition to their rolls. Those who remained in Mississippi were bolstered by a $75,000 appropriation from the Congress in 1918, which provided not only badly needed financial assistance but also federal recognition of an existing Indian community in the state. This formal recognition was more than a formality. In a symbolic sense, it paid tribute to Choctaw perseverance. It emphasized

the continuity of the Choctaw presence and increased the likelihood that Choctaw people would remain in the state. It also made
the tribe eligible for other federal programs in the future.

In Minnesota, the Nelson Act, a state law patterned after the
Dawes Act, drastically changed life on the White Earth reservation. The Anishinabeg lived here in a transitional zone between
prairie and forest, which allowed the people to have choices in
their economy and permitted development of both agricultural and
timber resources. The residents of White Earth comprised migrants from different bands from the northern part of the state and
Metis, or mixed bloods, the descendants of marriages between
Anishinabe women and English and French fur traders. This latter
group, with names such as Fairbanks and Beaulieu, brought bilingual skills and greater awareness of the workings of the larger
American society.

The Nelson Act not only divided White Earth, it also opened
the reservation to subsequent legislation that additionally harmed
the people. Minnesota representatives Moses E. Clapp and Halvor
Steenerson sponsored a bill that Congress passed giving lumber
interests the ability to purchase timber from holders of individual
allotments. Passage of the Burke Act inspired Clapp and Steenerson to gain congressional approval not to limit the sale, encum-
brance, or taxation of allotted lands on White Earth. Subjected to
new taxes and confronted by escalating demands for their lands,
the people of White Earth began to sell off parcels of real estate.
Soon much of White Earth was now owned or controlled by outsiders. In turn, the Anishinabe people were increasingly limited in
their access to wild rice, maple sap, and berries, as well as in hunting deer and fishing. These restrictions affected the reservation
economy, but they also had social and cultural repercussions. Traditionally, women had completed most of the harvesting and men
had accomplished most of the hunting and fishing. Denied access
to many of their traditional sites, the people became less cohesive.
Women and men were less able to teach these skills to their children,
and children grew up without the benefit of learning such customary
practices. Extended families thus were less likely to carry out seasonal work together, and families separated as individuals left the reservation to try to find more lucrative opportunities elsewhere.

Identities

Such a reversal of fortune sometimes encouraged overt or covert forms of resistance. In eastern Oklahoma, the Redbird Smith movement and the so-called Crazy Snake rebellion symbolized widespread resentment as well as reaffirmation of traditional identities. Born July 19, 1850, at the edge of Cherokee country, Redbird Little Pig Smith was a member of the Keetowah Society. The Keetowahs were cultural conservatives who had been an organized unit for centuries. They saw in allotment a tool that non-Indians might use to destroy Cherokee life. Redbird Smith attempted to lead the Cherokees toward a more complete recognition of traditional tribal values and practices. His followers sought to follow what they called the White Path, a balanced life that promoted personal harmony; they tried to keep the Sacred Fires burning at the sites for ceremonies. When Smith and others resisted allotment and the official tribal enrollment demanded by the Dawes Commission, they were arrested and forced to enroll. After Congress dissolved the Cherokee government in 1906, conservative "fullbloods" named Smith as their new chief. (In many Indian communities people of mixed ancestry were termed "mixed-bloods"; they were often, but not always, more willing to incorporate new social, cultural, and economic elements into their lives. "Fullbloods," whose ancestry was completely or almost fully within the tribe, tended to be more conservative in such choices.) Smith opposed allotment until his death in 1918, but the Keetowahs ultimately split over the issue, with some grimly accepting the land division as inevitable. Denied Smith's dream of a separate conservative Cherokee community, many fullbloods retreated into the eastern Oklahoma hill country and observed traditional ways with as little contact as possible with others who disagreed with them. In 1912 two thousand land allotments went unclaimed. Keetowah fires continued to burn.

Chitto Harjo, called Crazy Snake, led conservative Muscogee political revitalization in the Indian Territory at the turn of the century. He also resisted the kinds of changes being imposed upon his people. Like Smith, he denied the authority of the federal government to negate the sovereignty of the Native community. The acceptance of an allotment, Chitto Harjo contended, was a break with tribal custom, and those who did so would no longer be members of the Muscogee nation. Accordingly, his followers harassed and punished those who did take allotments. Finally federal officials, supported by U.S. cavalry, stepped in to quash resistance and for a time imprisoned in Leavenworth the man who had reasserted the power of traditional Native law. If overt resistance ceased, the sentiments in support of traditional authority remained present, even after Harjo's death in 1909. The Muscogee poet Alexander Posey paid tribute to him: ". . . Such will! such courage to defy/ The powerful makers of his fate!", wrote Posey. "Condemn him and his kind to shame!/I bow to him, exalt his name!"

Contemporary observers of Indian communities in the early twentieth century could be excused for gloomy prognostications of a bleak future. Federal policy had shown little shift in direction. Most Christian missionaries remained inflexible in their attitudes toward Native religious ceremonies. A rapidly expanding non-Indian population challenged and often appropriated Indian resources. In the lower forty-eight states, roughly two out of every three acres that Indians had owned or controlled prior to passage of the Allotment Act had been removed from the tribal estate. Even with those dilemmas, Indians resolved not to simply accede to the customary assumptions of the day. They were determined to weather this era and to move forward. The period did include victimization and despair, but also, ultimately, reasons for hope.

Native women and men searched for ways to make their constrained surroundings into meaningful and viable environments. To borrow historian Frederick Hoxie's useful concept, they sought to turn prisons into homelands. Such terminology is not overly melodramatic. Federal agents on the reservations served heavy handedly. A colonial mentality persisted. Indian peoples hated being dependent for rations, being told where they could live, and being commanded how they should worship. They turned to the elders and to younger leaders and to family relationships to find ways continue to observe traditional values.

No magical, instantaneous unity appeared on the reservations. The first generation or two of reservation life prompted different opinions about the future. Where allotment had taken place, for example, people were likely to reside in a more dispersed pattern. Many reservations now encompassed members of more than one band or even more than one tribe. For example, four of the seven western Lakota bands lived on Cheyenne River. At Fort Belknap, the Gros Ventres shared acreage with the Assiniboines. Although band and tribal distinctions and divisions remained, circumstances dictated the need for some degree of accommodation. How could the people save the land that they still held? Many communities concluded they had little choice other than to try to employ an imposed political system to work toward certain goals. To be effective the leaders of a tribal council or business council had to embody customary virtues, including wisdom, generosity, and the ability to speak well.

Cheyenne River revealed the kind of partial success that could be realized. The reservation was established in 1889. In 1900 the allotment process began, and eventually it pushed people to spread out across the reservation. A business council and a police force of Cheyenne River residents started to function. This initial version of a tribal council was comprised of representatives from different districts of the reservation. The federal government treated the reservation as a unit. The people living on Cheyenne River began to see themselves not only as Mnikowoju or Sihasapa but also as Cheyenne River Sioux. One should not overstate this point at Cheyenne River or elsewhere, for such identification depended upon how new institutions affected daily life. If the new political unit challenged the authority of an existing traditional governing system, especially one combining secular and religious power, then it was unlikely to succeed. If the council or committee did not consider the residents of an important area or was in some other way not wholly representative, then it decreased its chances for acceptance. If the unit did not seek goals upon which the community had reached consensus, then it shackled its promise.

At Cheyenne River, the new business council confronted an immediate threat. Non-Indian interests, well represented in the Congress by Senator Robert Gamble and Congressman Philo Hall, wanted to reduce or eliminate the reservation. Special Agent McLaughlin tried to engineer such a reduction, while Gamble and Hall introduced bills toward that end. The political leaders at

Cheyenne River could not fight off one cession of land. But other attempts failed to further reduce the reservation in size. Increasingly experienced negotiators from the business council such as Ed Swan and Percy Phillips traveled more than once to Washington, stalled, offered counterproposals, and manipulated, seizing upon the inefficiency of the Indian Office. Like their counterparts all over Indian country, these people battled against the odds to preserve some kind of land base for the future. These challenges could encourage the election of individuals who spoke English more fluently and who could represent tribal interests more effectively in this new era. These representatives often were younger men who had obtained more schooling.

The Indian Office tried to accomplish two conflicting goals. It preached self-sufficiency for the Indians at the same time it placated non-Indians who wanted access to Native lands. Federal officials embraced agriculture as a way to use those lands productively and to teach Indians the value of toil. More than a few Indian communities had rich and long-standing agricultural traditions. However, other groups had not emphasized farming or had perceived it to be work to be done by women rather than men; in these locales, the men balked at assuming a task they thought women should undertake. In addition, many reservations were ill-suited for agriculture. Aridity, short growing seasons, and the small size of allotments all conspired against successful farming. Under these circumstances, agents or superintendents—as head federal officials for a particular locale started to be called—faced severe challenges. The Reclamation Act of 1902 was designed to help non-Indians in the West, through funding for substantial dams and extended canals to be constructed throughout the region. Although non-Indian citizens often complained about federal assistance to Indians, they did not hesitate to take advantage of this aid for themselves. Indian communities that could have benefited greatly from such help struggled to obtain even small amounts of federal aid for similar but much more limited projects on their lands.

On the Fort Belknap reservation in northern Montana, the Assiniboines and Gros Ventres complained about off-reservation farmers and ranchers who diverted water from the Milk River before it could flow through their lands. Superintendent William R.

Logan complained to the commissioner of Indian affairs on June 3, 1905: "So far this spring, we have had no water in our ditch whatever. Our meadows are now rapidly parching up. The Indians have planted large crops and a great deal of grain. All will be lost unless some radical action is taken at once to make the settlers above the Reservation respect our rights. To the Indians it means either good crops this fall or starvation this winter."

Logan's complaint eventually brought the matter to court, where he pleaded his case on the basis of prior appropriation. This doctrine, recognized in Montana, held that the first users of water had the senior rights to the resource. Judge William Hunt of the U.S. district court decided that in agreeing to the terms of the treaty which confined them to the lands of Fort Belknap, the Indians were entitled to sufficient water to fulfill the purposes of that agreement. The treaty clearly indicated that the occupants of the reservation should "become 'self-supporting as a pastoral and agricultural people.'" It did not matter whether non-Indian farmers and ranchers such as Henry Winter (whose name was entered as "Winters" in court documents) had a prior claim to the water.

After the Ninth Circuit Court affirmed Judge Hunt's decision, the U.S. Supreme Court ruled on *Winters* v. *U.S.* on January 6, 1908. Justice Joseph McKenna spoke for the Court in his opinion. He stated: "The Indians had command of the lands and the waters—command of all their beneficial use, whether kept for hunting, and grazing, roving herds of stock, or turned to agricultural and the arts of civilization." McKenna then asked: "Did they give up all this? Did they reduce the area of their occupation and give up the waters which made it valuable or adequate?" He declared they did not. This declaration of water rights for Fort Belknap, which became known as the Winters Doctrine, marked a fundamental turning point in the national Native struggle to remain on their land. Not only did *Winters* buttress Indian claims to water rights, it offered additional testimony that Native peoples were not going to disappear.

The decision had lasting significance, but it made less of a difference at Fort Belknap than one might have anticipated. Superintendent Logan had encouraged non-Indians to reside on the reservation in order, he said, to encourage greater Indian productivity.

Logan also built up a sizable cattle herd of his own, even appropriating Indian cattle to bolster that enterprise. Therefore Logan had not been concerned just about Indian well-being when he complained about the diversion of water from the river. Moreover, five years after *Winters,* the Matador Land and Cattle Company of Texas gained a lease to most of the reservation and held that lease through 1927. Thus the hopes for continuing economic development by and for Natives at Fort Belknap proved largely unfounded, even though Gros Ventre and Assiniboine farmers and ranchers had made a promising start in the decade before the Supreme Court decision.

Cattle ranching elsewhere produced better results. Prevailing federal policies often worked against Native initiatives, but many reservations witnessed the emergence of an industry that made social and cultural as well as economic sense. Much of the remaining estate was well-suited for the grazing of livestock. In the Great Basin country, the Plateau area of the Northwest, in Oklahoma, on the northern Plains and in the Southwest, Indians began to work as cowboys and as ranchers. Becoming cowboys allowed them to remain Indians. That is to say, cattle ranching permitted them to stay on the land and to practice time-honored values. They fed relatives and strangers; they gave cattle as gifts. They formed ranching associations based on family and band ties.

Difficult winters, the leasing of ranges to non-Indians, and varying market conditions worked against full development of Indian cattle ranching, but some success stories could be reported. On the White Mountain Apache (or Fort Apache) reservation in central Arizona, Wallace Altaha, known also by his brand of R-14, became the most famous Indian cattleman of the region. By 1918 he owned 10,000 head of cattle, allowing him to purchase $25,000 worth of liberty bonds. Superintendent C. W. Crouse helped develop the industry by importing Herefords, which became the mainstay of Apache cattle ranching. The existence of Indian cattle raising also helped maintain or add to Native land bases. The creation of the main Tohono O'odham reservation in southern Arizona in 1916 was justified on the need for more land for the expanding cattle herds of the people.

Women participated in cattle ranching as individual ranchers, as spouses who worked with their husbands, and as members of extended families who raised cattle. Historian Clifford Trafzer's research on the Yakama reservation suggests that Yakama women generally played a larger role in the working of the tribal economy than previously has been assumed. From 1909 to 1912, for example, the women purchased more household goods, wagons, buggies, and hacks than did the men. They also bought more horses and more cattle. On the reservations in general, men certainly outnumbered women in their ownership of cattle and played the dominant role in livestock associations, but women were not absent from the picture. At Navajo, where the people primarily raised sheep rather than cattle, ownership of the flocks was vested in the women. The raising of sheep also empowered Navajo women because of their ability to weave wool. The raising of sheep or cattle throughout the Indian West mattered additionally because it offered children, often charged to tend the flock, responsibility and taught them discipline, while it underscored their importance as contributors to their families' welfare.

Raising livestock presented an opportunity for independent choice and action during an era in which the memory of military defeat, the reality of confinement, and the policy of forced assimilation all rankled. The sale of Indian-owned cattle might necessitate a trip away from the reservation. Such a journey was as likely to reinforce tribal identity as it was to diminish it. When the Hidatsa ranchers from Fort Berthold, North Dakota, traveled to St. Paul and Chicago in 1900 they saw surprising dimensions of the non-Indian world. Wolf Chief later recalled that in Chicago, in back of a hotel, "they threw away old foods they did not want any more on their tables." He saw "some poor women dirty and in rags take off the covers of cans, and they took the food to eat." The Hidatsas professed astonishment at this demonstration of a lack of generosity and caring among the Whites. "If an Indian man is hungry," mused Wolf Chief, "no matter what he has done or how foolish he has acted, we will always give him food."

Indian cowboys also sought fame and fortune in rodeo. The best-known Indian rodeo cowboy of this generation was a Nez

Perce man, Jackson Sundown, who earned renown for his bronc-riding ability at such major events as the Pendleton Roundup. Sam Bird-in-Ground (Crow) and George Defender (Standing Rock Sioux) also gained acclaim for their exploits. Will Rogers, the son of Cherokee rancher Clem Rogers, participated as a roper in rodeos at Madison Square Garden and elsewhere. Rogers later said the excitement of the rodeo encouraged him to try his luck in the world of entertainment, where his probing and amusing commentary made him a beloved national figure.

Cattle ranching provided a positive alternative to farming for many tribes of the interior; for coastal peoples the ocean offered another option to agriculture. The Makahs of the Olympic Peninsula in Washington state were successful whalers long before the United States became a country. They proved quite willing to incorporate useful new technology as they pursued not only whales but also fur seals. By the late nineteenth century they prospered sufficiently to employ White labor for their schooners. They dutifully planted a few potatoes, but potatoes seemed a luxury; the Makahs observed that it seemed much easier to obtain food from the ocean than from the earth. Money from sealing permitted Makahs in 1892 to buy Neah Bay's two food stores, the local trading post, and the one hotel. As U.S. laws began to severely restrict Native sealing, the Makahs moved into fishing for halibut. Despite massive numbers of competing non-Indian fishermen and additional restrictions on their participation in this maritime activity, the Makah people still fared quite well in the industry throughout the remainder of this period.

Indians seized upon various new institutions and tried to utilize them for their own purposes. For example, federal agents inaugurated a version of the county fair on reservations in order to advertise Native agricultural accomplishment. Thus in 1904 Samuel Reynolds started a fair in Crow country, but the Crows quickly realized such occasions could provide more than a procession of potatoes. They could also include parades, horse races, and rodeos. Crow Fair allowed the Crows a fine opportunity to be together and to have a great time. Of course such gatherings could serve commercial purposes as well. In North Carolina, the Eastern

Cherokee fair started in 1914 and soon allowed the people a useful venue for the sale of their crafts to neighboring non-Indians.

The Fourth of July also offered an opportunity for community celebration. Indians quickly realized that festivities organized ostensibly for patriotic purposes had a better chance of being endorsed than communal religious observances. At Rosebud in South Dakota, for example, a six-day spectacle in 1897 encompassed everything from Corn and White Buffalo dances to music by the Rosebud Cornet Band and a reading of the Declaration of Independence. For good measure, spectators observed bronc and steer riding and a mock reenactment of the Custer battle. Federal policy may have prohibited tribal religious rituals, but the program noted: "These dances having been prohibited, special permission has been granted to have these occur on this day for the last time." Employing the Fourth of July for their own purposes allowed Indian communities another occasion to establish their own priorities and to define who they were.

The Wild West shows yielded another avenue for travel and adventure during this transitional age. From the time Buffalo Bill Cody and his associates organized the first of these productions in 1883, critics assailed them as demeaning to Indian participants. Most of the Native individuals who joined the shows disagreed with this assessment. They relished the chance not only to travel and see new places, but also to ride horses and make more money than they likely would have made on the reservation. Some of the "show Indians," as they became known, journeyed more than once to Europe and visited many of the major cities in the United States. Most of them actually liked Cody, who demonstrated more respect for them than other show entrepreneurs. Defeating Custer one more time in reenactments, portraying Indian cowboys and cowgirls, and taking part in rodeo-like events all evoked enthusiasm from the show Indians, most of whom hailed from the Plains region. They saw the shows usually as an adventure and a new possibility to exhibit honor and courage. Like the Hidatsas who traveled to Chicago, their contact with the non-Indian world promoted rather than diminished their own sense of identity as Indians.

On the local and national level, more than a few Indians perceived the last years of the nineteenth century and the first years of the twentieth not as the end of an era but the start of a period filled with promise. Quanah, or, as he was generally called, Quanah Parker, exemplified this sentiment in Oklahoma. He seized upon changing times for his own benefit and the benefit of his people, the Comanches. Parker's surname came from his mother, Cynthia Ann Parker, who at nine years of age had been captured by the Comanches in 1836 and who had remained with them, becoming a member of the tribe. Quanah's father, Peta Nocona, a war chief, was not in camp on the day in 1861 when Texas Rangers recaptured Cynthia Ann Parker and returned her and her daughter to White relatives. Quanah never saw his mother and sister again. They both had died by 1870, three years after the Comanches had signed the Treaty of Medicine Lodge, which confined the tribe to a reservation in what became southwestern Oklahoma.

These lands, shared with the Kiowas and the Apaches, were in the path of the expanding Texas cattle industry. Quanah rose to a position of leadership on the reservation and by 1885 served as primary spokesperson for his people. In some ways, he remained a "traditional." Like a number of prosperous Comanche men, he was married to more than one woman. A cultural broker, Quanah interpreted the ways of one culture to another and tried to find ways to realize mutual understanding and advantage. As principal chief, he negotiated with the Texas cattlemen, acknowledged their power, and attempted to strike the best leasing deals he could. Before the Jerome Agreement went into effect in 1900, he and the Comanches enjoyed a brief interlude of prosperity. Quanah practiced the politics of delay, hoping to retard the ratification of the agreement as long as possible. However, as a pragmatist, he realized that he and others would have to adapt to changing circumstances. Quanah thus accumulated a substantial cattle herd of his own and did not hesitate to try to find means to improve his personal finances. He built a fine home with a big porch and stars painted on its roof. Yet as he adjusted to an economic order, he also played a vital role in promoting the expansion of the Native American Church. Over the course of his career, Quanah traveled to Washington nearly twenty times to represent the Comanches. He was appointed a tribal judge to rule on criminal offenses at a time when being married to more than one woman represented a criminal offense. A charismatic and complicated person, he is but one of many examples of Indian people during this era who utilized the new, often imposed, institutions in creative ways to maintain or establish flexible, viable contemporary Native identities.

Other Indians looked to the new century with emotions other than unmixed gloom. They appreciated their heritage, but they also believed Indians as individuals and as a group could realize bright tomorrows. Many were college graduates whose education and professional experiences had empowered them. Henry Roe Cloud, for example, did not see the world as did Henry Dawes, though they both had graduated from Yale University. In fact Roe Cloud also had gained a master's degree in anthropology from Yale as well as a degree in divinity from Auburn Theological Seminary. Roe Cloud and his colleagues recognized that all Indians had things in common and they understood that an Indian identity did not have to conflict with membership in a band or tribe. Using the model of the Indian Rights Association, they decided to form an organization not only for Native peoples, but with full membership limited to Indians. Assisted by Fayette McKenzie, who taught at Ohio State University, an original committee of six Native Americans met in Columbus, Ohio, in April 1911, to plan a conference for an association that would consider the needs and issues facing Indian peoples. The committee members were Laura Cornelius (Oneida), Charles Daganett (Peoria), Charles Eastman, Carlos Montezuma (Yavapai), Thomas Sloan (Omaha), and Henry Standing Bear (Sicangu Lakota). The group called itself the Society of American Indians. The group of six quickly expanded to eighteen, including Marie Baldwin (Anishinabe), Rosa B. La Flesche (Omaha), Arthur C. Parker (Seneca), and Henry Roe Cloud.

The Society of American Indians (SAI) appeared to present a valuable forum for Indians to meet and consider the Native present and future. Nonetheless, certain issues surfaced that divided the society's modest membership. Should the Bureau of Indian Affairs

(BIA) be abolished? Should Indians work for the bureau? Should peyote be prohibited? Montezuma argued that the bureau was beyond salvation and must be abolished immediately, whereas Parker initially was more moderate in his criticism. Sloan was an active member of the Native American Church, while Gertrude Bonnin, as mentioned, wanted peyote outlawed. Philip Gordon (Anishinabe), a Catholic priest, censured those who worked for the bureau; Sherman Coolidge (Northern Arapaho) was a minister, but disagreed with Gordon about the matter of employment. Almost from one annual conference to the next, the SAI's stance seemed to shift on some of these hotly contested points.

Such internal divisions limited the SAI's development. It had not built a membership base beyond several hundred people. It had not succeeded in developing grass-roots support from reservation communities. Most of its members remained people who had had access to more education and who had enjoyed more opportunities than the majority of Native Americans. Lacking a sufficient foundation either of adherents or financial benefactors, it could not directly engage in extended campaigns to right contemporary wrongs. Although it persisted into the 1920s, the SAI did not survive the decade. Such limitations frustrated Montezuma, among others. After the annual meeting in 1915 in Lawrence, Kansas, he muttered in his newsletter, *Wassaja:* "The sky is clear and we meet only to discuss. It is so nice to meet and discuss. There is nothing wrong. We meet only to discuss. It is so nice to meet and discuss. We can meet and discuss as well as the Mohonk Conference. . . . Meeting and discussing is so soothing and smoothing. Sh—! Sh—! Don't whisper about the Indian Bureau."

During World War I, Arthur C. Parker, the editor of the SAI's journal, *The American Indian Magazine,* as well as the society's current president, joined the armed forces and thus could not attend the 1918 conference in Minneapolis. In his absence, the SAI voted in favor of abolishing the BIA. It also elected Charles Eastman as president, retaining Parker as journal editor. When Parker did not reply immediately to new SAI secretary Gertrude Bonnin's query about whether he wished to continue as editor, she promptly extended her own duties to include editing the journal.

The society's leadership was primarily male, but women also assumed important responsibilities. Bonnin was one of the most articulate voices of Indian America in the early twentieth century. Born February 22, 1876, on the Yankton reservation, she accompanied Quaker missionaries to White's Indiana Manual Labor Institute in Wabash, where she enrolled for three years. Although she had been unhappy at the school, she returned to it at the age of fourteen to further her education. She then attended Earlham College; leaving because of illness before she graduated, she still obtained a teaching post at Carlisle and then attended the New England Conservatory of Music. A talented violinist, she also published a collection of essays and a separate collection of short stories. Bonnin detested Pratt, whom she once labeled "pig-headed," and others who pushed for rapid assimilation. She also fought for women, first to be included in the Society of American Indians, and then for them to take on major tasks within the workings of it.

Parker was also a significant figure. A member of a distinguished Seneca family, he had grown up on the Cattaraugus reservation (in upstate New York) and in New York City, where he studied with anthropologist Franz Boas at Columbia. Parker left the university before receiving his undergraduate degree, yet went on to become a well-regarded scholar, contributing studies of Iroquois history and culture. Parker never lost sight of his identity both as a Seneca and as an American Indian. He, like others in SAI, appreciated some of the ironies of the present day. English now presented a common language for Indian peoples. Development of regional and national transportation networks and mail systems increased the chances for Indians to see and communicate with each other. In other words, developments that initially seemed to hasten assimilation did not necessarily further that prospect.

World War I

Service in World War I created another bond among many Indian men and women. Native participation in the war had been encouraged by federal officials and assimilationists who believed the war would accelerate assimilation and permit Indians to demonstrate their ability to contribute to American society. Although many Indians had not yet been granted citizenship and were not eligible for the draft, they were asked to register with the selective service, and over 16,000 Indians served in the war, a rate twice that of other eligible Americans. Those who went overseas encountered commanding officers whose reading of history convinced them that Indians were "natural" scouts. General John Pershing remembered the service of Apaches as scouts against other Apaches and more recently as trackers in the campaign against Pancho Villa. Indians also had served in the Oklahoma National Guard on the south Texas border in that same campaign. Pershing thus formed a unit of Apaches to scout in France.

Pratt and SAI leaders argued against such segregated entities, contending that Native soldiers could best exhibit their talents and their patriotism in integrated units. Why not permit Indians to be bakers, teamsters, sharpshooters, aviators, engineers, artillerymen, and hospital aides? Native soldiers served alongside other Americans in the war, but they also filled such units as the 36th Division, which included many Indians from Texas and Oklahoma, especially from the Five Tribes. Company "E" of the 142nd Infantry Regiment was almost all-Indian.

Indian soldiers gained many awards for heroism. Sergeant Alfred Bailey (Cherokee) received posthumously the Distinguished Service Cross. Corporal Nicholas E. Brown (Choctaw) also died in battle and received a Croix de Guerre. Private Joseph Oklahombi (Choctaw) had the Croix de Guerre bestowed upon him by Marshal Henri Pétain. Historian Michael Tate wrote that Pétain praised Oklahombi "for single-handedly crossing 210 yards of barbed wire entanglements, wrenching a machine gun away from its German crew, and capturing 171 German prisoners with the same gun," then holding the position for four days. In addition, two Choctaws from the 142nd Infantry pioneered the use of an Indian language for coded radio communications. Their success inspired formation of a unit of Indian code talkers, with twenty-six different Native languages at their disposal. *The American Indian*

Magazine in 1919 reported with great glee upon this development in an article entitled, "Played Joke on the Huns."

As they would in later wars, Indians debated about fighting for a country that had treated Native peoples shamefully. Those who did enlist frequently spoke to the need to prove Indian patriotism and capabilities. Still others saw in the conflict a different opportunity. Plains Indian soldiers earned honor by counting coup in battle through touching or striking the enemy. Others participated in appropriate tribal ceremonies upon their return home. Some WWI veterans were welcomed as warriors into the old, traditional warrior societies. Historian Tom Holm (Cherokee-Muscogee), a veteran of the war in Vietnam, argued that such a person "abided by the treaties signed between his people and the federal government; most importantly he had taken part in those time-honored tribal traditions linked to warfare. In short," Holm concluded, "he was a warrior and whether clad in traditional dress or olive drab, he had reaffirmed his tribal identity."

Not all Indians endorsed the war effort. Some reaffirmed their tribal identity, they said, through opposing registration for the selective service or conscription. For example, Parker reported "a systematic attempt on the part of some Indians to discourage the idea of registering on the ground that Federal law or ruling requiring registration did not apply to wards." The Indians to whom Parker referred were Iroquois, who did not oppose war but opposed any infringement upon Iroquois sovereignty. Unhappy with leases that had eroded their land base, these Iroquois saw registration as the latest in a series of assaults upon their own control of their lives. If individual Iroquois wanted to volunteer, they reasoned, that was up to them, but service should be voluntary. In the same sense, when the Oneidas and Onondagas of the Six Nations chose to declare war on Germany, that action also should be permitted.

In eastern Oklahoma the war ignited new and reignited long-standing grievances over federal and non-Indian treatment of Indians. Some members of the Five Tribes angrily joined the Green Corn Rebellion, an agrarian uprising organized by unionists and socialists. The rebellion protested people being uprooted from the land, but it also expressed the view that poor men should not fight in a war that would benefit rich men. Near Henryetta, Oklahoma, about 200 Muscogees participated in a protest over the issue of conscription. One of their leaders, Ellen Perryman, contended: "The Indians are not going to the slaughter fields of France." "To Hell with the Government and the Allies . . . ," she added. "They are nothing but a bunch of Grafters and Sons of Bitches." Although she was not imprisoned, Perryman was charged with violating the Espionage Act for advising Indians not to register for and to resist the draft.

Ellen Perryman and Joseph Oklahombi both hailed from the same part of Indian America. Their varied responses to World War I underlined the various ways in which different Native Americans could react not only to the war but to this entire era, which had brought so much social and economic change. In the end, the first two decades of the twentieth century had verified what Indians, regardless of their perspectives, had known all along. They were not going to disappear, and they would be Indians all of their lives.

CHAPTER TWO

Confronting Continuation, 1921–1932

In December 1922, Carlos Montezuma decided to return home to a place where he had never lived. A physician, he knew that he had little time remaining. He boarded the train in Chicago one final time to make the long, familiar journey to Arizona to be with his Yavapai relatives. Montezuma was born in the 1860s, when tribes still could and did conduct raids on their enemies. Kidnapped by Pimas, the young Montezuma was sold to a non-Indian and raised in the Midwest and the East. He completed medical school in Chicago and eventually entered private practice there. As an adult, he traveled west to become reacquainted with relatives now living on the newly founded Fort McDowell reservation. He had witnessed an era in which his people had begun to transform their reservation into home, into a place that mattered, into a base to be safeguarded for future generations. Although he severely criticized the Bureau of Indian Affairs for its management of reservation life, his continuing association with his relatives at Fort McDowell had taught him that these communities must not be abandoned. During his life Montezuma helped his people stay, to ward off attempts to remove them from their small enclave. He got off the train in Phoenix and traveled out to Fort McDowell, where he refused the care of other doctors. Within a month he was dead. He was buried on the reservation that had never been his residence but had, in his final years, become his home.

In the last issue of his newsletter, *Wassaja,* Montezuma had provided his own epitaph. It addressed the concerns of the present, but it also underlined the certainty he and other Native Americans shared that Indians had a future: ". . . if the world be against us, let us not be dismayed, let us not be discouraged, let us look up and go ahead and fight on for freedom and citizenship of our people. If it means death, let us die on the pathway that leads to the emancipation of our race; keeping in our hearts that our children will pass over our graves to victory."

The final act in the dramatic life of Carlos Montezuma continues to inspire his people, but it also demonstrated, as early as the 1920s, that Indian reservations would remain. What kinds of lives were possible for their residents? Even with the damage caused by the allotment era, even with the onslaught of assimilation, Native peoples persisted. However, their lands, their schools, their health care all needed to be improved. In the 1920s, Americans had to confront the fact of Indian continuation. A national debate ensued over the future status of these first nations.

Failed Policies

The need for significant alteration of prevailing federal policies had been articulated by members of the Society of American Indians (SAI) and other critics. As the decade began, these dissenters did not have far to look for examples of ongoing problems with the administration of Indian affairs. The Osages and Muscogees of Oklahoma, the Pueblo Indian communities of the Southwest, and the Mescalero Apaches of New Mexico offered telling cases in point of why major changes had to occur.

The Osages were one of many tribes who had been moved to the Indian Territory. Their new home happened to be situated on one of the great oil fields in the region. Oil had been discovered under Osage land in 1896. Although the surface lands on the reservation fell prey to allotment in 1906, the subsurface rights remained an "underground reservation." Thus individuals, by virtue of membership in the tribe, were eligible to share in the sudden wealth. During the 1920s, despite impressive mismanagement and almost instantaneous corruption in the leasing of the fields, royalties on the sale of oil still came flooding into the Osages. Before the Great Depression and the plummeting of oil prices, they appeared to possess more wealth than one could possibly imagine. Other Americans were quick to learn of the "oil Indians," who reportedly were squandering their new-found fortunes on fancy cars and endless parties.

That fleeting image soon was replaced by a more familiar and enduring one—of Indians being overrun by outsiders seeking to obtain their own wealth from Native lands. In the matter of a few years—years marked by the marriage of Indian and non-Indian partners for reasons other than love, acts of violence, and a score of "unsolved" murders—the Osages lost most of their money and most of their control over their lands. The Oklahoma court system proved willing to facilitate this transfer of wealth. Attorneys representing non-Indian interests found ready allies in judges who quickly stamped approval on devious schemes to defraud the Osages. William K. Hale and his nephew Ernest Burkhart were two of a multitude of migrants who schemed to obtain wealth in Osage country. They eventually plotted to murder members of the family into which Burkhart had married in order to gain their inheritance. Osages were killed by bullets, poison, and explosives, before the Federal Bureau of Investigation took charge of solving a mystery that local authorities seemed unwilling and unable to untangle. Even after the oil boom ended, the oil resources that had not been depleted continued to prove a mixed blessing for the Osages. The tribe still struggled with an internal factionalism fueled by the problems of inheritance.

Nor were the Osages alone in facing problems resultant from the sudden influx of oil money. The Muscogees also occupied lands with considerable petroleum deposits, the discovery of which made some tribal members extraordinarily wealthy, while

leading to the dispossession of many more. Jackson Barnett (Muscogee) for example, became rich because of oil discovered on his
land. Soon after his financial status was public knowledge, he was
lured into the car of Anna Laura Lowe. Lowe, a former prostitute,
proceeded to get Barnett drunk, drive him to Coffeyville, Kansas,
marry him, and claim his wealth. Eventually Lowe's interest in
Barnett's estate was bought off by Commissioner of Indian Affairs
Charles Burke, who took control of Barnett's assets. Burke si-
phoned off $550,000 in Lowe's direction, landed $137,500 for her
attorney, and a fast $550,000 to the Baptist Home Missionary
Society, which was instructed to pay Barnett a yearly sum of
$20,000. This arrangement appeared less than ideal to the U.S.
congressional committee that investigated the matter in the late
1920s, to the legal guardian appointed for Barnett, and to a judge
to whom the guardian had appealed. Oil had brought wealth to
eastern Oklahoma, but relatively little of long-term benefit ac-
crued to Native peoples of the area, whose mineral holdings had
brought them little other than misery.

The Pueblo Indians of Arizona and New Mexico had resided
on their lands for centuries. Following the war with Mexico, the
Treaty of Guadalupe Hidalgo in 1848 brought U.S. claims of authority to the region. The granting of statehood to Arizona and
New Mexico territories in 1912 intensified further pressure by
non-Indians upon Native community lives and lands. Events of the
1910s and 1920s forced Pueblo Indians to realize that this new
presence, the federal government of the United States, could have
a major impact upon their religious traditions and their ability to
control their territory.

Leading federal officials still were influenced by the sentiments of Christian missionaries and their supporters within the
ranks of leading philanthropic organizations. Indian Rights Association president Herbert Welsh sounded the alarm in 1920 about
the "corrupting" influences of the Hopi Snake Dance. Welsh alleged that this ritual encouraged sexual permissiveness among its
participants. Welsh's colleague, Matthew K. Sniffen, editor of the
Association newsletter, *Indian Truth,* quickly followed up with assertions of the "immoral" tendencies encouraged by traditional

dances at other pueblos. Protestant missionaries who resented the Catholic ascendancy in Pueblo country joined the chorus of complaint. Seizing upon Indian religious ceremonies as obstacles that had prevented the tide of assimilation from fully washing over Native peoples, assimilationists argued that only through new restrictions upon Indian religious observances could proper progress be achieved.

In Commissioner of Indian Affairs Burke, such proponents had a steadfast ally. A former Congressman from South Dakota, Burke had no sympathy for the persistence of Indian traditions. Blithely disregarding constitutional separations between church and state, he ordered all Indian students at federal boarding schools to attend Christian church services on Sunday. Then he issued Circular 1665, on April 21, 1921, threatening participants in all Indian religious ceremonies with fines or imprisonment. Just to make sure no one misunderstood his intentions, Burke presented an addition to Circular 1665 on February 14, 1923, in which he proclaimed that many dances should be banned or at least held less frequently. The commissioner targeted certain dances as being so degraded that only those Indians fifty years of age or older could be permitted to indulge in them. Forty-nine year-olds evidently remained tender and vulnerable; Burke tried to send them and their younger counterparts to the sidelines.

In the midst of the Burke blockade, other developments vied for the attention of the Native peoples of New Mexico. As commissioner of Indian Affairs, Burke reported to the secretary of the interior. In the Harding administration, this person also happened to be a westerner. Albert Bacon Fall of New Mexico had a particular interest in Native lands in his state. An attorney, he had been an active participant in New Mexico territorial and state politics. In 1906 he purchased the Three Rivers Ranch, 106,000 acres of which adjoined the Mescalero Apache reservation. Joining forces with other wealthy New Mexicans, Fall succeeded in building a small empire of private, state, and federal lands totaling over a million acres. His influence and power encouraged his selection in 1912 by the state senate as one of the first two U.S. senators to represent New Mexico. Mescalero water resources were critical to

his Fall's overall plans for developing his allied holdings. He ma-
neuvered to obtain access to Mescalero water, but he had gained
only temporary and partial use of the resource when he became
secretary of the interior in 1921. By that time, Fall had suffered
various financial difficulties that prompted him to take more des-
perate measures. When Ernest Stecker, a longtime BIA employee,
objected to expanding Fall's diversion of reservation water, Fall
transferred him to another reservation. Fall also had pushed for allotment of Mescalero and for the opening of tribal lands more
completely to timber and mining interests. In 1919 Congress approved opening executive order reservations—those reserves established by presidential initiative rather than by congressional action—to mining. Of seventy-three leases granted at Mescalero
during Fall's tenure as secretary of the interior, ten were obtained
by Fall's daughter-in-law, son-in-law, and his ranch manager. Only an
outcry from the IRA forced Fall to exclude Mescalero from the law.

Fall had tried yet another means to diminish the Mescalero future. Immediately after he became a U.S. senator, he sponsored
two bills in Congress that would have established national parks in
the state. One of the two parks was to be carved out of Mescalero
land. Commissioner of Indian Affairs Robert Valentine objected to
one bill that called for the inclusion of Mescalero land in one of
the proposed parks; the other park failed to materialize because
the Bureau of Reclamation had other plans for the area around El-
ephant Butte. Fall thus failed, but when he assumed the post of interior secretary, he tried again, this time working through friends
in the region to advocate new versions of the previous measures as
well as other similar schemes. Corrupt, but not lacking in determination, the secretary of the interior seemed on the verge of ultimate triumph when a defender of Indian rights appeared to help
foil his plans.

Collier and the Pueblo Indians

This newcomer was John Collier, whose activities during the
1920s in New Mexico launched a remarkable and unlikely career.
Collier is best known for his own ideas and actions as commis-

sioner of Indian affairs during the administration of Franklin D. Roosevelt, but his activities a decade before the New Deal had prompted his selection for the post. The son of a former mayor of Atlanta, Collier had left the South to work in New York City in the early twentieth century. Collier's interests in the fate of foreign immigrants to the city found an outlet in working for the People's Institute. The People's Institute attempted to aid immigrant workers in the city through a variety of programs, ranging from cultural presentations to efforts to improve living conditions. Collier was impressed by the vitality and determination of immigrants to New York, but he worried about what they lost in coming to a country that seemed so insistent on their abandonment of different traditions and customs. He also agonized over the impact of urban life on all residents of the city. It appeared to Collier, as it did to many observers of the era, that the city denied its residents a real and supportive sense of community and individual self-worth. Collier's ideals did not always mesh with his modest administrative abilities or the political realities of New York. After encountering a series of disappointments to his often ambitious plans, he left the city, uncertain about his future. He worked in 1920 for the California State Housing and Immigration Commission before being forced to resign his position before year's end. Collier had gained the improbable assignment of directing the commission's community-organization program, but it soon became evident that his notions of community did not mirror those of powerful nativist groups in the state such as the Sons of the Golden West.

Collier then impulsively accepted the invitation of Mabel Dodge, to come visit her at Taos, New Mexico, where she now resided. Collier had known Dodge in New York. She was one of many people who had been drawn in the late 1910s to the extraordinary country of northern New Mexico. Dodge had divorced her husband, initiated a relationship with a man from Taos Pueblo, Antonio Luhan, and married him in 1923. She loved her new surroundings and spared no effort in recruiting a bevy of others, from Collier to D. H. Lawrence, to travel to Taos. Collier arrived there with his family less than six weeks after he had resigned his post in California. He remained in Taos for five months before going back to California. When Kate Vosburg of Azusa, California, contributed $10,000 to sponsor his proposed study of reservation conditions, Collier returned to New Mexico in September 1922. Nearly half a century later, he died in the Taos area which had become the center of his world.

In the life of Taos Pueblo itself, Collier discovered a group of people who had managed to combine the benefits of shared community values and beliefs with respect for the integrity of the individual. He concluded that Taos had over the centuries evolved into something that was precious and should be maintained. Taos Pueblo also offered something valuable to the United States; it could teach Americans that preservation of Native custom and tradition did not necessarily yield negative consequences for the mainstream society. Collier realized that he had stumbled into a situation that posed tremendous danger to all Indian nations of New Mexico. He therefore initiated a zealous campaign designed to save Indian lands.

The specific matter that launched the Collier crusade involved a bill concocted by Fall and proposed to Congress by New Mexico senator Holm Olaf Bursum. Bursum's bill was prompted by disputes over non-Indian land and water claims to the Pueblo estate. In essence the bill legitimized most claims of non-Indians who had resided for some time on Pueblo lands. It threw Pueblo water rights and land jurisdiction into the state court system, where the Indians obviously would be at a considerable disadvantage. The Pueblo peoples protested this usurpation, but Bursum had not been elected to represent Indian concerns.

Collier visited Pueblo villages, discussed the current situation with individuals and various governing bodies, and added to his rapidly increasing storehouse of knowledge about Pueblo history and culture. When he obtained a final version of the Bursum bill, he was armed and ready to respond. Collier and Stella Atwood, chair of the Indian welfare committee for the General Federation of Women's Clubs, wrote articles sympathetic to the Pueblos' position for *Survey,* an eastern magazine. Collier also penned a series of essays for *Sunset* magazine of California. In "Plundering the Pueblos," published in the January 1923 issue of *Sunset,* Collier demonstrated a flair for dramatic assertion, at times romantic over-statement, as well as his conviction of the importance of Indians to America. "The Pueblos of Zuni, Santo Domingo and Taos live on today," he proclaimed, "mysterious and colorful and vital from the ancient world." Now they faced a great challenge. "Can the Pueblo Indian communities today survive even if they receive justice?" "The answer," Collier suggested, "lies in history":

They have already survived four centuries of contact with the white man's world. Even those Pueblos whose condition is most piteous—Tesuque and San Ildefonso, starving, and riddled with preventable and curable disease—have not yet lost their own souls. Still through the veins of their members runs that fierce joy expressed in a dance and song which have lost none of their splendor. Still, and increasingly, they produce objects of beauty—vases and rings and graceful adobe dwellings. Still the members of the tribe are faithful to the tribe, and the old industry continues in the face of discouragements which would disintegrate most white communities. . . . They have as much to teach to the white man as they have to learn from him. They belong to the future as much as to the past. They are a national asset; and the Bursum bill, which is a blow at them, is a blow at an innocent, helpless and priceless part of America's cultural life.

On November 5, 1922, the All Pueblo Council convened at Santo Domingo and signified its opposition to the bill and its willingness to dispatch representatives to Washington, D.C., to plead their case. Two months later Fall resigned, driven from office by the Teapot Dome scandal. Collier and the Pueblo delegates traveled to Washington via Chicago and New York, galvanizing opposition to the Bursum Bill along the way. They and Atwood appeared before a Senate committee, demonstrating the potential possessed by Indians and their allies to speak out effectively in a national arena.

Collier had forged personal and political connections across the country. His efforts clearly established the foundation for both his own future, including an extended term as commissioner of Indian Affairs, as well the possibility of a serious reexamination of federal Indian policy. During the remainder of the 1920s, he continued to lobby and fight for the rights of Native peoples to maintain their cultures and retain their remaining land and natural resources. When Burke convinced Montana representative Scott Leavitt to introduce a bill in 1926 that, among other provisions, outlawed traditional Indian forms of marriage and divorce, Collier lead a successful campaign to prevent its passage.

Rights, Opportunities, and Identity

Throughout the lower forty-eight states and the territory of Alaska, Native peoples worked in this era to realize rights and gain opportunities. In Alaska, the Alaska Native Brotherhood (ANB) had been founded in Sitka in 1912; a related, although significantly less influential organization, the Alaska Native Sisterhood was founded three years later. The ANB had been started by thirteen people, twelve of whom were Tlingit. Its membership remained concentrated in southeast Alaska and mostly limited to the Tlingits and Haidas, but by 1920 it was beginning to mature into an organization that could more effectively become engaged in issues affecting all of Alaska's aboriginal peoples. In that year William Paul, a Tongass Tlingit, began to assume a leadership role in the ANB. Paul had attended Carlisle and gone on to gain a law degree, becoming the first Alaskan Native attorney and, in 1924, the first Native elected to the territorial legislature. Through his successful defense of his great-uncle, a Tlingit leader who had been charged with a felony for voting in a local election, Paul established the right to vote for all Alaska Natives. In 1929 Paul and the ANB also filed legal claims to title to ancestral Tlingit lands, thus initiating the modern land claims movement in Alaska. The 1920s thus marked a crucial period of growth for the ANB and the emergence of William Paul as an important Native leader within Alaska.

At the other end of North America, Native groups in the East, like the Nanticokes of Delaware and the Mashpees of Massachusetts, asserted their rights as separate communities. Because they were perceived as persons of color, if not always acknowledged as Indians, Nanticoke children generally attended separate schools and Nanticoke Christians worshipped in separate churches. The beginning of the 1920s marked a reassertion of Nanticoke identity, with the election of William Russel Clark as chief and the incorporation of the Nanticoke Indian Association under Delaware law. Through their incorporation, charter, and bylaws, the Nanticokes obtained a form of state acknowledgment of their status as Indians and established a precedent followed by other Indian groups in the Carolinas, Rhode Island, and Virginia. The Nanticoke Indian Association soon began to sponsor an annual festival or powwow.

Until the twentieth century, by virtue of their location, the Mashpees had remained largely apart from non-Indian towns and from other Indian groups. The new century, however, brought with it a steady increase of non-Indians living or vacationing on Cape Cod. As the Mashpees started to confront the specter of this demographic transition, they realized a cultural revitalization through which their identity as Indians was reaffirmed. Members of the tribe sought out other nearby Indian groups in Gay Head and Herring Pond to form in 1928 a new organization—the Wampanoag Nation. The organization soon held its first powwow at Mashpee, building upon the annual summer homecoming, an event more than two centuries old. The August event had something for everyone. The first day included a speech by Harvard University president A. Lawrence Lowell (a summer resident of the area), a peace pipe ceremony, and speeches emphasizing Wampanoag identity. Day two began with a commemoration of the death of the great seventeenth-century Wampanoag leader, King Philip, and concluded with a ten-mile race and baseball games pitting the Mashpees against the Narragansetts and the married Mashpee women against the single Mashpee women. In addition to a beauty contest—won, perhaps predictably, by a Mashpee contestant—the final day included games, songs, and dances combining elements and features of Mashpee and other Indian groups' traditions. Although neither tribe, like other New England tribes, was federally recognized, these gatherings brought their people together during a challenging transitional era, and demonstrated both to themselves and to outsiders the firm determination that these communities would not disappear.

A continuing Indian presence was recognized in the passage in 1924 of the Citizenship Act, which finally granted citizenship to all American Indians. By the time the law passed, roughly two out of every three Native Americans already had been accorded this status, including those who had taken allotments or who had served in World War I. Citizenship in and of itself surely did not change the economic difficulties plaguing many Indian communities, and many Indians regarded the matter as irrelevant because of their perspectives on sovereignty. Yet because its absence had been so insulting and because it had been singled out as a specific goal to be achieved, gaining U.S. citizenship mattered very much to many individuals. However, citizenship itself neither magically assimilated Indians nor guaranteed them full rights as Americans. Upon becoming citizens Indians did not automatically discard their separate languages or other cultural traditions, as the assimilationists had assumed they would. And, as many minority individuals can attest, citizenship by no means opened all the doors to Indians desiring to participate fully in American life. Voting offered a telling case in point. After 1924, though all Indians were citizens, they remained restricted in their ability to exercise the franchise other than in tribal elections. Such restrictions obviously reinforced tribal loyalties rather than reduced them. Western and midwestern states discouraged Indian voting in nontribal elections in ways not unlike the manner in which southern states denied the vote to Black voters. Voters had to be "civilized," said California, Minnesota, North Dakota, Oklahoma, and Wisconsin, leaving interpretation of the definition of who was and was not civilized up to voting officials at the local level. Voters had to be taxpayers, said Arizona, Idaho, Nevada, New Mexico, Utah, and Washington; since reservation lands were not subject to state property taxes, Indians, officials in these states contended, should not go to the polls. For good measure, Arizona, Nevada, and Utah specifically declared reservation residents ineligible for participation in the electoral process. If Indian participation in World War I had been needed to prompt the final granting of universal citizenship, then Native contributions to World War II would have to be recognized before full voting rights could become a reality in all states. Returning Indian veterans in Arizona and New Mexico helped eliminate the final official restrictions in 1948 in these states. In Maine a comparable victory was achieved in 1954.

The attempt to establish equal rights for Natives accompanied the ongoing need to develop and diversify Indian economies. Cattle ranching remained as a viable option for many Native communities in the West, even though the leasing of reservation lands worked against the evolution of what can be termed a successful Indian cattle industry. A determined individual agent, however, could make a difference. On the San Carlos reservation in Arizona, for example, the arrival of James B. Kitch in 1923 opened the door to rapid expansion of Apache cattle ranching. Kitch learned that half of the families at San Carlos already had become involved in this pursuit, but they only owned 2,500 head of cattle and leasing had limited further expansion. Through Kitch's persistent efforts through the remainder of the 1920s and much of the 1930s, non-Indian ranchers were denied extension of their leases or, in some instances, had their permits revoked, and Apache cattle ranchers were thus able to expand the quantity of their herds and were encouraged to improve the quality of them as well. This transition was not accomplished without a fight, for by the mid-1920s the ranching industry in general had confronted falling prices for beef and rising costs of doing business; lessees complained bitterly about both the curtailment of their access to reservation lands and growing competition from their Indian neighbors.

Tourism and the Arts

The growth of tourism in Indian country also offered possibilities for economic development. Native Americans were no more enthusiastic about the newcomers who ventured into their midst than were non-Indian residents, but they began to appreciate the opportunities for financial gain the travelers represented. As national and regional transportation systems continued to improve and expand, many urban and suburban Americans started to explore previously isolated terrain. The mass production and new affordability of the automobile combined with the development of paved highways to prompt a new wave of intraAmerican tourism. In North Carolina, the sale of Eastern Cherokee crafts increased significantly, so that by the end of the 1920s the community realized at least $5,000 a year from the sale of baskets to tourists. In addition, the major transcontinental railroads vigorously promoted travel about their routes to destinations in or near Indian country.

Through this era Indian communities did not benefit as directly from the tourist trade as they would later in the century. However, many recognized the potential for financial gain, especially from the sale of various forms of Native art: pottery, baskets, weavings, jewelry, paintings, and so forth. Often the very existence of the tourist trade inspired the transformation of pots and baskets used in everyday life into products designed specifically for commercial sale. In California, for example, small tribes such as the Chemehuevis and Pomos became noted for their exceptionally fine baskets. Individual artists, such as the great Washo basket weaver Daotsali, gained a reputation not only in the immediate vicinity of their homes, but regionally and eventually nationally. Even at the beginning of the 1900s there existed two quite different but lucrative markets for the inexpensive curio souvenir and the painstaking product that reflected the highest level of talent. Marketing proved crucial to the distribution of Native art, as owners of trading posts and other stores sought to cultivate not only the business of the passing tourist but also that of the discriminating purchaser who might never venture far from home. Entrepreneurs like Juan Lorenzo Hubbell, whose trading empire extended from his headquarters at Ganado, Arizona, succeeded in developing good markets in both inexpensive and fine Navajo weavings. Customers could order Navajo rugs based upon the illustrations they reviewed in catalogs or could visit and inspect the products first hand. In either instance, people such as Hubbell played a vital role in the process, not only in brokering the exchange but even in encouraging the use of new designs or colors.

Tourism within Indian country often was linked with travel to the national parks or monuments which bordered reservations and, indeed, had often been carved from Native lands. The great hotels of such national parks as Glacier, Grand Canyon, or Yosemite featured the work of Indian artists, usually from the immediate area, but occasionally from farther afield. The Great Northern Railway used the Blackfeet as a romantic symbol to draw tourists to Glacier, praising in its promotional literature the "tribesmen who live in the very shadows of the 'Shining Mountains' and whose traditions have so enriched the area." Starting in 1928 and continuing for thirty years the railway employed on its calendars portraits of the Blackfeet by artist Winold Reiss. Nowhere was this linkage more striking nor more successful than the partnership between and among the Santa Fe Railway, the Harvey Houses (a chain of hotels, noted for their good restaurants), the BIA, and the national parks and monuments of Arizona and New Mexico. The Santa Fe used Pueblo motifs and images of such pueblos as Taos in its advertisements, trying to lure the easterner or midwesterner to visit the "Land of Pueblos." A typical advertisement spoke of the traveler being able to witness "age-old ceremonial dances, or fascinating rituals" as well as "watch the Indians making pottery and silver-and-turquoise jewelry." The patented "Indian detours" run by the Fred Harvey Company allowed tourists to stay in good hotels, enjoy fine meals, and journey to Pueblo villages or other Indian communities. The company organized these side trips to encourage visitors to venture into country they otherwise might have bypassed.

Infusion of tourist dollars into the Pueblo villages inevitably prompted a fundamental transition in their economies, from subsistence to cash. Pueblo farming could not maintain an adequate financial base for the people. Throughout the United States small farms had declined in their viability. In New Mexico Anglo and Hispanic land claims and occupations restricted the acreage villagers could use. Arts and crafts thus offered a badly needed stimulus. The experience of San Ildefonso Pueblo constitutes a dramatic illustration.

Prior to 1900 little about San Ildefonso pottery distinguished it from the ware produced by other villages. The ready availability of tin and enameled containers discouraged most villagers from making pots out of clay. After the arrival of the Santa Fe Railway in the late nineteenth century, the early tourist trade actually undermined the quality and the size of San Ildefonso pottery; most travelers preferred small, cheap pots, which made good souvenirs. Then in 1907 the School of American Research of Santa Fe, supervised by Edgar L. Hewitt, an archaeologist of Tuscarora descent, began to conduct work near San Ildefonso. In the course of the excavations, Hewitt and his co-workers, including San Ildefonso laborers such as Julian Martinez, uncovered pieces of old pots dating back hundreds of years. Hewitt was struck by the artistry of the designs on these pots, as was Martinez's wife, Maria. Hewitt asked Maria Martinez if she could recreate the polychrome pottery. As it turned out, she could. So commenced a veritable revolution in the world of Pueblo art.

Maria and Julian Martinez worked together. She became a master in creating the pot itself—reaching new heights in regard to shape, firing, and finish; he decorated the pot, using his artistic ability to adapt pre-contact and nineteenth-century designs. He was also inspired by the pioneering work of Nampeyo, the great Hopi-Tewa potter. In 1919 Maria and Julian Martinez began to redefine the look of San Ildefonso pottery by producing the black-on-black ware that would gain international renown. They did not keep their methods to themselves, but shared them with other potters in the village. By 1925 the appearance of San Ildefonso pottery was established. The Santa Fe Indian Market, set up in 1922, provided a showcase for the work of artists from San Ildefonso and elsewhere; construction of a bridge over the Rio Grande in 1924 allowed potential buyers to have access to the potters in the village itself. Maria Martinez at first was astonished at the prices her work began to command. When collector Henry Dendahl asked her how much she wanted for a large, particularly beautiful pot—now in a Santa Fe museum—she told him, "Oh, you can give me whatever you want." When he gave her $40 and three shawls, she recalled, she nearly fell down. Maria Martinez earned over $5,000 a year from her work by the 1930s, making her wealthy indeed by the income standards of the era. Her success, both artistically and financially, helped inspire many other aspiring Native artists.

Work, Community, and Government

Despite such positive advances, the overall economic picture on many reservations remained discouraging. Some Native Americans chose to leave their home communities for seasonal employment as agricultural laborers or for more permanent off-reservation jobs. Historian Kurt M. Peters (Blackfeet) learned that in 1901 his grandfather, then fifteen years old, left home to go to work for the railroad. He continued in his railroad section maintenance job for the next half a century. Many Indians who lived near the lines of the great western railroads were recruited to work for them. SAI member Charles Daganett served for a number of years as the Indian Office's national employment supervisor. He helped negotiate contracts with individual Indians to do the hard work on the railroad that many other Americans did not find desirable. In Pueblo communities such as Acoma and Laguna, working for the Santa Fe railway evolved into an ongoing means to keep families together and to earn needed income. Men and women who assumed such jobs sometimes formed "colonies" of Native people in the off-reservation main railroad towns, from Winslow, Arizona, to Richmond, California.

Mohawks from Caughnauwaga in Quebec and Akwesasne in New York began their migrations off their reservations and into North American cities, beckoned by available construction work on bridges and buildings. The use of steel in construction made possible the skyscrapers of New York City and other major cities; the Mohawks earned a reputation for their proficiency in working fearlessly upon "high steel." A new tradition had become established. Everywhere you looked in New York City you saw structures that the Mohawks helped to build, from the George Washington Bridge to the Empire State Building. As more Mohawks began to settle their families in a Brooklyn neighborhood, the local grocery stores soon featured a new item on their shelves— Quaker white enriched and degerminated corn meal—preferred for the making of a traditional Mohawk bread. The new downtown of Caughnauwaga, the people said, now could be found in Brooklyn.

In Nevada, Northern Paiutes and Western Shoshones also engaged in work for wages in order to bring in needed cash, but also as a means to keep family and relatives together. Although they had considerable interest in developing their own farms and ranches, Paiutes and Shoshones were hamstrung by federal policies that pushed for development of regional lands at the expense of the needs of the indigenous occupants. Passage of the Reclamation Act in 1902 clearly benefited new and recent non-Indian migrants to western Nevada more than it did Indian community members, who often worked for the farms and ranches belonging to these latecomers. However, Northern Paiutes in the Fallon area attempted with some success to combine wage labor with traditional subsistence activities. The money they earned from part-time jobs enabled them to purchase needed material items, actually giving them back more time for hunting and gathering, activities that yielded valuable foods but, equally significant, helped develop important aspects of Native culture, such as associations with kin and lessons learned from older relatives. Among the Western Shoshones scattered across the northern half of the state, fandangos allowed hundreds of people to congregate for traditional pastimes such as round dances, songs, handgames, and feasts, as well as athletic competition, including racing, on foot and on horse back, rodeos, and baseball. Baseball games matched different Shoshones communities or pitted Shoshone teams against White teams. In 1921, at one fandango, the Battle Mountain Shoshone team defeated the White team from the same town.

In the 1920s, Natives continued to pursue other games handed down from one generation to the next. Sadie Brower Neakok, an Inupiat (Eskimo) woman from the Barrow, Alaska, area recalled that in the summer, following chores, young people would "all gang up down on the beach with all kinds of competitions done with bones or old spike nails, heavy objects. . . . You each had five pieces of stick or five rocks that, every time you win or come closer than your opponent, then that rock went to your side; you play until all the rocks on are one side or another. . . ." Grownups often joined in, with married people sometimes competing against the unmarried.

More remote areas like Barrow, removed from earlier gold rushes, still reflected more uninterrupted continuity with past economies and societies, but even in northern Alaska commercial activities had an impact. Commercial whalers reduced the whale population and introduced new forms of technology to whaling and hunting. Some of these non-Indian whalers married Inupiat women. Sadie Brower was the "mixed-blood" daughter of Charles Brower and Asianggataq. She grew up in a world where, even with attendance at school and church in the village, one could enjoy maktak (dried seal meat) in summer and hear stories in the winter, the appropriate time to relate such accounts. An old man, Suakpak, enthralled youngsters with tales about animals and "boogie men stories" designed to scare and enlighten.

In one Indian community after another in the 1920s, one witnessed, then, a mix of new people and old customs; one saw Native peoples attempting to find a proper way to navigate through the complicated currents that swirled around them. The old customs had great staying power, but the new economic forces unleashed through the allotment era did threaten to fragment what once had been a cohesive world. Large, multigenerational households helped maintain languages, for example, and served as a kind of buffer against imposed, sudden change. Nonetheless, at Crow and elsewhere, as Frederick Hoxie has observed, there were "crossing trajectories of cultural growth and economic decline." Reduction of reservation acreage through cession, allotment, and eventual sale, combined with leasing, eroded Indian efforts to become economically more self-sufficient. Frustrated by limited opportunities, more than a few Native individuals departed the reservation for extended periods of time. In some instances, they never returned.

Thousands of Indians migrated to urban areas in search of employment. The main thrust of urban migration did not occur until after World War II, but Native Americans moved into towns bordering reservations and into cities throughout the twentieth century. SAI leaders such as Gertrude Bonnin, Carlos Montezuma, and Arthur C. Parker chose life in the city. So, too, by the 1920s had a host of other less prominent individuals.

These urban migrants did not necessarily seek anonymity or assimilation in their new surroundings. Many Native people joined urban organizations that promoted a sense of continuing Indian identity, emphasizing a new commonality as Indians rather than specific tribal identities. In Minneapolis, Indians joined a club associated with the American Indian Association and Tepee Order, a fraternal society. However, the proximity of Minneapolis to Anishinabe country and the particular economic problems besetting Minnesota Anishinabe reservations encouraged the formation of other groups, such as the Twin Cities Chippewa Council. Some who moved to the city chafed at federal restrictions over reservations and individual options on these lands. In Minneapolis and elsewhere many such migrants lobbied for per capita distribution of tribal assets. This tendency resurfaced in the termination era following World War II.

The reservation remained home for most American Indians during the 1920s. In this setting, Indian communities struggled with economic development, the evolution of tribal government, and the provision of health care. As the example of Cheyenne River demonstrates, the existence of a tribal council could make a major difference in addressing central issues facing the people. The process of election to the council mattered considerably in the kind of power council members might wield. On the Wind River reservation in Wyoming, home to the Northern Arapahos and Eastern Shoshones, each tribe separately selected its representatives. Wind River had three governing entities—separate councils for each tribe as well as a joint business council. On such reservations, the joint councils naturally labored against divisions between the two Indian groups; however, common concerns such as leases, payments, and looking after the resources of the reservation, could bind a joint council together.

On some reservations in the 1920s or with newly established councils in the 1930s, religious societies or other preexisting ceremonial organizations influenced the authority the new councils attempted to assume. At Wind River, a Drum Ceremony provided the forum for the selection of council representatives. On this occasion, important in its own right for its symbolic linking of the people with the Creator, elders or a councilman acting under the authority of the elders chose the new members. These people, of course, had to have a high regard for traditional religious practices and the ongoing traditions of the people, including the role of elders. Men such as Henry Lee Tyler and Robert Friday served on the Arapaho Council throughout the 1920s. Tyler had gained his initial education at Fort Washakie on the reservation and then left for three years to attend Genoa Indian School in Nebraska. Friday had attended both Carlisle and Haskell. Their command of English as well as Arapahoe were perceived as assets. Tyler and Friday also remained adherents to traditional religious ceremonies. The leadership of these talented men allowed a returned student to put to use new linguistic skills and an awareness of the outside world to try to reach goals that remained consistent with a more conservative social order.

Wind River was hardly unique in this regard. Some returned students had become converts to Christianity and their attempted assumption of authority would be greeted differently, but in many Native communities, individuals comparable to Tyler and Friday played the role of cultural broker. This transition could not occur overnight and obviously was subject to a host of local variables. Among the Southern Arapahos in Oklahoma, Jesse Rowlodge followed a path not unlike that of Tyler and Friday. He grew up in a traditional family, but left to attend Haskell in 1904, after completing the first six grades in the local boarding school. By the 1920s, recently married and having gained experience as a BIA employee and a farmer, he was ready to engage in tribal politics. Rowlodge participated in both the Sun Dance and peyote ceremonies and belonged to a Christian church, but his multiple religious affiliations only widened his circle of allies and friends. During the decade, Rowlodge was one of a number of well-educated Arapaho men who went to Washington to try to assert the needs of his tribe. The transition toward a greater role for such individuals and for a more authoritative role for the general council did not occur without some division; the old chiefs and people loyal to them were not always pleased with the emergence of this new form of political power. Such divisions sometimes fostered factionalism within the council and worked against its overall influence.

Moving Toward Reform

Even the restructured councils had little effect on one of the major problems facing reservations: inadequate health care. In fact, the desire to improve health conditions in large measure helped inspire the cry for reform of prevailing federal policies. Tuberculosis and trachoma, an infectious eye disease, had persisted on reservations from the turn of the century. A penny-pinching Congress acknowledged the problem, but failed to approve sufficient funding to effectively halt incidence of the diseases. Albert Fall's successor as secretary of the interior in 1923, Hubert Work, had served as president of the American Medical Association. Distressed at what he had learned about contemporary conditions in Native communities, he pushed Congress to increase its appropriation. Congress responded to Work's plea, nearly doubling the amount from $370,000 in 1923 to $700,000 in 1926. However, the increase in funding did not result in immediate improvement in health care. A much publicized but experimental approach in treating trachoma proved largely futile, and government officials refused to change prevailing approaches to other diseases.

Work attempted to respond in other ways to the growing clamor for reform. Soon after he assumed his position, he appointed a Committee of One Hundred to review the contemporary status of American Indians. The group ranged in its eclectic membership from William Jennings Bryan to John Collier, and from Pershing to Kroeber. The IRA was well represented. Indians participated in the committee. Arthur C. Parker was named as its chair and, among others, Henry Roe Cloud, Sherman Coolidge, Charles Eastman, Philip Gordon, and Thomas Sloan contributed to its efforts. In its quick survey and response to Work and the new president, Calvin Coolidge, the committee pointed out the need for more Indians to attend colleges and universities, for better health care programs on the reservations, and for other such improvements, but could concur on no specific recommendations. Clearly a more comprehensive survey was required.

For this assignment Work turned to the Brookings Institution. Accustomed to studying entities from the Patent Office to the Alaskan Engineering Commission, the Institute was an obvious choice for a detailed examination of a bureaucracy. Institute staff member Lewis Meriam directed the study and the ensuing report, formally entitled *The Problem of Indian Administration,* but soon known simply as the Meriam Report. Meriam and his nine principal associates, including Henry Roe Cloud, devoted seven months to field work before organizing and compiling their findings, which they presented to Work on February 21, 1928. The report considered eight subjects: policy; health; education; economic conditions; family and community life and the activities of women; migration; legal aspects; and missionary activities. With an index, it totaled 872 pages.

Meriam's report represented a ringing indictment of federal Indian policy. "An overwhelming majority of the Indians are poor, even extremely poor," it began. Indian health compared badly to that of the rest of the U.S. population. Living conditions included a poor diet, inadequate housing, and limited sanitary facilities. Indian families generally had low incomes. The allotment policy had failed. An adequate public health system had not been developed. Boarding schools were characterized by dietary deficiencies, overcrowded dormitories, student labor, inadequate medical care, and an inappropriate curriculum. Leasing of Indian lands must be curtailed. Taken in sum, *The Problem of Indian Administration* hardly could have been more damning in its assessment of how the federal government had failed to carry out its trust responsibilities. Its lack of bombast and its dimensions helped insure its reputation as a serious, thorough study. At the same time, its very title spoke to its emphasis and its inherent limits. The report analyzed the failures of the BIA to achieve its goals, but it did not question fully the ultimate nature of those objectives. In the end the Meriam Report appeared far more critical of bureaucratic inefficiency and incompetence than of the assumption that Indians should be fully assimilated into American life.

The subsequent administration of President Herbert Hoover in certain respects presaged the forthcoming "Indian New Deal." For example, the new director of Indian education, W. Carson Ryan, had been on Meriam's staff and appreciated the need for change. Ryan, who would continue in his post during the first years of Collier's term as commissioner, wished to reduce the number of boarding schools and the percentage of Indian students who attended these institutions. He also sought to establish community schools that reflected the needs and concerns of the particular locales in which they were situated. These were laudable objectives, but Ryan found it difficult to move quickly to achieve them in full measure. Thus, by the beginning of the 1930s, the reformers had little patience with his seeming lack of progress. Ryan did succeed in closing a few boarding schools and in converting a few others to day schools, but the growth in the number of Indians attending school meant that by 1933 there were more Native children in boarding schools than there had been in 1928. To make things more difficult, congressional representatives resisted school closures in their districts. When Ryan proposed closing two of the oldest and most well-known boarding schools, Haskell and Chemawa, he met considerable resistance as well from Indian communities whose children had attended these institutions; Haskell and Chemawa remained open. In other matters, Commissioner of Indian Affairs Charles J. Rhoads and Secretary of the Interior Ray Lyman Wilbur mirrored the president in their reluctance to embrace anything other than cautious, incremental progress. As this period drew to a close, Native Americans could only hope that better days lay ahead.

CHAPTER THREE

Initiatives and Impositions, 1933–1940

Alice Lee Jemison could not believe it. John Collier was going to be the next commissioner of Indian affairs. The young Seneca woman declared in no uncertain terms that this was a very bad idea. Writing for the *Buffalo Evening News* early in 1933, she wrapped up her anger and frustration in one gloriously long, indignant sentence: "We are weary unto death," she groaned, "of the propaganda for a continuance of the bureau to further 'protect' the Indian which is spread by the so-called Indian Defense Association and other societies which are sponsored by wealthy people in the name of charity, many of whom have never seen an Indian, would not know one unless he had on full tribal regalia, have absolutely no knowledge of reservations or actual conditions thereon, but who think they know exactly what is best for the Indians."

Born in 1901 in Silver Creek, New York, adjacent to the Cattaraugus Seneca reservation in New York, Jemison was the daughter of a Seneca mother and Cherokee father, who had both attended Hampton. She was proud of her Seneca heritage and confident of her own ability and the ability of other Indians to make their own way in the world without federal assistance or intervention. Jemison expressed her anger at a government that did not respect Iroquois sovereignty and did nothing about the contamination of Cattaraugus Creek or tuberculosis at Cattaraugus. Married at the age of eighteen, separated at twenty-seven, she abandoned hopes of becoming an attorney in order to work to support her two children and her mother. Through the years she gained employment as a beautician, a Bureau of the Census employee, a clerk, a confectionery store manager, a dressmaker, a factory worker, a farmer, a free-lance journalist, a housekeeper, a paralegal researcher, a peddler, a political lobbyist, a practical nurse, a secretary, and a theater usher. She knew what it was like to be poor, to be out of work, and to do a job she would prefer not to do. Influenced by the writings of Carlos Montezuma, she had promoted the candidacy of Joseph Latimer, Montezuma's attorney, for commissioner of the Bureau of Indian Affairs. If Latimer got the position, she believed, he would do what Montezuma had always recommended: abolish the BIA. If John Collier thought Indians all over America were going to welcome him with open arms as the next commissioner, Alice Lee Jemison would soon let him know otherwise.

Collier's Perspective

When John Collier was appointed commissioner of Indian affairs in 1933, he became the head of the very agency of which he had been so disapproving. Changing how the BIA did business represented a major challenge. Many federal employees remained wedded to assimilation, and they were not about to change their minds. Non-Indians with vested interests in Indian country—primarily those who had access to Indian land or wished to convert Indians to Christianity—worried about any significant change to the situation they had enjoyed for so long. More than a few Indians assumed that nothing good could come out of Washington; if the commissioner of Indian Affairs proposed something, nothing positive lay behind it. In addition, the long era of Americanization had affected the perspectives of many Indians. Native Americans who had moved away from more traditional beliefs or surroundings saw Collier as a person attempting to move the clock back rather than forward.

Collier did not make any strong distinction between the different problems faced by different Indian peoples. In 1934 he told members of the Iroquois nations—the Cayugas, Mohawks, Oneidas, Onondagas, Senecas, and Tuscaroras—that federal policy toward it "should become exactly what the policy is toward the Blackfeet, the Sioux, the Papagos, the Pueblos, or the Navajos." Alice Jemison and other Iroquois, however, did not see themselves as members of just another Native confederation. Their pride in their unique history and heritage encouraged a resentment toward Collier, given his apparent willingness to lump them together with other peoples, with whom, correctly or incorrectly, the Iroquois felt they had little in common. Collier failed to realize the degree to which different Indian peoples had not only different histories but also different perspectives and different needs.

But the new commissioner did appreciate the resilience of Indian cultures and the potential that Native communities had to retain or revive their languages, beliefs, and values. Collier thus differed from his predecessors in his judgment of the place of Native Americans in national life. He was a cultural pluralist before the term "cultural pluralism" became a part of the American vocabulary. However, he also often believed the ends justified the means, and he proved willing to impose his ideas in much the same way as assimilationists had in previous generations. Because of the length of his tenure, his activist nature, the power he wielded, and the complicated and enduring legacy of the era, Collier demands extended attention in any analysis of the 1930s. After his departure from office in 1945, no commissioner, or no non-Indian for that matter, would ever play such a dominant role in Indian affairs.

After Collier became commissioner he moved promptly to try to put some of his ideas into practice. Aided by his associates, including Assistant Commissioner William Zimmerman, Solicitor Nathan Margold, and Margold's assistant Felix Cohen, Collier wanted Indian tribes "to develop their own life in their own patterns, not as segregated minorities but as noble elements in our common life." In *Indians of the Americas,* Collier later spoke of Indians as "perduring" and emphasized how Indian communities over time had demonstrated their ability to flourish when they had received the right kind of "social rain." The new commissioner intended to provide that necessary nourishment. Even given the damage of the past half century, tribes could experience new prosperity if certain objectives could be realized. Indian land bases had to be consolidated and expanded. Indians must enjoy all the freedoms, including religious freedom, that other Americans possessed. They must also be able to govern themselves more fully, develop their economies, and be able to articulate their own sense of who they were and who they could become. All dimensions of Indian cultures, including language, art, and belief, should be fully supported.

Analysis of Collier as commissioner has been largely limited to the Indian Reorganization Act of 1934, the central piece of legislation to be passed during his administration. It also emerged as a considerably modified version of Collier's ideals, for it did not encompass all of what Collier tried to achieve or what this period represented.

Cultural Considerations

In 1934 the BIA issued the following order: "No interference with Indian religious life will be hereafter tolerated. The cultural history of Indians is in all respects to be considered equal to that of any non-Indian group. And it is desirable that Indians be bilingual—fluent and literate in English, and fluent in their vital, beautiful, and efficient native languages." This statement offered a striking contrast with the federal philosophy of the past half century.

As a result of Collier's order, specific steps were taken to bolster Indian religious freedom. Now the Native American Church could hold its ceremonies as it wished. When Senator Dennis Chavez of New Mexico introduced legislation in 1937 to prohibit the interstate transportation of peyote, Collier organized sufficient opposition to kill the bill. The commissioner and his aides for education, Carson Ryan and then Willard Beatty, worked to reduce the percentage of Indian students attending boarding schools, where students often had been compelled to attend Christian church services. They also prohibited federal employees from forcing Indian children to go to such services. Indian communities were free to conduct traditional ceremonies without harassment by the BIA; this freedom encouraged the revival of the Sun Dance and other ceremonies that had been outlawed in the past. Freedom of worship did have its ironic consequences, because not only had the doors been opened to the Sun Dance, but as well to the pentecostal and evangelical churches and the Church of Jesus Christ of Latter-day Saints, who largely had been shut out of the division of Indian country for missionary work more than half a century before. These groups quickly became much more active in their missionary efforts and enjoyed some immediate success. Their presence, in turn, contributed to an overall increase in competing missionary activity on various reservations.

The BIA encouraged the development of new written versions of various Indian languages. John Harrington, Robert Young, and others labored to create orthographies that could be used in bilingual curricular materials. By 1940 linguists such as Edward Kennard and Young had begun to work with Native linguists like William Morgan (Navajo) to develop bilingual materials for the schools. Series such as "The Little Herder" and the "Singing Sioux Cowboy" by Ann Nolan Clark were published in bilingual editions and illustrated by Native artists. Now Navajo, Sioux, and Pueblo Indian pupils could read about children from their own communities. In *Little Herder in Spring,* the text read:

THE HOGAN	HOOGHAN
My mother's hogan is dry	Shimá bighan góne' hóółtsaih
against the gray mists	'ahbínígo
of morning.	'áhí bee halbáa ndi.
My mother's hogan is warm	Shimá bighan góne' honeezdo
against the gray cold	'ahbínígo
of morning.	hak'az bee halbáa ndi.
I sit in the middle	Hooghan shináz'áago
of its rounded walls,	hoogahn góne' sédáh

walls that my father built
of juniper and good earth.
Walls that my father blessed
with song and corn pollen.
Here in the middle
of my mother's hogan
I sit
because I am happy.

shizhé'é gad dóó łeezh
hoogahn yee 'áyiilaayígíí.
Shizhé'é hooghan tádídíín yee
da'azhdlishígíí.
T'áá kwe'é
shimá bighan góné'
sédáh,
shił hózhóǫgo biniinaa.

Many Indian languages remained without a modern orthography by the conclusion of Collier's term, but a start had been made and a principle underscored. Through the newsletter published under Beatty's term as director of education, BIA teachers also were encouraged to be supportive of cultural pluralism. Anthropologist Ruth Underhill and others wrote articles clarifying the value of traditional Native customs or comparing the evolution of Indian practices or rituals with celebrations such as Easter, which Underhill labeled "our heathen festival."

Native artistic expression gained strong support. Through the provisions of the Works Progress Administration, Indian artists painted murals in public buildings and in new tribal buildings like the Navajo Tribal Council chambers in Window Rock, Arizona. Forty-five Indian painters and other artists from New Mexico painted murals and made pottery, rugs, and other works of art for Indian community centers, hospitals, and schools. Monroe Tsatoke (Kiowa) participated in the painting of murals for the Oklahoma Historical Society building in Oklahoma City. Other prominent Oklahoma Indian artists, including James Auchiah (Kiowa), Acee Blue Eagle (Muscogee), Woody Crumbo (Muscogee-Potawatomi), and Stephen Mopope (Kiowa) worked on other structures. In New York Arthur C. Parker directed a very successful Seneca Arts Project, largely underwritten by Works Progress Administration funds. It featured the work of important artists such as Jessie J. Cornplanter, the best Iroquois mask carver of the day, and painter Ernest Smith.

A new Indian Arts and Crafts Board under the direction of Rene d'Harnoncourt offered support. D'Harnoncourt was a forceful and energetic administrator. He encouraged more vigorous efforts to publicize and sell Native work. He also contended that Indian artistic expression should be allowed to evolve, rather than remaining frozen in place in regard to form and style. The Golden Gate International Exposition of San Francisco in 1939 and a special exhibition at the Museum of Modern Art in New York in 1941 exhibited and advertised the best contemporary Native work. The New York exhibit underlined that Indian artists of the day were as gifted as those of previous generations. The board also helped different tribes start their own arts and crafts enterprises.

Other developments fostered Native art. In 1930 the Hall of Indian Arts was inaugurated at the Museum of New Mexico in Santa Fe. The hall exhibited the work of outstanding contemporary Indian artists. In 1931 the Exposition of Indian Tribal Arts took place at the Grand Central Galleries in New York, and the work of San Ildefonso painter Oqwa Pi toured nationally to visit a number of museums, including the Museum of Modern Art in New York and Joslyn Museum in Omaha. The exposition featured work from fifty different private, university, and museum collections and displayed the talent of Southwestern painters such as Fred Kabotie (Hopi), Awa Tsireh (San Ildefonso), and six Kiowa artists—Tsatoke, Mopope, Jack Hokeah, Asah, Bou-ge-tah Smokey, and Auchiah.

In 1932 Santa Fe Indian School hired Dorothy Dunn as an art instructor. The school immediately emerged as a major center for the training and developing of Native artists. Noted New Mexico painter Olive Rush helped coordinate the first multitribal murals painted on the walls of the dining room. Prominent Indian artists, including Julian Martinez and Jack Hokeah, joined with eight student artists on this impressive endeavor. Later in the year the painting studio at the school began, with forty students ranging in age from fifteen to twenty-two. Primarily from the Southwest but also including Natives from the Plains and elsewhere, the student body included in its ranks artists such as Pablita Velarde (Santa Clara) and Andrew Tsihnahjinnie (Navajo). By the third year the studio had attracted more than four times its initial enrollment, as Sioux, Omaha, Kiowa, Klamath, Cherokee, Salish, Cheyenne, and

Arapaho students joined the others. From this extremely talented contingent, Allan Houser (Chiricahua Apache) and Oscar Howe (Yanktonai Dakota) became two of the most highly regarded Native artists of the twentieth century.

Dorothy Dunn at the Santa Fe school and Oscar Jacobson in Oklahoma were significant mentors of these painters. The studio school painting style later drew increasing criticism; some complained that students had been limited in their freedom of artistic expression. The whole question of patronage and non-Indian influences upon Native art, to be sure, continued through the remainder of the century. The two-dimensional representation style of the studios of the 1930s was idealized and may well have imposed upon or funneled Indian expression. Students from the Santa Fe program varied in their reflections upon their experience. Houser, for example, later contended that Dunn "trained us all the same way. . . . Her style lacked originality and creativity." Yet others claimed they "had lots of freedom." Perhaps the studio's greatest limitation may have derived from its very success, for later in the century some Indian painters fought against the creation of what became defined as "traditional" or "true" Indian art. These artists felt that such a narrow definition had solidified into a kind of rigidity that did not allow new forms of painting always to be fully appreciated as equally legitimate. On the other hand, as Hulleah J. Tsinhnanjinnie (Seminole-Muscogee-Navajo) has said, the "rather peculiar times" of the 1960s and 1970s may have encouraged an overreaction. It was certainly unfair and insensitive— Hulleah Tsinhnahjinnie called it "internalized racism"—to label fine artists such as her father, Andrew Tsinhahjinnie (whose name was spelled differently), and Harrison Begay, Pablita Velarde, and other "traditional painters" as individuals who worked in a "Bambi style." Today there is renewed appreciation for the quality of the work of the artists of the 1930s and the kind of foundation they established for future generations.

In a related sense, the 1930s saw two major Native writers explore themes of Indian identity and cultural continuity and change and create a legacy for Indian writers of the future. As A. LaVonne Brown Ruoff and other students of modern Indian literature have observed, John Joseph Mathews (Osage) and D'Arcy McNickle (Salish-Kootenai) wrote impressive and influential novels that helped establish a common theme of twentieth-century Indian writers of fiction: "the quests of mixed-blood protagonists to find their places in society and . . . the importance of oral tradition to the survival of tribalism."

Born in Indian Territory in 1894, Mathews journeyed to Norman to attend the University of Oklahoma. After serving in World War I in Europe as a military pilot, he resumed his studies in geology and graduated Phi Beta Kappa. Mathews declined a Rhodes scholarship and yet attended Oxford, graduating in 1923 with a degree in natural sciences from Merton College. Although he had enjoyed great success as a student, he understood the kind of alienation and despair Native Americans could experience in a university setting. In *Sundown,* published in 1934, Mathews presented the memorable character of Challenge Windzer, a mixed-blood who experiences all the potential and problems inherent in Osage life of this era. Mathews's first book, *Wah'kon-Tah: The Osage and the White Man's Road* (1930) became a Book-of-the-Month Club selection and sold 50,000 copies in the first year after its release. In 1938 Mathews helped his people establish the first tribal museum in the country. He enjoyed a long, happy, and distinguished life as a resident of Osage country. "Being Indian," Mathews once said, "isn't in looks, in features or color. Indian is inside you."

D'Arcy McNickle seconded such sentiments. Of Cree descent, but brought up as a member of the Confederated Salish and Kootenai community on the Flathead reservation, he attended the University of Montana and, briefly, Oxford University. He settled in New York City in 1926 and began work on a novel set at Flathead. Not unlike *Sundown, The Surrounded* was based to a significant degree on the author's own life experiences and observations. McNickle's novel told of Archilde Leon, a mixed-blood young man who knows many struggles and disappointments. The book won considerable critical acclaim following its publication in 1936, but not a considerable audience. McNickle was more prominent in the 1930s as an associate of John Collier. He contributed to

Indians at Work and as a government employee journeyed to articulate the New Deal program to many Native communities. Through his travels, McNickle gained an appreciation for the common challenges facing Indian peoples, which later encouraged him to play a central role in the founding of the National Congress of American Indians.

Education, Health Care, and Land Use

In three other areas—education, health, and control of land—Native peoples achieved some headway in the 1930s, even if much more remained to be accomplished. Native determination to obtain better education, improved health care, and increased power over their own estates, together with altered federal policies, prompted these relative advancements.

The enthusiasm that Collier, Beatty, and Ryan shared for a bilingual, bicultural approach to Indian education did not translate into an instantaneous shift of teaching philosophies at all BIA schools. Some teachers and principals welcomed the attempted transition, but many others resisted it. Beatty employed *Indian Education,* summer workshops, and others means to push for his goals, yet he could not require all employees to swear full allegiance to new objectives. Low salaries, isolated (in the eyes of most non-Indian teachers) locations, and the overall demands of the job caused high teacher turnover rates. Indian resistance to other bureau programs often crossed into the educational arena.

However, the situation within the federal schools did not remain static. The government closed some of the older boarding schools and began to construct community day schools in their stead. The opportunity for more Indian children to remain at home pleased many parents and pupils, even if the nature of the curriculum remained a topic of considerable disagreement. Passage of the Johnson-O'Malley Act in 1934 permitted state departments of education to contract with and provide funds for local public school districts that enrolled Indian children. Only four states during the 1930s worked out such contracts with the Department of Interior: Arizona (1938), California (1934), Minnesota (1937), and

Washington (1935). Although bureaucratic obstacles loomed, Johnson-O'Malley helped increase the percentage of Indian children attending public school.

Not all Indians wanted all boarding schools closed. They identified formal high school instruction with the boarding school and approved of the progress such institutions had made since the early days of Carlisle. Students no longer marched; boys and girls were more likely to sit together in the dining room. At Santa Fe students started the Mide-Wi-Win or Indian Club in 1933 in order to encourage Native dances, songs, and food. Boys at the school took pride in winning state championships in boxing and baseball. At Chilocco and at other multitribal schools, K. Tsianina Lomawaima (Muscogee) asserted, "student life was more richly textured than a simple opposition to non-Indian authority might indicate." She added: "Age, tribe, family life, native language, and other salient factors operated meaningfully to subdivide students while survival, shared experience, resistance to authority, and an enrollment in an 'Indian' school knit them together." In the 1930s students were more likely to enroll at Chilocco when they were older. If they also came from more stable family backgrounds, they tended to be far more positive about their experience than had their counterparts in the 1920s. In those final years before the start of World War II, Lomawaima concluded, Native pupils assumed greater power over the nature of their experience at Chilocco: "Native people made Chilocco their own. Chilocco was an Indian school."

Health care gradually improved during the 1930s, although significant problems persisted. By decade's end, an effective treatment had been introduced against trachoma, and some Indian Service administrators realized the benefit of working more cooperatively with traditional religious leaders to encourage Indians to seek appropriate medical treatment. When a new hospital opened in Fort Defiance, Arizona, in 1938, for example, the director of medical care invited a Navajo, Pete Price, to perform the Blessingway ceremony. However, medical missionaries and doctors from Christian evangelical backgrounds still echoed the sentiments of Rehoboth, New Mexico, hospital director Dr. Richard H.

Pousma, who proclaimed that people who encouraged Indian religious ceremonies were "idiotic, exceedingly stupid, and ignorant of conditions among the Indians." Many physicians agreed with the sentiments emblazoned on a sign in front of the Presbyterian mission hospital in Ganado, Arizona: Tradition, it announced, is the Enemy of Progress. Nonetheless, as roads continued to be built and the general isolation of many Native communities reduced, more people started to use hospitals and clinics. A slowly growing number of Native individuals became nurses; a few became physicians.

Indian communities had paid a terrible price through land allotment. Formal cessation of allotment mattered. By the end of the 1930s, statistics demonstrated Indians at last had stemmed the inroads upon their various land bases. Through the Indian Reorganization Act, land allotment had become a thing of the past. Although the act did not grant specific authority for consolidation of the lands splintered by allotment, and western congressional representatives still blocked appropriation of sufficient funds for substantial land purchases, the BIA had succeeded in adding about 4 million acres to the Native estate. The gains on individual reservations, however, were generally piecemeal in character and modest in amount.

The New Deal's Civilian Conservation Corps (CCC) included funds for building dams and reservoirs, fences, roads, and wells. On many reservations, the CCC—Indian Division—provided modest but badly needed salaries for labor and tangible results. The program offered more to men than it did to women, who tried to find employment through arts and crafts, the tourist industry, agriculture, and domestic labor in neighboring communities. The people of the Tohono O'odham reservation, for example, welcomed the money and the new wells, but new fences did not always meet with approval, for they disrupted traditional land use by local cattle ranchers.

In the days of the dust bowl, soil conservation assumed a high priority, but the Tohono O'odham, Navajos, and other tribes did not generally share the perspectives of federal employees who claimed that the herds had to be reduced if the soil was to be preserved. The subsequent crusade by federal employees to reduce the number of cattle owned by the Tohono O'odham and sheep owned by the Navajos mirrored national patterns, but such federal interference was unexpected and unwelcome. The livestock reduction program caused considerable confusion and, ultimately, great anguish. The Native communities did not believe they had overgrazed the land, arguing that prolonged drought, insufficient grazing acreage, and restricted water sources were responsible for soil erosion. They truly hated having their animals destroyed; to them the cattle and sheep were not simply economic commodities but valuable entities in the workings of their social and cultural order. Collier believed livestock reduction had to be carried out to halt soil erosion and to allow Indian communities to carry on traditional livestock raising, albeit on a reduced scale. But Collier's motives and methods were not understood nor accepted by the people themselves. Navajo elder Descheeny Nez Tracy said: "All was going well, and the people had increased their livestock very rapidly, when along came John Collier and stomped his big foot on our sheep, goats and horses—and crushed them before our eyes." The world would never again be the same. "We believe," Tracy contended, "that is when the rain went with the sheep. If it hadn't happened we would have rain and green ranges with sheep grazing all over. Now we only have small units to our permits, and the sandstorms erase a herd's hoof prints in seconds."

The Indian Reorganization Act

The original version of the Indian Reorganization Act (IRA) or the Wheeler-Howard Act—for its initial sponsors, Senator Burton K. Wheeler of Montana and Congressman Edgar Howard of Nebraska—ran to forty-eight pages. The bill included four titles concerning Indian self-government, education, land, and a Court of Indian Affairs. In regard to self-government, each Indian community would be granted a charter through which it would be responsible for a progressively greater degree of its own affairs. Approval by the people of the charter would institute a new body that would have significant authority over local affairs and would protect the community from undue exercise of power by the federal government. In addition, the bill called for the government to take a more active role in training Indian people for employment within the BIA. This second title also emphasized the importance of maintaining traditional Indian cultures. In the third title further allotment of tribal lands was prohibited. So-called surplus lands that had been opened for non-Indian occupancy and had not been purchased would be returned to the tribal domain. Additional lands would be added to reservations, especially with a concern for consolidating the fractionated acres created through the legacy of allotment. Finally, a Court of Indian Affairs would be established through which many important cases now adjudicated elsewhere in the federal court system could be considered. This provision attempted to devise a means whereby cases involving Indian peoples could be heard more promptly, fully, and sympathetically.

Responding to the uncertainties expressed about this legislation, Collier quickly scheduled ten congresses across the United States in March and April 1934. Through these sessions Indian people could learn more about the bill, raise questions about it, and, Collier hoped, become more supportive of the proposal. The congresses began in Rapid City, South Dakota, on March 2–5. With the exception of a belated gathering in Hayward, Wisconsin, on April 24, the remaining meetings took place in rapid-fire succession, all in the month of March. The other eight sites included, in chronological order, Chemawa, Oregon; Fort Defiance, Arizona; Santo Domingo, New Mexico; Phoenix, Arizona; Riverside, California; Anadarko, Oklahoma; Muskogee, Oklahoma, and Miami, Oklahoma. Collier attended seven of these sessions. Other than in Hayward, no congress occurred east of the Mississippi River. This neglect of eastern Indian communities did not increase the bill's chances for acceptance in the East, especially in Iroquois country, where Jemison and her allies immediately proclaimed their steadfast opposition.

Many Indians who attended the congresses marveled at the idea of a commissioner actually willing to leave Washington, but the novelty of the sight of the commissioner did not guarantee a positive reaction to what he presented. At Rapid City, Plains Indians who had endured the ravages of land allotment and cession worried aloud about the immediate future. A Northern Arapaho spoke of his people as being circled by a predatory wolf. Antoine Roubideaux (Sicangu Lakota), later recalled the active opposition of the Catholic Church and other denominations toward the bill, because the churches "knew if the Indian people went under this '34 Act, they would lose control of the Indian, you know." Such opponents alleged that "that was a socialistic form of government that John Collier was trying to set up" and raised the specter that Indians "would go back to their old ways." By contrast, George Yellow from Lower Brule hailed an end to allotment, which had permitted the Whites to steal "everything except the soles of my shoes." The Blackfeet adopted Collier into the tribe and bestowed upon him the name of Spotted Eagle, for they said he would erase the spots on the reservation created through the division of land by allotment.

In the end, divisions over the proposal followed rather predictable lines. Conservative Christians and old-line assimilationists, among them many veteran BIA employees, lobbied against the bill. They realized that Collier was trying to unravel all they had accomplished over the past half century. Their voices were heard by many congressional representatives who resisted any kind of separate status for Native Americans. The version of Wheeler-Howard ultimately approved by Congress and signed into law by President Roosevelt on June 18, 1934, was watered down considerably from Collier's original recipe. Collier took solace in what remained: allotment was dead; surplus unsold lands were returned to the tribal domain; Native lands could not be sold or leased without specific tribal approval; and tribes could form their own governments, with their own constitutions, but only if they voted to approve all the provisions of the Indian Reorganization Act. Ten million dollars had been put aside for a revolving credit fund for economic development. However, prior allotments remained intact and the Indian court system had been eradicated from the final bill. The powers of the tribal government had been reduced, and the secretary of the interior maintained a veto power over decisions it made. The specific mention of the effort to help foster and maintain Indian cultures had vanished.

Oklahoma Indians gained exemption from the act's provisions; Alaska's Native villages and groups also were omitted. The act potentially might benefit federally recognized Indian tribes who had maintained at least some kind of land base. Once bestowed, federal recognition formally acknowledged a community as an "Indian community" making it eligible for federal services and trust protection. For other Native communities, particularly in the East and South but as well scattered around the West, who failed to gain this recognition and who presently did not possess a viable land base, the Indian Reorganization Act essentially offered little hope for a future renaissance. The act presented a strict definition of Indian identity based exclusively on blood quantum. Those who were one-half "Indian blood" fell under its provisions as individuals, even if their tribes were not considered eligible for recognition.

In the wake of the passage of the Indian Reorganization Act, Indian communities faced a significant, often divisive, question. Should they agree to form governments organized under the act's provisions? The referendum on this fundamental issue had to be held within a year. This deadline did not allow enough time for voters to gain a full sense of what implementation of the act might mean specifically for them. The vote was to be on the basis of majority rule rather than the consensus many groups preferred. Boycott the proceedings and one might feel satisfaction, but such action would not be counted as a "no" vote. In fact, under the terms governing this specific election, it would be counted as a "yes" vote. This arrangement may have allowed the act to be approved on some reservations where it otherwise might not have been, but such deception called into question the overall legitimacy of the process through which many tribal governments were established. Other concurrent developments clouded the process. For example, Navajo sentiment about Collier had already been affected by the livestock reduction program. And within the particular reservations, competing communities or constituencies saw the formation of new governmental units as the chance to obtain power or the chance to have authority wrested away. Once voters understood that rejection of the IRA did not mean termination of trust status, they could cast their ballots based on other criteria.

Observers of the referenda and historians who followed came up with wildly varying counts of the particular votes and perceived the importance of their outcomes in sharply different ways. In New York the Iroquois sentiment had been registered quite clearly. Almost half of the eligible voters took part and over 80 percent of them disapproved of the Act. The people of Allegany voted against it 298–37. The other reservations also said "no" to Wheeler-Howard: Cattaraugus, 475–101; Onondaga, 206–17; Akwesasne, 237–46; Tonawanda, 175–42; and Tuscarora, 132–6. Alice Jemison helped organize opposition, but her task had been made easier by the historic distrust of the BIA by the New York Iroquois and the degree to which the Iroquois tribes of the state saw their own status as separate and distinct. Those Iroquois who had migrated westward had not had the same historical experience and saw the IRA in quite different terms. Thus the Oneidas of Wisconsin voted affirmatively. Well-developed factions within the Wisconsin group saw it as a chance to assume control. Most of the people were extremely poor and many were willing to endorse any proposal that might ameliorate their circumstances. The IRA passed at Oneida 688–126, although 56 percent of the eligible voters did not exercise their right to vote. The practice of counting no vote at all as a vote in favor of the measure helped swing close elections, especially on smaller reservations. The Santa Ysabel reservation in California was counted as giving the Act a 71–43 margin of approval, but only nine persons there actually voted for Wheeler-Howard. On many reservations residents actually voted and did so enthusiastically and overwhelmingly in favor of the IRA. Local conditions and historical precedents influenced the direction of the particular outcomes. Before, during, and after the referendum, many voters remained confused about the nature of the vote. Others claimed later that they would have voted the other way had they better understood what was at stake.

Eventually the Indian Reorganization Act gained approval by 174 Indian tribes and bands, while 78 others voted against the measure. The largest tribe, the Navajos, narrowly defeated the

IRA, 8214–7795. The vote totals reflected Navajo unhappiness with stock reduction as well as the enmity toward Collier felt by Jacob Morgan of Shiprock, New Mexico. In addition, the commissioner had failed to deliver on his promise of expanding the Navajo reservation eastward and Navajo voters in that area also expressed their disappointment at the polls. Collier could not blame the results on voter apathy, for 98 percent of the eligible voters on Navajo cast ballots.

Most of the large reservations favored the IRA. But at Crow, Fort Peck, and Klamath, all noteworthy for long-standing internal divisions, the measure failed. The Crows voted overwhelmingly against the IRA, even though the reservation's new superintendent, Robert Yellowtail, was a member of the tribe and campaigned for it. Yellowtail was not universally popular, but even some of his friends and political allies could not bring themselves to support the measure. James Carpenter complained the IRA maintained the federal government's power and ignored Crow rights. The Crows, Carpenter argued, would be "serfs" under the IRA.

A considerable number of small groups also wound up casting negative votes, including many of the California Indian communities. Rupert Costo (Cahuilla), a prominent opponent of Collier and the IRA, helped lead the campaign in California. Costo viewed the IRA as "the last great drive to assimilate the American Indian." He believed that under the new law the secretary of the interior would became more powerful. Costo also took a great dislike to Collier, perceiving the commissioner as a man who manipulated Indian people and one who made promises he did not intend to keep.

An examination of the response to the IRA on several reservations clarifies its initial effect. The Jicarilla Apaches of northern New Mexico voted to accept its provisions. Jicarilla historian Veronica Velarde Tiller noted that this affirmative vote allowed the tribe to give up allotments, buy the Wirt trading post from outsiders, obtain new sheep and cattle, and adopt conservation programs. "All of this," she concluded, "amounted to a visible increase in individual and tribal income, which, in turn, improved social conditions on the reservation. As a result, the Jicarillas changed from a dying, poverty-stricken race to a prosperous people with a thriving livestock economy."

The Jicarillas had voted for the IRA in part because the federal government had made a vigorous, and largely successful, attempt to add to the reservation land base by purchasing adjacent lands from non-Indians. The tribal council established under the IRA reflected local group settlements and permitted a majority of the first council members to be people who supported traditional religious observances and customs. Some were descendants of traditional leaders. In addition, the council included the five wealthiest men at Jicarilla: John Mills Baltazar, DeJesus Campos Serafin, Grover Vigil, Lindo Vigil, and Laell Vicenti. Council membership comprised both people who had many years of formal education and people who had never been to school.

The Jicarilla Apache Council also functioned effectively. It helped make a difference in the daily lives of average citizens. Through a loan from the federal revolving credit fund, the tribe purchased the old Wirt trading post and transformed it into the Jicarilla Apache Cooperative Store. The cooperative store not only mirrored tribal ownership but encouraged more people to get into the livestock business. In addition, the government sponsored a very popular and successful herd of about 1,000 sheep. This herd helped support tribal elders. It became known as the Old People's Herd. On San Carlos, a comparable herd of cattle established at this time was called the Social Security Herd.

Of course not all tribal councils experienced comparable success. Divisions within a reservation community could doom a council's efforts or the very existence of a council could exacerbate existing intratribal factions. The tribal council for the Anishinabe community at Keweenaw Bay on Michigan's Upper Peninsula consisted of six representatives from the L'Anse district on the reservation's eastern shore and six from the Baraga side of the bay. Local interests naturally encouraged six-to-six votes. Divisions within Lac Courte Oreilles in northern Wisconsin kept it from reaching agreement upon a tribal constitution.

Hopi and Pine Ridge present instructive cases in point of how the IRA could create havoc or worsen existing splits on reservations. At Hopi, traditionalists generally boycotted the vote and others who voted in favor of the IRA did so because they anticipated specific benefits from the government in return. Among other things, the Hopis expected the government to expand their livestock herds and their land holdings and to keep the Navajos from using the Keams Canyon school and hospital. When the government did not fulfill these expectations, the council began its life under a considerable cloud. After four years, marked by disagreement and ineffectiveness, the council was disbanded in 1940. A decade passed before attempts began to revive it.

On Pine Ridge the new tribal council ran directly into the existing dichotomy between fullbloods, who generally lived in the more isolated stretches of the reservation, and the mixed bloods, who primarily lived in and around the small towns. Those who assumed power through the tribal government tended to be mixed bloods. Council members were known in English as the New Dealers, in Lakota as Oon-tey-cha, the new way of life. Those on the outside were called the Old Dealers. Traditionalists who believed the council did not represent them tried to ignore the entity and did not accord to it any degree of respectability or authority. That authority they reserved for individuals at the local level who shared their values and customs and continued the old ways of looking out for the well-being of others.

If tribal councils struggled with the matter of incorporating or representing different groups, they also usually floundered in regard to the inclusion of women. Men constituted the vast majority of membership on the councils in the latter half of the 1930s and into the 1940s. Women were not entirely absent from the political process but were not equal partners in it. Nell Scott (Northern Arapaho) offered one exception to the rule. First elected to the business council in 1937, she served on it for thirty years, frequently as its chair. The daughter of an Arapaho woman and a white man, Scott hailed from the section of the Wind River reservation almost entirely occupied by Shoshones. Scott's mother was divorced and had chosen to reside in this location, obtaining allotments there for her family members. Although she did not speak

Arapaho and later married a non-Indian, Scott emerged as a powerful force in tribal politics. She devoted her life to the well-being of the people of Wind River, and over the course of her long career she earned the respect of both tribes. Scott's knowledge of English and the outside world made her especially effective in transitional times. She knew how to interpret the world beyond Wind River—often through a joke which demonstrated her understanding of non-Indian behaviors and tendencies—as well as how to deliver needed services to her constituents.

Tribal councils in the 1930s confronted the problems in the national economy. Generally lacking legal counsel, the councils possessed limited means to combat inequities in attempted Native development of natural resources. Indians often had to compete with non-Indians for access to these resources, and state and local interests frequently restricted the ability of Natives to take advantage of such resources. In Washington, for example, the state government worked against Indian participation in the fishing industry, at either the commercial or subsistence level. In the first decades of the twentieth century tribes such as the Lummis faced severe restrictions. By the time of the Indian New Deal, destitution had replaced self-sufficiency, with the Lummis limited to fishing only on reservation waters, where non-Indians also fished, and denied jobs in the canneries.

The advent of the New Deal did not improve the lot of the Lummis. In November 1934 voters in Washington approved Initiative 77. This law banned traps, fish wheels, and set nets. The state moved to strongly discourage Indians from using any form of fish trap. The Lummis and others also rejected the idea of fishing seasons as another imposition of state authority. Tensions increased in Washington about the rights of Native fishers, even though Indians actually took a very small percentage of the catch.

Elsewhere the faltering national economy also did not encourage greater economic independence for tribes. Critics charged that the IRA simply increased dependence upon Washington. Supporters pointed with pride to examples such as the Red Shirt Table Development Association on Pine Ridge, where federal support had made possible everything from a new day school and new housing to more cattle and irrigated farming. Those who opposed it complained that such intervention bound the people all the more to the government.

Alaska and Oklahoma

The Native peoples of Alaska and Oklahoma had been excluded from the IRA, but in 1936 Congress passed legislation providing new regulations affecting these areas. The Alaska Reorganization Act (ARA) permitted villages which chose to do so to organize governments and establish cooperative businesses. Some Indian communities used the funds available through the Act to establish canneries important to their economies. However, the diversity of the Native population, long-standing conflicts among some of the Natives, and non-Indian opposition stymied the potential of the ARA. They also contributed to the problems inherent in land use in the region that would become progressively more apparent in the years after World War II.

The Oklahoma Indian Welfare Act also encouraged the establishment of tribal governments and constitutions. Many Oklahoma Native communities decided to organize under the provisions of this act. These included the Caddos, Cheyenne-Arapahos, three towns of the Muscogees, Absentee Shawnees, Eastern Shawnees, Iowas, Kickapoos, Miamis, Pawnees, Peorias, Poncas, Potawatomis, Sac and Foxes, Senecas, Tonkawas, the Wyandots, and the United Keetowah Band.

However, some Oklahoma Indians also played an important role in opposing the Indian New Deal. Joseph Bruner (Muscogee) chaired the American Indian Federation (AIF), a right-wing organization that linked Collier with Communism. Although many observers ridiculed the AIF, it appealed at the time to Indians who favored an emphasis on individualism. Prominent participants in the group included Jemison, Jacob Morgan, Fred Bauer (Eastern Cherokee), and Thomas Sloan. The AIF was established in response to the Collier commissionership; when Collier resigned his post in 1945, the AIF soon disbanded.

Land Bases and Recognition

In the 1930s those Indians who lived on reservations generally were better positioned to gain assistance from the federal government than were Natives living off the reservations. In Nevada, for example, the western Shoshones and Paiutes living at Duck Valley (Western Shoshone) received the benefit of the Civilian Conservation Corps–Indian Division program, whereas others who resided in Nevada's tiny Indian "colonies" in the state's towns were less affected. Duck Valley gained a new hospital, a new community gymnasium, new roads, and additional fencing and water sources for cattle. Nothing comparable came to the colonies. By the early 1940s, however, the government created several new reservations within Nevada through the purchase of land—primarily that owned by White ranchers—and residents from the colonies of Elko and Battle Mountain, and elsewhere moved to these new sites. South Fork (eventually 13,638 acres), Yomba (4,681 acres), and Duckwater (3,642 acres) represented important additions to the Indian land base in Nevada.

BIA efforts to expand, consolidate, or create Native land bases naturally did not always succeed, but some victories were recorded. In Florida, the Seminoles had provided a classic instance of "support" for the IRA. Only twenty-one of the approximately 500 tribal members had voted on the measure, but since all twenty-one voted in the affirmative, the measure passed. The BIA established Big Cyprus reservation in 1911 and the Hollywood reservation in 1926. The difficult times of the thirties prompted some Seminoles to move to these new land bases in order to take advantage of federal programs. Divisions remained, however, among the people. Many individuals attempted to remain off the reservations and tried to capitalize on the burgeoning tourist trade in the Everglades. In the 1930s the federal government also obtained the site for the Brighton reservation, northwest of Lake Okeechobee. This substantial land base of over 30,000 acres proved to be good cattle country, and the federal government funded the start of a tribal herd of 1,200 head. The election of trustees to serve on the cattle enterprise offered Seminole women their first chance to vote directly in a tribal election. Creation of a reservation such as Brighton would not have been possible in later years, with the vast influx of newcomers and rapidly escalating real estate prices that characterized postwar Florida. In Nevada, Florida, and other locations, the Collier administration took advantage of the depressed market conditions of the period to establish needed land bases.

Many smaller and more isolated Indian communities in the 1930s saw the possibility of financial assistance and support for their identity as separate Native entities from the federal government and accordingly sought formal federal recognition. This attempt to receive such status almost always meant an extended struggle. East of the Mississippi, with few exceptions, tribal communities had little land, a declining number of Native language speakers, and an increasingly diverse character. Eventually some of these communities received state recognition. Thus in Virginia, North Carolina, and South Carolina, for example, small Indian groups held reservations dating back to colonial or antebellum times, even without federal designation as tribes. Others owned or used lands over decades or centuries and defined themselves as members of Indian communities, regardless of whether the state or national government might deign to accord recognition. The movement to gain such status accelerated after World War II and gained additional impetus in 1978, when the BIA established procedures to petition for recognition through a new Branch of Federal Acknowledgment and Research.

Federal officials were not eager to assume responsibilities for groups that appeared more marginal, especially if these communities were located outside of the West. Given the focus of Collier's and Ickes's attention on that region and on the considerable number of existing groups already eligible for the IRA, non-western, non-recognized entities faced an uphill fight. One of the most intriguing of these groups lived primarily in North Carolina. The Lumbees did seek formal federal recognition in the 1930s, with Collier's backing, but Ickes's opposition doomed their chances. "It would appear," Ickes stated, "that the Federal Government is under no obligation whatsoever to this group of people." Part of the problem lay with the particular nature of this group's identity, as well as the usual combination of forces opposing a change in the status quo. Local Whites wanted to continue to have access to inexpensive labor, and a few Lumbees did not think a reservation would improve their lives Although the Lumbees themselves had always considered themselves as Indians, their legitimacy as a Native entity had not always been accepted by outsiders, including many of the Eastern Cherokees. Lumbee scholars Adolph Dial and Linda Oxendine concluded that their people are an amalgamation of the Cheraws, an eastern Siouan group, and remnants of other tribes who moved to the swamps of eastern North Carolina. Most Lumbees resided in Robeson County, in southeastern North Carolina, although some also lived in South Carolina. In North Carolina, the Lumbees had been classified from 1835 to 1865 as "Free Persons of Color," from 1865 to 1885 as "non-White," from 1885 to 1911 as "Croatan Indians," from 1911 to 1913 as "Indians of Robeson County," and after 1913, against the opposition of the Eastern Cherokees, as the "Cherokee Indians of Robeson County." They were determined, under whatever name, to gain proper recognition and strenuously resisted the efforts of the state to classify them as African Americans. This resistance prompted the creation for them in 1940 of Pembroke State College for Indians—now Pembroke State University—and since 1953 open to all students.

The 1930s, therefore, yielded a chapter in an ongoing story that would take on intriguing turns as the century progressed, not only in regard to the Lumbees, but among many other communities, both east and west of the Mississippi, as well. In the state of Washington, landless tribes vied unsuccessfully for federal recognition. Snoqualmie and Steilacoom leaders, for example, had been encouraged by the wording of the Indian Reorganization Act, but because these groups lacked reservation land, BIA officials balked at extending them recognition.

By the end of the decade, as a reviving economy cooled America's commitment to many New Deal programs, the "Indian New Deal" slowed its momentum; the start of World War II essentially brought it to an end. Despite the appropriate criticisms that could be lodged against its flaws and imperfections, D'Arcy

McNickle emphasized how crucial it had been to end allotment, to add 4 million acres to the tribal land base, to provide, however modestly, some credit financing to Native concerns, to promote a bicultural, bilingual approach in education, and to support Native art and religions. Collier, McNickle acknowledged, "was limited in what he could do. He could not substitute his will and vision for Indian will and vision." But even with his faults and limitations, he had been the first commissioner who understood that Indians would not disappear, that Indian societies could adapt, change, and respond to the challenges presented by the modern age.

CHAPTER FOUR

The War, Termination, and the Start of Self-Determination, 1941–1961

The 1940s and 1950s brought extraordinary change to Indian country. World War II provided for thousands of Indian men and women a new opportunity to perceive and experience American society. Service in the armed forces and work in war-related industries permitted individuals to gain a heightened sense of the demands, biases, and priorities of the United States. However, the wars years were followed by termination, a movement to divest the federal government of its trust responsibilities for Indians, an effort that also mirrored American demands, biases, and priorities.

Ruth Muskrat Bronson (Cherokee) spoke out in 1957 against the renewed pressures for assimilation this period engendered:

More than one theorist has stated that "the solution to the Indian problem" is the absorption of the Indian into the culture, race, and society of the European-oriented American way. Shouldn't the Indian have something to say about this? Should the Indian be forced to give up his beliefs, his way of conducting his affairs, his method of organized living, his kind of life on the land he is part of, if he chooses not to? Shouldn't the Indi-

ans have the same right to self-determination that our government has
stated, often and officially, is the inalienable right of peoples in far parts
of the world? Do we apply a different set of principles, of ethics, to the
people within our own borders? . . .

Born in a rural Cherokee community in Indian Territory,
Bronson graduated from Mount Holyoke College in 1925 and devoted her life to what she termed "the Indian cause." She worked
for years for the BIA, laboring to increase educational opportunities for Native students. Then, in 1944, she began to play a central
role in the life of a new organization, the National Congress of
American Indians (NCAI), that had been established by Indian
people to address the needs and concerns of Native Americans. As
national secretary for the NCAI, she helped insure its survival and
maturation into an important medium through which pressing issues could be confronted. As the above quotation indicates, Bronson also offered an articulate and determined voice against the tide
of termination of federal trust responsibility. People like Ruth
Muskrat Bronson prepared the foundations for the modern Indian
movement toward greater self-determination, a movement that
gained greater and more immediate force because of the dangers
and discrimination that the new policy of termination posed.

The story of this period begins with the outbreak of war.
Twenty-five thousand American Indians served in the armed
forces during World War II and more than 550 of them were killed.
Clarence Spotted Wolf knew he might not survive the war. A private in the U.S. Army, the young Gros Ventre from Montana was
sent overseas. Fully recognizing the danger he was in, he wrote to
his family:

If I should be killed, I want you to bury me on one of the hills east of the
place where my grandparents and brothers and sisters and other relatives
are buried. If you have a memorial service, I want the soldiers to go
ahead with the American flag. I want cowboys to follow, all on horseback. I want one of the cowboys to lead one of the wildest T over X
horses with saddle and bridle on. I will be riding that horse.

Private Spotted Wolf lost his life in Luxembourg on December 21, 1944. He did not know the satisfaction or hear the accolades Native men and women received from their many contributions to the national effort. But he would be remembered, and his particular story would be told. There are many American Indian narratives from the war and, of course, no single one is representative of that collective experience. Many of those stories involved struggle and death. Some emphasized tragedy, some survival, others triumph. Now, more than fifty years after the war's end, they continue to be repeated, and they still hold lessons about the significance of the war years. They suggest that in some ways the era yielded a kind of turning point in the modern Indian experience. In *Speaking of Indians,* published in 1944, Ella Deloria (Yankton Sioux) observed: "The war has indeed wrought an overnight change in the outlook, horizon, and even the habits of the Indian people—a change that might not have come for many years yet." However, this period also often accentuated or emphasized trends already under way in individual lives and in the communities Native peoples called home.

American Indians had not been completely isolated before 1941. Many had left reservation environments to attend school; others had gone to the city to work. Federal programs had left their mark on tribal government, land use, education, and health care. Nonetheless, the war allowed countless thousands of Indians to perceive and experience the larger society of America. These perceptions and experiences, in turn, affected individual and group decisions about life in the postwar era.

World War II and Its Consequences

Although many Native Americans rushed to volunteer for the war effort, others resisted the demands of the Selective Service Act of 1940. Now that all Indians were citizens, they all faced the draft. Even the Iroquois in New York who supported the United States cause, for example, questioned the authority of the federal government to force men to fight. They took the matter to court. However, in *Ex parte Green*, the United States Court of Appeals for the Second Circuit denied Iroquois protestations. The federal government catered to the Iroquois sense of separation by encouraging a group of individuals from the Six Nations—Louis David and Peter Oaks (Mohawk), Jesse Lyons (Onondaga), Hilton Nicholas and William Rockwell (Oneida), and Uly Pierce (Cayuga)—to come to Washington, D.C. and to issue a separate Iroquois declaration of war against the Axis. That the men acted as individuals rather than as official representatives was largely ignored in the flurry of media publicity surrounding the event.

Other Indian nations divided over the matter. Tohono O'odham village leader Pia Machita, about ninety years of age, denied the legitimacy of the Gadsden Purchase, which had brought his people's lands into the United States in 1854. To signify his disclaimer of the Indian Reorganization Act he had flown the Mexican flag over his village for six months. In 1940 he urged young men from his district not to register for the draft. Another local man, Leandro, provided the same counsel. Machita and Leandro were both arrested and sent to Terminal Island in California and then transferred elsewhere to serve time for their defiance. Tribal chairman Pete Blaine and BIA administrator Wade Head intervened to shorten their terms of incarceration. In the meantime other Tohono O'odham quickly voiced support for the war, and the tribal council purchased $10,000 of war bonds in 1942.

At Hopi a group of young men from Hotevilla declined to register for the draught in 1941. James Pongonyuma and Dan Katchgonva argued in behalf of the men before a judge in federal court: "We have a stone tablet. . . . It says that there will come a time when there will be great trouble involving many nations. The Hopi are to show their bows and arrows to no one at that time." Unpersuaded, the judge sentenced the five men to a year and a day in prison—a term later reduced. By contrast, tribal council chairman Byron Adams informed Arizona governor Sidney Osborn that the Hopis were "100 percent with the nation." Thomas Banyacya went to prison three times during the war because of his resistance to the draft. After the war he became a leader of the traditionalist movement at Hopi.

The overall response by Indian men and women to the needs of wartime reflected both nationalism and tribalism. World War II let Native Americans demonstrate their love of country. It also yielded the possibility for men to display valor and courage, much in the way their ancestors had in other battles during prior centuries. Nowhere was this display more evident than in the Plains tribes. From the Assiniboines, Blackfeet, and Lakotas in the north to the Kiowas and Comanches in the south, Plains Indians revived warrior traditions and societies. For example, Cecil Horse, a Kiowa man, looked on with pride as his son John, who had been awarded a bronze star and a purple heart, later received from his people a war bonnet and a give-away ceremony in his honor. Nevertheless many men from the Plains, including at least one hundred Sioux, perished during the war. Others, like Walter Amiotte, suffered severe injuries. Amiotte, a tank driver for the Forty-first Armored Division in the Normandy invasion, lost part of his leg when his tank was hit and overturned. Among the other casualties was Osage Clarence W. Tinker, the commanding general of the air forces in Hawaii, killed at Midway. Altogether about 25,000 Indians joined the armed forces, including 21,767 in the army, 1,910 in the navy, 874 in the marines, and 121 in the coast guard. Hundreds of Native women served as nurses, as "Wacs" and "Waves." Natives fought in integrated units all over the world, earning a variety of medals and awards, including the Silver Star, the Distinguished Service Cross, the Navy Cross, and the Purple Heart. Lieutenant Ernest Childers, a Muscogee from Broken Arrow, Oklahoma, gained the Medal of Honor. Ira Hayes, a Pima from Bapchule, Arizona, was immortalized as one of the marines photographed on Iwo Jima raising the American flag. Navajo men in the marines formed the Codetalkers and used their language as the basis of an effective code during the campaign in the Pacific; hundreds of others from the tribe fought in Europe. In the wake of the Japanese attack on Pearl Harbor, Alaska mobilized a Native militia, primarily Inuit, to protect the territory. The Eskimo territorial guard companies, as they were called, shot down Japanese balloons carrying incendiary bombs and worked hard to build up civil defenses in case of invasion.

Not all of these stories had happy endings. Only nineteen years old when he enlisted in the marines, Hayes struggled with the unanticipated and unwanted attention brought by the glare of publicity. Ultimately he lost a long battle with alcoholism and died in 1955 at the age of thirty-three. William Tsosie (Navajo) survived the horrors of the landing at Omaha Beach, but the memories of D-Day haunted him thereafter, as did his recollections of the German concentration camps. Robert Nez (Navajo) was taken as a prisoner of war by the Germans and after sixty-five days in captivity escaped and went on to participate in other battles. It took years, he said, for him to "finally accept life again," following a period of heavy drinking and nightmares. As they were in World War I, Indians were still stereotyped as "natural" scouts, and they frequently drew dangerous assignments that exposed them to even greater danger than they might otherwise have encountered. Secretary of the Interior Harold Ickes had rhapsodized about such "inherited talents"—their "endurance, rhythm, a feeling for timing, co-ordination, sense perception, an uncanny ability to get over any sort of terrain at night, and better than all else, an enthusiasm for fighting."

Nonetheless, thousands of Indians who served in the armed forces in World War II clearly returned with a heightened sense of pride in themselves and received a lasting tribute from grateful Americans in general and from members of their home community in particular. Their exploits in "the good war" are still celebrated in parades and reunions; they are still commemorated in displays at tribal museums across Indian country. When the Navajo Codetalkers marched in the presidential inaugural parade on January 20, 1997, the event simply marked the latest in a long series of tributes Native veterans had received. Among the Delawares and countless other Native peoples, tribal rituals and ceremonies were invoked to safeguard those in the armed services when they were away and to cleanse them when they returned home. The veterans often had positive stories to relate, reflecting a sense of accomplishment and a tangible sense of a mission achieved.

The experience frequently reaffirmed prevailing Native values. For Codetalker Cozy Stanley Brown, the success of the code, the ability of the Navajos to help other Americans, underlined his sense of being a member of his tribe. "We were Code Talkers for four months at Guadalcanal," he recalled. "That was the time we took advantage of our enemy. It was like the old saying of our elderly Navajo people, 'Only the Navajos had the whole world in their hands,' or 'the Navajos created the earth.'" But the war also reinforced for Brown that there were ways to behave and ways not to behave. A young man from Crownpoint, New Mexico, had not paid attention to such teachings. He was always "acting silly" or "being prankster" and saying things you should not say, like, "I'm getting fat, and I eat too much. It would seem like the enemy would butcher me at any time." That night he was killed.

The war experience also underlined the responsibility the veterans felt for working for constructive social and political change. Across the United States they returned to problems that needed addressing and that they felt more empowered to confront. In this recognition, they were joined by other Natives whose lives and perspectives had also been altered during the war years. These individuals included the thousands who had gone to work in war-related industries as well as the thousands who had remained at home and had assumed new responsibilities. A great many in this latter cohort were women. Some had sought new surroundings or new tasks; others had had little choice in shouldering novel tasks in order to feed, clothe, and house themselves and their family members.

The women and men who were employed during the war frequently worked under trying conditions. Previously industry had been an almost entirely male domain. Women who went to work in such environments were almost never in charge and were subject to criticism and ridicule by men who resented their presence in the workplace. "Minority" women and men also faced prejudice and discrimination in a variety of forms, ranging from salutations of "chief" to more hostile responses. However, the need for a paycheck had to be weighed against such reactions. Working in a war ordnance depot offered more money than the usual employment to which Indians, especially women, had been relegated. Many Native women entered or remained in the realm of domestic service workers, where they received less pay or were not necessarily exempt from bias. However, the opportunity to work in new areas of employment allowed higher numbers of Indian women to become clerical workers, for example, when prior to the war only a few had ventured into such jobs. In addition, the disparity between off- and on-reservation employment possibilities and salaries encouraged many people to ponder relocation to urban areas after the war ended.

Indian workers had to deal with a variety of adjustments during this transitional era. For many, their war-time job represented the first time they had ever worked or worked on a full time basis for an hourly wage. Their employers expected them to follow a kind of schedule that for many seemed rigid and unyielding. Even with labor shortages, employers had little sympathy for employees who showed up late for work or who returned tardy after a weekend back home. They generally had even less sympathy for the cultural demands and expectations upon Indian workers to be present for a ceremony or to go home immediately when a family-related problem suddenly occurred. War-time housing was not always ideal, and transportation to and from work continued to be problematic. At the same time, most Indians were used to dealing with hardship, and the Great Depression that had gripped the United States in the 1930s had affected Indian country as well. When Patty Loew (Bad River Anishinabe) asked her grandfather what life was like during the Depression, she evoked a chuckle. "It's always depression on an Indian reservation," he had replied. Rationing during wartime thus did not seem like an altogether unprecedented situation. Like other Americans, Indian families grew "victory gardens." If anything, they were more accustomed than non-Indians to sharing what they had.

On many reservations hunting and fishing continued to be essential means to provide or augment individual and family food supplies. In a time when Indians rarely had access to legal counsel, they had to endure state restrictions upon Native hunting and fishing on reservations, quite apart from rights that soon would be contested off reservations. In Wisconsin Indian men and women were subjected to a sentence of one to six months in jail for "violating" state conservation laws, because they and their families seldom could produce the $158 fine usually imposed on "poachers."

Indians who sought off-reservation employment, of course, did not always venture into the city. In the American West, the demand for seasonal farm labor persisted, and Indians found jobs picking cotton or harvesting fruit. Cotton farmers in Arizona who in 1938 had denied any need to hire Tohono O'odham workers, four years later eagerly searched on the reservation for potential employees. Given language and other cultural barriers, misunderstanding as well as exploitation emerged. Native workers, including children, had to ride for hours standing in the back of trucks that took them to their jobs in the fields. Those who did not commute frequently lived in terrible housing, and endured inadequate sanitation, a lack of schools, and other problems. Agricultural extension service and U.S. employment service employees sometimes attempted to intervene to stop abusive labor practices, but their efforts could not quickly alter such a widespread and exploitative labor system.

Whether in field or factory, Indian employees generally had to combat overwhelming homesickness. They were accustomed to seeing members of their extended family on a daily or at least frequent basis. Native workers also missed the sight of traditional landmarks—the mountains or mesas, the creeks or lakes—that had offered a sense of place. They longed for others who spoke their particular tribal language or who listened to the same kind of music or who told the same kind of jokes. Of course other Americans struggled with wartime transitions, but the cultural and social distance Indians had to travel rivaled and sometimes exceeded that of their counterparts.

The war years also brought unwanted intrusions on Native lands. The federal government imposed two of the internment camps for Japanese-Americans on reservations. Such camps were constructed on the Colorado River and Gila River reservations in Arizona by the War Relocation Authority. Collier had pressed for such use of Native land because he thought the Indians would inherit facilities constructed for this temporary purpose. The arrival of 20,000 Japanese-Americans at Colorado River and another 5,000 at Gila River, together with personnel charged with running the camps, expropriated Indian land and disrupted community life. To house its citizen prisoners, the government hurriedly constructed makeshift buildings. Soon after the war, most of these shoddy structures were torn down. A surviving warehouse might become for a time a place for dances at Colorado River, but for the most part, other than obtaining some lease money, the Indian communities gained nothing from the imposition.

Other war-time demands affected Indian reservations and lands. On Pine Ridge over 400,000 acres were appropriated for a gunnery range. Most of this land was owned by individuals—a legacy of the allotment era—and those living on the acreage were compelled to sell their property both quickly and cheaply. Not until the mid-1950s, after more than a decade of protest, did the dispossessed Oglalas obtain more substantial payment, but the land remained severed from the reservation.

In another instance, the Unangan (Aleuts) were evacuated from their homes following the Japanese invasion of the Aleutian Islands and their capture of Attu. While the Japanese took the inhabitants of Attu as prisoners to Japan, the United States ordered that the remaining Unangan, who lived in villages west of Unimak Island and in the Pribilofs, be incarcerated in southeast Alaska. Although federal officials ordered the evacuation of these people ostensibly to protect them from danger, they permitted some individuals who were not Unangan and Unangan who resided in the easternmost portion of the islands to remain in their homes. The conditions the Native internees faced at the internment camps in Alaska mirrored those endured by the Japanese Americans incarcerated in the lower forty-eight. In the Unangan's case, however, the hardships imposed on them by flimsy housing and inadequate provisions of food and health care were intensified during the fierce winters. Many of the old people and children died. Moreover, once the war was over, U.S. officials gave low priority to a prompt return of the internees to their home communities. Some Unangan feared they would have little to return to and chose to remain in southeast Alaska, while others finally were able to go home. There they discovered, to their horror, that in their absence American military personnel had stolen their personal property, trashed most of their homes, and absconded with irreplaceable religious icons from their Orthodox churches. The people of Attu were even denied permission to return from Japan to the Aleutians. The overall situation resulted in economic loss and a very traumatic cultural disruption.

The events of the 1930s and early 1940s thus emphasized that Indian communities had entered a new age, one that would not allow the degree of separation some had experienced in the past. Changes in the workings of the regional and national marketplace, transportation, and communication drew Indian nations more fully into the patterns of American life. Once again, their mineral resources invited exploitation by outside interests. Experiences in the armed forces and in industry had underscored the need for a more complete command of the English language. The appropriation of their land by non-Indians and the discrimination they met in surrounding communities emphasized the necessity of gaining legal counsel. The war years thus set the stage for an unprecedented push for the industrial development of Indian lands, for more extended schooling for a higher percentage of Native children, and for the obtainment of attorneys by the tribes.

The NCAI, the ICC, and Legal Representation

Changing times highlighted the need for some kind of national organization that could address common needs and concerns. In 1944 eighty people from more than fifty tribes gathered in Denver, Colorado, to found the National Congress of American Indians (NCAI). A number of the key participants had worked for the BIA during the Collier administration, had traveled widely, and believed deeply that through collective action Indians could confront more effectively the challenges of contemporary American life. Some of the most significant founders included Ruth Muskrat Bronson, D'Arcy McNickle, Ben Dwight (Choctaw), Archie Phinney (Nez Perce), Charlie Heacock (Sicangu Lakota), Lois Harland (Cherokee) and Erma Hicks (Cherokee). McNickle worked particularly hard to persuade people to make the journey to Denver. Dwight chaired the proceedings and Bronson served as the organization's executive secretary during its formative years. They recognized that the new association had to move beyond the accomplishments of the Society of American Indians. The NCAI could not be largely composed of middle-class, well-educated individuals. It had to develop support at the tribal level; it had to do more than "meet and discuss." Thus the Congress's first president, N. B. Johnson (Cherokee) noted with considerable satisfaction after the initial meetings in Denver, Browning, Montana, and Oklahoma City, that those in attendance comprised "a cross-section of Indian population: old and young, full-bloods, mixed-bloods, educated and uneducated Indians from allotted areas and others from reservations."

Bronson recognized that the fledgling organization needed to address voting rights in Arizona, New Mexico, and Maine, Social Security benefits for all Indians, tribal land claims, and safeguarding the Indian estate. With membership dues set at one dollar, the NCAI began on perilous financial footing. Bronson sought necessary donations, volunteered her time, and created the Legal Aid and Service Bureau at 1426 35th Street Northwest, her home address. Although Dan Madrano (Caddo) first had been chosen as secretary, he resigned by early 1946. At the NCAI's third annual meeting, in August 1946, Bronson was formally designated national secretary, a post she had occupied for quite some time. Her modest yet determined demeanor and her unfailing dedication to the organization were vital to its survival and its maturation.

Many Native women played key roles in the NCAI during these early years. Lorene Burgess (Blackfeet) served on the executive council in 1945. Ataloa (Chickasaw), May Dornback (Yurok), Amanda H. Finley (Cherokee), Leona Hayes (Chickasaw), Marie Hayes (Cherokee), Cora Welch Irgens (Blackfeet), Josephine Kelly (Lakota), Willamette LaVatta (Shoshone-Bannock), and Anita Sky Eyes (Cherokee) took on various assignments, ranging from the annual meeting and membership development to creating educational materials and working as regional secretaries. Helen Peter-son, a Cheyenne by birth who grew up on and was enrolled at Pine Ridge, and Elizabeth Roe Cloud (White Earth Anishinabe) prepared to take on major leadership responsibilities in the near future. Indian men may have appeared to dominate the organization in its first years, but it is evident that without Bronson and her compatriots, the NCAI would have been far less effective or ambitious.

The NCAI took on urgent issues throughout the United States. Bronson journeyed to southeast Alaska, where she learned from Haida and Tlingit representatives about their anxieties in regard to natural resources. The Three Affiliated Tribes (Arikara, Hidatsa, and Mandan) of Fort Berthold, North Dakota, needed more voices to speak out against the notion of the Garrison Dam, a massive project on the Missouri that would flood Indian lands. The winds of termination were already starting to sweep across Indian country. In 1946 it specifically appealed to Congress and the Truman administration "not to enact legislation or promulgate rules and regulations thereunder affecting the Indians without first consulting the Tribes affected." An Indian claims commission, proposed but thwarted during the Indian New Deal, appeared to offer the opportunity for Native peoples to gain compensation for lands and resources taken from them unfairly and without proper compensation. Bronson and other NCAI leaders therefore testified in favor of establishing the Indian Claims Commission.

The commission created by Congress in 1946 ultimately embodied contradictory impulses and objectives. Indians saw in it the means to confront long-standing grievances and to force the federal government to acknowledge that millions of acres of Native land had been taken illegally or improperly. After all, the 370 treaties signed between 1784 and 1871 had encompassed 720 cessions of land. Although Indians had been pledged almost $800 million in return, they had in a great many instances either not received the amount they had been promised or had obtained insufficient value from what they had surrendered. A decade after the formal conclusion of treaty making, the Choctaws became the first Indian nation to challenge the United States in the federal court of claims. By the time the Indian Claims Commission had been established, a total of 219 claims had been filed, but only thirty-five had resulted in any compensation. Although $77 million had been awarded by the ICC, to Native Americans the total represented a down payment for what they should have received.

However, federal policy-makers were not wracked by guilt and did not perceive the commission as a means to dispense untold millions of dollars with few questions asked. They recognized the need to expedite the hearing of the claims, but they also saw the commission as an integral part of a more comprehensive goal: removing the federal government as fully as possible from its traditional position of trustee for the Indians. Once some version of justice had been handed out, the government would be free, as one common phrase expressed it, "to get out of the Indian business." The ICC and termination, in sum, were linked. When he signed the legislation creating the commission into law, President Harry Truman expressed his hope that the act would "mark the beginning of a new era for our Indian citizens. . . . With the final settlement of all outstanding claims which this measure insures, Indians can take their place without special handicaps or special advantages in the economic life of our nation and share fully in its progress."

The Indian Claims Commission (ICC) was supposed to hear and rule on not only all pending claims but hundreds of new ones inspired by its creation. Of the 176 tribes or bands eligible to file claims, almost all did so, and many filed more than one grievance. A total of 370 petitions ultimately were presented, usually involving lands claimed by individual communities. The commission therefore had to determine whether Indian groups had appropriately claimed occupation and use of specific territories, whether they had been unjustly dispossessed of these lands, and if they had, how much compensation they should be awarded. The ICC had an initial charter of a mere five years. However, the slow nature of the work extended the ICC's life span until 1978. As Indian communities discovered, the creation of the commission did not guarantee any compensation or a prompt hearing. Nor were all those who served on the ICC exactly free from bias. Arthur Watkins, who as a U.S. Senator from Utah had been a leading proponent of termination, was chosen in 1960 to replace a retiring member of the unit. The claims process employed a lot of lawyers and provided work for social scientists, but the commission gave little credence to the oral histories of the tribes or the testimony of elders based upon such histories. Tribes found themselves mired in protracted proceedings that emphasized contentiousness rather than consensus. In order to have any hope at all of obtaining some compensation, however meager, Indian communities had to not only hire attorneys but invest these newcomers with unprecedented degrees of power and authority. Eventually over $800 million was awarded, but attorney fees swallowed a substantial portion of that sum.

Almost all Indians believed that the ICC did not serve them well. Most wanted the return of their lands more than the money bestowed. Few, if any, thought the financial compensation sufficient, because the commission tried to ascertain the value of the lands at the time of their usurpation rather than their current worth. The Black Hills yielded one of the most publicized and significant examples. In 1942 the U.S. Court of Claims had denied a Sioux claim, filed in 1923, for the unjust taking of their lands in western South Dakota. Although the ICC initially decided the Sioux could not press a renewed claim to it, the U.S. Court of Claims ordered the ICC to reconsider this decision. The ICC eventually decided that the Sioux had not been compensated sufficiently and awarded them $17.5 million. After this decision had been appealed by the U.S. government, the U.S. Supreme Court finally ruled in 1980 that this amount should stand, plus interest. However, the eight Sioux communities who took part in the suit refused to accept the money. Their position had not changed since 1923, or, indeed, since 1877, when the land was seized in violation of the terms of the Fort Laramie Treaty of 1868. They believed you could not put a price upon sacred ground. They wanted the Black Hills returned to them. As of 1997, this objective had not been realized, but the Sioux held their position.

In another instance, two Western Shoshone sisters, Mary and Carrie Dann, carried on for decades an ill-fated battle that grew out of dissatisfaction with the claims process. As had many other groups, the Western Shoshones had hired the Washington, D.C., firm of Wilkinson, Cragun, and Barker to represent them. Fifteen years after this firm had been employed by the Shoshones, the Claims Commission ruled in 1962 that certain Shoshone lands had been "taken" through the "gradual encroachment" of non-Indian settlers. Regardless of how the Shoshones might interpret their rights under the 1863 Treaty of Ruby Valley, they could only try to gain financial compensation for this loss rather than regain control of the land. Attorney Robert Barker chose to work with those Shoshones who would be willing to accept the money. The process thus obviously embittered many people and caused divisions among the Shoshones. Eventually in *U.S.* v. *Mary and Carrie Dann,* the federal government charged the sisters with illegally grazing their cattle on Bureau of Land Management land. Mary and Carrie Dann and their allies argued that the people had never surrendered their territory. Although the Danns won a temporary victory at the Circuit Court, the Supreme Court ruled in 1985 against their cause.

When the tribes decided to hire attorneys for the claims process, firms such as Wilkinson, Cragun, and Barker corralled a number of contracts, occasionally involving potential conflicts of interest in measuring the territory occupied or used by one Indian claimant versus another. Law firms in the nation's capital were well positioned to undertake this potentially lucrative mission, for federal offices and records were within easy reach. Some Indian nations, however, chose an individual attorney or a firm outside of Washington in order to facilitate more direct and frequent contact between themselves and their lawyers.

Regardless of their selection of legal representation, the eventual consequences of the claims process for Indian nations often proved more significant than at first might have been imagined. Tribal attorneys were poised to occupy center stage in tribal affairs. Not only did their potential success or failure cast a significant shadow over reservation life, but their involvement in the life of that community did not end at the commission's door. They had positioned themselves to become advisors to the tribal chairman or council, offering counsel on everything from economic development to the functioning of the tribal government itself. Depending on the character of the parties involved and the questions facing the particular Indian community, an attorney or a firm could soon occupy a place of great power. Many attorneys were dedicated professionals who zealously and effectively represented tribal interests; others were indifferent to the people's pressing needs and devoted insufficient time to them, were not very competent, or even could be swayed by payments made to them by companies desiring access to reservation resources. In any event, the presence of attorneys unquestionably altered the workings of tribal life.

The Termination Era

A weary John Collier resigned as commissioner of Indian affairs in January 1945. Although Collier and a small number of associates remained in Washington, during the war the offices of the bureau were moved (in 1942) to the Merchandise Mart in Chicago, where they remained until war's end. Reform had been halted not only by separation of most BIA personnel from the nation's capital, but as well by the absence of necessary funds, materials, and employees to continue to develop programs on reservations. The campaign to convert more of the boarding schools to day schools faltered in the face of prevailing conditions. School buses lacked gasoline and drivers. Many reservation roads became quagmires after snow or rain, but there was no money for improving roads, let alone building new highways, or, for that matter, new schools. Paul Schmitt, a school principal in Toadlena, New Mexico, also was responsible for supervising other Indian Service schools in the vicinity. But neither he nor the students could get to their schools. One mid-January morning, he wrote a letter to one of his daughters, describing the local situation: ". . . the snows and rain continue. Roads are impassable. I have not been to Cove, Red Rock, and Burnham since before Christmas. Only Nava is accessible and only Nava has operated its bus since the holidays. Sanostee has some 25 or 30 pupils walk in. The other schools are closed until the snows melt and the roads improve. This will mean late sessions in the spring, on into June, or the shortening of the term." Schmitt knew the likely outcome. "Probably the latter," he concluded, "because in so many instances Navajos move to the mountains or other areas where grazing is better." The winter weather in northwestern New Mexico was not going to change, so only with better transportation and roads could Navajo children have greater, more continuing access to education. That prospect awaited another day.

Collier's successor, William Brophy, had his hands full. The claims commission had been established and legal counsel frequently had been obtained, but the results of the claims process were yet to be determined. In some states Indian veterans were being denied the right to vote. Native individuals who had gained new horizons during the war years pondered the options for their home communities. What kind of economic development could be achieved? What kind of access to education would their children have? What responses would the federal government make to charges by critics such as O. K. Armstrong that the Collier years had inflicted "a collectivist system upon the Indians, with bigger doses of paternalism and regimentation"? To Armstrong, writing in 1945 for the *Reader's Digest,* the answer seemed simple. "Set the Indians Free!," he entitled his article. He urged Congress to "emancipate" the Indians by removing "restrictions" that stood in their way. Free from the roadblocks imposed by federal trusteeship, Native American communities would be liberated to achieve new heights now denied them. America, he argued, should not foster segregation but integration. Others owned lands privately rather than in common. The idea of a reservation had become outmoded. Employing rhetoric and logic eerily comparable to the language and reasoning of Indian policy reformers during the late nineteenth century, Armstrong called for a new era in Indian affairs. The Indians had proved their mettle during the war; they were ready to become full-fledged Americans. However, this effort to terminate federal trust responsibility spelled potential disaster for Indian America.

Two interrelated developments marked the period from war's end until the beginning of the 1960s. The first helped encourage the second. The drive toward terminating federal trust responsibility for Indians caused immediate harm and sometimes lasting damage, to certain Indian communities. However, the threat of federal withdrawal helped galvanize the beginnings of the modern Native American movement toward self-determination. Indian individuals and groups responded forcefully to reaffirm their rights and to find new means to realize them. Federal policies, then, did have negative consequences, yet Indians during this time also constructed the foundation for a movement in the 1960s that, like the African-American civil rights movement, had its origins in the prior decade.

Passage of concurrent resolution 108 in Congress in 1953 officially launched termination, but the resolution followed years of discussion and debate. The goal of withdrawing federal services from and federal protection of Indian communities fit well with the more conservative postwar mood in the United States. Republicans were more likely to favor turning Indian affairs over to the states, but momentum for termination developed during the Truman administration. Critics called for "liberation" of the Indians from the shackles of federal paternalism. They perceived reservations as antiquated relics of a bygone age. If reservations could be eliminated, their acreage fully divided into property, and individual Indians freed from the restraint of federal bureaucracy, they professed, Indians would be better able to reach their full potential.

Not all Native Americans disagreed with this prescription. Some fully subscribed to the idea of assimilation, while others bitterly resented the kind of control BIA officials still appeared to maintain over tribal councils. With the postwar economic boom centered in urban America, more than a few Indians saw the cities as places where opportunity beckoned. Yet most Native Americans wanted relocation to be voluntary rather than required. They recognized that the young could migrate to the city more easily and effectively than could older people. Indians knew that relocation could sever connections to the land and relationships among extended family members. They resented the heavy-handed tactics and simplistic thinking embraced by congressional proponents of "reform." In the process of resisting an imposed direction, Native persons increasingly began to chart a direction of their own, one that emphasized pride in tribal and Indian identity and a conviction that Indians were entitled to a wide range of rights.

After authorizing the Indian Claims Commission, Congress demanded an overhaul of the Bureau of Indian Affairs. An ailing William Brophy did not appear before the Senate Committee on Civil Service, chaired by William Langer of North Dakota. After being subpoenaed to appear, Assistant Commissioner William Zimmerman substituted for Brophy. Zimmerman felt trapped between the demands he knew the committee members would make for reducing the bureau's size and responsibilities and the widely varying conditions of different Indian reservations. Rejecting the notion that all Indian communities should be equally subject to withdrawal of federal protection, Zimmerman offered a kind of compromise. In his testimony before the committee on February 6, 1947, he divided Indian communities into three groups and listed four categories that might be used to determine their preparedness for altered status. One group could manage immediately without federal services. A second could move toward the end of trust status after a ten-year period of limited protection. A third should have a longer period than ten years before federal protection should be withdrawn. The four categories included the degree of acculturation of a tribe, its economy, its stance toward termination, and the attitude toward and ability of the state in which it was situated to take on the duties the federal government previously had assumed.

Unwittingly, Zimmerman had furnished advocates of termination with the kind of ammunition they needed. They immediately zeroed in on the first group of tribes he had delineated and made them immediate targets for termination. Included in the first group of tribes were those on whom the ax of termination eventually fell, including the Klamaths of Oregon and the Menominees of Wisconsin. Others, such as the Salish-Kootenais of the Flathead reservation in Montana, avoided termination, but only after a protracted campaign to do so. But all these Native peoples were put on notice. In 1947 Hugh Butler, a Republican senator from Nebraska, offered bills to end federal trust responsibility for not only the Menominee and Flathead reservations, but also for the Hupas of

California and various small reservations in that state, the Osages of Oklahoma, the Potawotamis of Kansas, the Turtle Mountain Anishinabeg of North Dakota, and the various Iroquois reservations in New York.

This list reveals something else at stake besides cutting federal spending and "liberating" American Indians. The Klamaths, Menominees, and Salish-Kootenais had reservation lands containing valuable economic resources. Once federal protection had been withdrawn, non-Indian outside interests were more likely to control or own the valuable timber and real estate of these three communities. Thus economic interest as well as ideology entered into the picture, just as it had during the allotment era.

Comparable economic interests affected the debate over the status of Indians in southeast Alaska. Tlingit and Haida land rights had been brushed aside in 1907 with the creation of the Tongass National Forest. The tribes had fourteen villages within the national forest's boundaries. After World War II, they persisted in their fight to participate in the development of an expanded timber industry in the Tongass. Representing the NCAI, Bronson traveled to the region to met with tribal leaders, who were trying to withstand the tremendous economic pressures. The Tongass Act of 1947, sponsored by Senators Butler and Watkins, however, verified the degree of non-Native power and the relative powerlessness of the affected Indian communities. Both the Forest Service and leading Alaskan politicians, including territorial governor Ernest Gruening, backed the construction of pulp mills in the forest. Gruening saw rapid development of Tongass resources as another vital step in Alaska's march toward statehood. Although the Tlingits and Haidas filed a land claims suit with the Indian Claims Commission, they were defeated in this particular confrontation. William Paul took some satisfaction in the fact there at least had been a battle. At the NCAI's fourth annual convention in Santa Fe in December 1947, D'Arcy McNickle emphasized the "need for Indians to stand together against the forces that would deprive them of their rights, their liberties, and their lands."

By the end of the 1940s, McNickle and other Native Americans knew too well that BIA officials would not join in that stand, but rather, join the forces to which McNickle referred. Brophy had resigned, to be followed by acting commissioner Zimmerman, and then a brief appearance by John R. Nichols as commissioner. During his eleven months in office, Nichols supported the rapid withdrawal of federal protection and failed to protest as Congress gave civil and criminal jurisdiction over the Agua Caliente reservation near Palm Springs to the state of California. Like other states, California had little respect for the notion of Indian separation or sovereignty. In May 1950 Dillon Myer succeeded Nichols. Myer had previously served as director of the War Relocation Authority, the agency in charge of interning Japanese Americans. He had butted heads with Collier during the war and now he was eager to reverse Collier's former policies.

Myer had taken a particular dislike to James Curry, an attorney who not only advised the NCAI but by the end of 1950 many Indian tribes, including the Pyramid Lake Paiutes. The Paiutes were embroiled in a highly publicized fight for their land and water rights. Myer attempted to restrict any tribe's ability to hire counsel and to limit any attorney so hired to a three-year term. After the NCAI, the American Bar Association, and other organizations howled in protest, Secretary of the Interior Oscar Chapman decided Myer had gone too far and revoked his proposed regulations.

Before leaving office at the start of the Eisenhower administration, Myer did his best to expedite the process of termination. Under his direction, the BIA targeted the Klamaths, the Menominees, the Osages, and the Sioux tribes of the Missouri country for prompt withdrawal of federal protection. Indian nations protested such plans, but Meyer believed these changes were necessary. Myer did not serve as commissioner long enough to finish the assignment he had undertaken, but he charted the course that his successor, Glenn Emmons, followed.

With the election of Dwight Eisenhower and a Republican Congress in 1952, the process of termination accelerated. Emmons, a banker from Gallup, New Mexico, was ideally suited to preside over the dissolution of the tribal estate. He was, if nothing else, an advocate of private property and free enterprise; two years after his arrival in town, he organized Gallup's first chamber of commerce. Emmons fully endorsed the views of Orme Lewis, a Phoenix attorney who had been appointed assistant secretary of the Department of Interior for public lands management. Lewis concluded that Indians "are Americans and ought to become a part of us for their own good and for the benefit they can give us," and emphasized he had "utterly no patience with those who think more about Indian culture than they do about Indians." "The world is made up of people who overran others, as a result of which we have great nations," he argued. "America is an outstanding example of that. . . ."

Attorney Felix Cohen observed the shift in thinking that had occurred during the postwar years. "Like the miner's canary," he wrote in 1953, "the Indian marks the shifts from fresh air to poison gas in our political atmosphere; and our treatment of Indians, even more than our treatment of other minorities, reflects the rise and fall in our democratic faith." "Here, as in other parts of the world," he added, "the undermining of that faith begins with the glorification of 'expert administrators' whose power-drives are always accompanied by soft music about 'the withering away of the state' or the ultimate 'liquidation' of this or that bureau."

Dimensions of Termination

The Indians were about to be overrun, because ending trust protection was deemed good for them and, in part, because the federal government now was controlled by people determined to reduce its scope, slice its expenditures, and return as much power as possible to the states. In 1953, Lewis tabbed an old political friend and ally, Phoenix banker Carl Bimson, to head a committee to study both withdrawal of trust status and reduction of the BIA's budget. The findings and recommendations of Bimson's committee reinforced several key objectives: to transfer powers from the BIA to the states or to other federal agencies; to reduce the emphasis on boarding schools; to relocate people to the cities; to eliminate the trust status held by reservations.

The passage of Public Law 280 in 1953 constituted a crucial victory in the crusade to transfer power. California, Minnesota,

Nebraska, Oregon, and Wisconsin took over criminal and civil jurisdiction on Indian lands, except for the Red Lake reservation in Minnesota, the Warm Springs reservation in Oregon, and the Menominee reservation in Wisconsin. Iowa and Washington later chose to assume some jurisdiction and Alaska assumed jurisdiction when it became a state. Historian John Wunder later labeled Public Law 280 "the most successful legal attack on Indian rights and sovereignty since the adoption of the Constitution." Eisenhower hesitated before signing the law, noting that it did not depend on Indian consent and that it mirrored an "un-Christian" spirit.

When Public Law 280 went into effect, it posed real problems for Indian communities. In Nebraska, state officials chose not to enforce the law, leaving the task to the counties. The counties backed off as well from assuming any substantial responsibility. The Omaha and Winnebago reservations in eastern Nebraska quickly were overrun by criminal activity and unprecedented violence. In Indian America, according to Joe DeLaCruz, a Quinault who later served as president of the NCAI, "we had conflicts with the states and counties over highways. We also had confrontations over our children and the rights of our children. States used Public Law 280 to impose their educational practices on our children." Hank Adams (Assiniboine) recalled when he was fourteen years old he attended with his stepfather a meeting of the Quinault tribal council in Washington. The tribe voted almost unanimously to oppose the extension of state jurisdiction over it. However, Adams remembered, the next week, the tribal council chairman, the tribal attorney, and the BIA superintendent "met at the agency and petitioned the state of Washington to assume jurisdiction over the reservation." "That action," he charged, "was a violation of Quinault sovereignty, and it revealed a fundamental problem between Indians and the federal government. Invariably, external forces contrive to get what they want at the expense of Indian people, Indian rights, and Indian sovereignty." Soon thereafter the tribal chairman committed suicide. The chairman, Adams believed, had felt guilty about "violating the tribe's governing institutions and the will of the Quinault people." It all made a lasting impression on a fourteen year old, who in the 1960s and 1970s became a nationally known activist for Indian rights.

Another example of the transfer of power came with the delegation of Indian health care responsibilities from the BIA to the Public Health Service (PHS). The PHS established a special division, the Indian Health Service, to assume this new assignment, which began officially on July 1, 1955. A PHS survey then revealed what everyone already knew: the government had not fulfilled its trust responsibilities in this realm. The transfer did result in an infusion of badly needed funds into the system, but major systemic problems remained. Moving the job from one bureaucracy to another did not offer a miraculous cure. At the same time, from a standpoint of the delivery of health services, the move made sense and yielded the possibility that more satisfactory health care might yet be realized.

The need for change in regard to educational opportunities for Indian students could not be denied. Boarding schools too often provided the only option for rural reservation students. These schools emphasized immediate, applied vocational training at the high school level, to the exclusion of preparation for college. For many reasons development of public schools on the reservations appeared to be needed, but funding remained a major hurdle. Without the same forms of taxation, how could such schools be constructed and maintained? The answer started to emerge through passage of two public laws originally designed to deal with the issue of providing education for military dependents. Public school districts had balked at shouldering the additional expenses for such children on military bases, so Congress had agreed to subsidize existing school districts or provide funds to establish new ones for this purpose. In 1953 these laws were amended to include comparable assistance for the schooling of Indian children on reservations. Public Law 815 thus provided money for the construction of new Indian public schools and Public Law 874 yielded funds for operating those schools.

These laws now made public education for Indians a goal that could be achieved, even though many states were less than enthusiastic about the prospect. State education officials often stalled, attempting to continue with the old system of funding through the Johnson-O'Malley Act of 1935 than with the more recent legislation. Johnson-O'Malley encouraged the continuation of control at the state and non-Indian district level, because funding through its auspices targeted Indian children enrolled in existing schools. Public laws 815 and 874 raised the possibility of schools under Indian control and the diminution of the Johnson-O'Malley funds. School boards had come to rely on and frequently had employed these funds for purposes other than the well-being of its Native students. The BIA had simply contracted with state departments of education, bypassing any form of Indian participation, let alone control. Now new alternatives existed.

The BIA also started to reduce its overall role in education. In 1952 it closed all of its remaining schools in Idaho, Michigan, Washington, and Wisconsin, and in the following year it shut down an additional nineteen boarding and day schools. The federal presence in education remained prominent in Alaska and on large reservations such as Navajo. But even on Navajo, the pendulum began to swing more toward public education. Passage of the Navajo-Hopi Rehabilitation Act in 1950 had set aside additional funds for construction of both new highways and new schools. Although it would not occur overnight, the transition away from significant reliance on boarding schools had started to take place. In the next generation, the old off-reservation boarding high schools began to close, as more and more Indian students attended public schools, either on or off of reservations. By 1970, 70 percent of all Indian children attended public schools, 25 percent attended federal schools, and 5 percent attended private or church-related schools. Those who still attended federal schools, for the most part, resided in one of three locations: Alaska, the Navajo nation, and the Dakotas.

The migration of Native Americans to the cities also had a major impact on the demographics of Indian education. A growing number of Native children found themselves in urban classrooms, where they generally constituted a minority population. The 1960 U.S. Census reported over 30 percent of Indians resided in urban areas. In some instances, migrants to the city concentrated in one part of town, forming an identifiable Indian neighborhood, as in the case of Chicago's Uptown. More frequently, and particularly in western cities such as Los Angeles or Phoenix, Native families scattered to smaller core population centers. In such dispersed circumstances, Indian children often confronted the same dilemmas of other urban children of color: older school facilities, higher turnover rate among teachers and students, and a greater preoccupation with order than with instruction. BIA officials were preoccupied with the potential economic benefits to be brought by urban migration and concentrated their efforts on job placement. They paid little attention to the matter of education for the children of relocatees. Once Native families moved to town, they resided in public school districts. Indian parents hoped that a move to the city might bring increased educational opportunities for their children. But by this time teenage students usually were more distant from their elders and from older relatives who encouraged responsibility in individual behavior. They struggled with new peer group influences. "Maybe the schools are better here," said one woman who had moved to Chicago, "but half the time my kids just don't go to school. They start out, but they never get there—or else I guess they leave before school is out. I don't know what to do with them."

The attempted withdrawal of federal trust responsibility encouraged the parallel notion of withdrawal of Indians from reservation to the city. Going from rural enclave to urban residence represented another variation on the pervasive theme of "liberation." Senator Watkins expressed the congressional conventional wisdom in 1957 when he argued: "Secluded reservation life is a deterrent to the Indian, keeping him apart in ways far beyond the purely geographic." Watkins believed that erasing all distinctions between Indians and other Americans offered the route to true freedom and equality. "Following in the footsteps of the Emancipation Proclamation of ninety-four years ago," he concluded, "I see the following words embellished in letters of fire above the heads of the Indians—THESE PEOPLE SHALL BE FREE!"

House Concurrent Resolution 108 passed Congress unanimously and without debate. This resolution, approved on August

1, 1953, by the House, called for certain tribes to be terminated from trust status and singled out certain states in which termination was to be applied. The tribes earmarked for termination included the Klamaths of Oregon, the Potawotamies of Kansas and Nebraska, the Salish-Kootenais of Montana, the Menominees of Wisconsin, and the Turtle Mountain Anishinabeg. In addition, California, Florida, New York, and Texas were to have trust status eliminated for all of its Indian communities.

Resolution 108 offered a blueprint but did not determine precisely where termination would take place. Opposition from the Salish-Kootenais and from Montana representatives such as Senator Mike Mansfield derailed termination at Flathead, while the protests from four Paiute bands in Utah were not acknowledged by Watkins. In addition to the Paiute communities in Utah, other Indian reservations met a comparable fate through congressional decision in 1954: the Menominees, the Klamaths, the Alabamas and Coushattas in Texas, the Uintah and Ouray Utes in Utah, and various small bands and tribes in western Oregon. Over the next five years, various "rancheria" Indian communities in California, the Peorias, Ottawas, and Wyandots of Oklahoma, and the Catawbas of South Carolina were also terminated. The ax last fell in 1962 on the northern Poncas of Nebraska. Some groups did not have their trust status actually eliminated until the 1960s. In the most publicized cases, Menominee and Klamath termination went into effect in 1961, seven years after they had been singled out for this transition. For these two reservations, as elsewhere, termination proved disastrous. Without federal protection and with corresponding needs for funds to provide local services, Indian reservations were forced to sell land previously held in trust. As a result, of termination, over 1 million acres of Native land would ultimately be "liberated" from Native ownership. The social, cultural, and economic consequences of termination quickly became apparent in the 1960s. Ironically, termination punished the very Indian communities that had enjoyed some degree of self-sufficiency and that had possessed considerable promise for further development.

Other threats to the Native future appeared during this time. Various federal agencies built new dams designed to assist in the production of electrical power, the control of floods, and the provision of recreation. Some of these projects inundated Indian lands and Native peoples were uprooted from traditional residences and economies. In the Northwest, the Bonneville Dam on the Columbia River eradicated the Indian dip-net fishery at the Cascades and the Grand Coulee erased the dip-net fishery at Kettle Falls. Worst of all, the Dalles Dam, also on the Columbia, eliminated the cherished fishing site of Celilo Falls. Following the demise of Celilo Falls in 1957, the government paid a settlement to members of the affected tribes, but the money could not replace the social and cultural significance this site had possessed for generations. The massive Pick-Sloan plan, carried out on the Missouri River by the Bureau of Reclamation and the Army Corps of Engineers, caused massive devastation for the Indian peoples of the northern Plains. Fort Randall Dam, Oahe Dam, and Big Bend Dam flooded over 202,000 acres of Sioux lands on the Cheyenne River, Crow Creek, Lower Brule, Standing Rock, and Yankton reservations. The Three Affiliated Tribes of North Dakota also had productive lands and towns disappear following the construction of Garrison Dam. Their tribal headquarters at Elbowoods vanished, to be replaced by New Town; the resulting lake, dubbed Lake Sakakawea, separated the southern part of the reservation from the rest of Fort Berthold. Carl Whitman and other reservation leaders fought the doomed fight against Pick-Sloan, just as did Frank Ducheneaux at Cheyenne River and his associates in Sioux country. Whitman and Ducheneaux received more than one lecture about standing in the way of "progress," even though the money promised by the federal government did not represent fair compensation, quite apart from the fact that no amount of money could substitute for what had been lost. South Dakota congressman E. Y. Berry figured prominently both in the overall push for termination and for the construction of the dams. Indeed, Berry professed to see a beneficial result that would ensue from dissolving Indian trust lands and submerging them as well. With the new freedom and the new money, he suggested, these reservations "may be able to get out from under the yoke of the Indian Bureau before too long."

Nor were such catastrophes confined to the West. A comparable tragedy occurred on Seneca lands in New York, where the Kinzua Dam, constructed by the Army Corps of Engineers just south of the New York–Pennsylvania state line, flooded more than 9,000 acres of Native land. The Senecas of the Allegany reservation lost Cold Spring Longhouse, a vital place in their ceremonial life. Their land under water, 130 families had to move to new homes. Federal officials saw the new housing tracts at Steamburg and at Jimersontown as improvements, but the Senecas themselves mourned the loss of their old residences. The dam would not be formally dedicated until 1966, but the decision had been made in the 1950s. Once again, "rehabilitation" funds were presented by Congress, but what did money mean in the face of the loss of the people's cherished longhouse and their homes and lands?

Urban Migration and Relocation

The urban migration of American Indians, as has been noted, did not begin in the 1950s; it had been ongoing throughout the twentieth century. The experiences of individuals during World War II, however, did accelerate the movement into the city. Commissioner Myer's own personal transition from county extension agent to Washington bureaucrat influenced his conclusion that the United States was becoming increasingly urban and that the Indian future lay in the city. He established in 1951 a Branch of Placement and Relocation, with a new office in Chicago and an expansion of existing offices already serving Navajos in Denver, Los Angeles, and Salt Lake City. By February 1952 Indian relocatees were being funneled through this program. In its first year, 1,785 people participated. They received limited funding for initial transportation, housing, and living costs in their new urban environment. From these beginnings, the federal relocation program expanded to other cities, such as Dallas and Cleveland. Many people were deliberately placed a long way from home, not unlike the early boarding schools, so as to discourage prompt or easy return to reservation communities.

Orme Lewis spoke for many in the Eisenhower administration and the Congress when he said it was "nuts" to maintain the separation of the reservation. Lewis knew from his own experience in Arizona that reservations could be cultural enclaves, the environments of which worked against the goal of assimilation. For Indians to be "rehabilitated" they needed to move. Such a philosophy was also reflected in the inauguration of the Indian Placement Program by the Church of Jesus Christ of Latter-day Saints. Over the next quarter of a century more than 60,000 Native students were taken from their homes and placed with Mormon families elsewhere.

The experiences of Indian migrants to the cities did not always live up to the optimistic projections accompanying relocation. As historian Kenneth Philp has suggested, not all Native Americans came to the city because the BIA forced them to do so, nor did all suffer dire consequences through such decisions. Social and economic problems on reservations and in other rural areas where Indians lived encouraged more than a few people to leave. Land allotment and cession had splintered many such locales. On the reservations individuals with particular skills could not necessarily put them to full use; individuals with particular ambitions could not necessarily realize them. Indians in the 1950s thus continued a pattern evident in the years before World War II, when the first generation after the implementation of allotment frequently chose new locations. Charlotte Wilson Heth (Cherokee) remembered:

Younger people in the 1930s, often still in their teens, moved to the smaller cities and towns near their homes to get work as unskilled laborers and domestics in order to support their families. . . . In my own family, my grandfather moved his family a few miles from his allotment to a very small town where his father lived, and finally to Sallisaw, the largest town in the county. He was a handyman, gardener, butcher, barber, and cook. In town he could use these skills to support his family. Out in the country, he could not.

Heth's mother, at the age of sixteen, moved to Muskogee in 1930 to find work and assist her parents in buying a home. When Heth was two, her parents moved on to Tulsa, so that her father could obtain a better job. "Finally," she noted, "as might be predicted, my parents moved to Los Angeles in 1964 to find work, only to return to Oklahoma as soon as they could retire in 1978."

The story of her family suggests that the era of relocation from the end of the 1940s to the end of the 1950s must be placed in a larger context of ongoing migration. Not only did many Indians come voluntarily to the city, but urban migration did not always mean permanent exile from the Native community. Just as they did in later years, many Indians moved back and forth from reservation to urban centers, did their best to visit family members "back home," and encouraged relatives to visit them during the period they remained away.

For all who came to the city, the matter of urban migration mirrored the push of reservation economic underdevelopment and the pull of potential prosperity in urban areas. Much of the criticism surrounding relocation centered less on the actual choice and more on the process surrounding that decision. Many Indians conceded the current need for some people to seek to regenerate their fortunes in an alternative setting. The overriding issues for these people were what kind of assistance they received in getting started in the city, what kind of jobs they could obtain, and what social services were available to them. Testimony from urban migrants attested to a great variety in their experiences. Nonetheless, those who had received more formal education or who already possessed a marketable skill, not surprisingly, tended to fare better. Bureau personnel spoke of job training and continuing aid, but most Indians who came to the city through the federal program reported they had received little of either. They explained they had been given a one-way bus ticket, were offered a little initial help with finding a job and housing, and then largely were left on their own. Their situation resembled that of the person who has never been swimming and who is tossed into the pool by a well-meaning "instructor," who then commands the thrashing "swimmer" to swim. A lot of Indians believed the government simply left them to drown. More than a few found urban life traumatic. Many had not previously encountered stoplights, elevators, telephones, and a world ruled by the insistent ticking of the clock. They often wound up living in substandard housing. Some struggled with alcoholism.

However, being left to drown did not always result in drowning. Navajo anthropologist Jennie Joe commented that many of those who had difficulty in the city also had difficulty on the reservation. Those who hailed from troubled family circumstances or who were not well grounded in their own tribal culture, or both, she said, "usually report continuous personal and other situational problems and these difficulties appear to follow them whether they are in the city or on the reservation." For example, many adults who had been raised in boarding schools had not had much of an opportunity to learn good parenting skills. However, the problems that emerged or reappeared in the city demanded immediate attention and Indians knew they could not rely on federal officials to provide timely or appropriate assistance. They thus began to establish organizations of their own to try to deal with common needs and concerns. The Chicago Indian Center, for example, was established in 1953. Through Indian centers, churches, and associations, urban Indians often discovered not only that they were not alone, but that they could gain counsel and camaraderie. The racism and discrimination they encountered sometimes inspired greater solidarity, greater understanding of a common multitribal identity as Indians, as opposed to an identity tied to a particular reservation, community, or tribe. A thirty-three-year-old man reported that up in Wisconsin Oneidas might fight with Menominees, but in Chicago "we're all good friends. When we get to the city we begin to think of ourselves more as Indians. Here we all stick together."

Toward Self-Determination

The more publicized movement for Indian rights of the 1960s, therefore, began in the previous decade. The National Indian Youth Council (NIYC), founded in 1961, traced its origins to the annual conferences of the Southwest Association on Indian Affairs, starting in 1956. In the Saint Francis auditorium in Santa Fe, Indian high school and college students met and talked. This assemblage became the Southwest Regional Youth Council, which met annually until the NIYC's inauguration. Anthropologist Alfonso Ortiz (San Juan Pueblo) credited "a core group from these youth councils, augmented later by alumni of D'Arcy McNickle's

Indian leadership training programs" for founding "the NIYC in Gallup after the American Indian Chicago Conference was held in June [1961]."

That conference in Chicago brought together about 500 Indians from nearly 100 communities all over the United States. Two anthropologists, Sol Tax and Nancy Lurie, helped with the necessary arrangements to have the group convene from June 13 to June 20 at the University of Chicago, where Tax taught. Supported by the NCAI, the meeting allowed an eclectic mix of young and old, including some from tribes not yet recognized by the federal government, to gather and to hear each other's views. The "Declaration of Indian Purpose," which emerged from the conference opposed termination and Kinzua Dam and addressed the needs of Indian tribes for better education and medical care as well as economic development. For many individuals the conference encouraged or reinforced their sense of commonality among Indian people and the corresponding interest they had in speaking out for the achievement of a brighter Native American future.

Urbanization and the continued expansion of contact between and among Indian communities during this era also inspired the growth of two other major modern pan-Indian institutions: the Native American Church and the powwow. In the 1950s the annual meeting of the Native American Church began to take place for the first time outside of Oklahoma. The NAC convention convened in 1953 in Macy, Nebraska, on the Omaha reservation, followed by gatherings in Tama, Iowa, Wisconsin Dells, Wisconsin, and Scottsbluff, Nebraska. Navajo migrants to the San Francisco Bay Area and Denver helped promote the NAC in these locations. The powwow also expanded as a common meeting ground for Indians of all tribes. The powwow circuit continued to develop in the Plains, and Indians in urban locales began to plan and establish their own powwows. For some smaller Indian communities outside of the Plains region, the powwow began to emerge as a means through which a recognized form of Indian expression and celebration could occur. In the wake of lost traditions, a new tradition was being established.

Such cultural revitalization, of course, ran contrary to the assimilationist spirit that fueled the fires of termination. And there were other signs suggesting that Indian identity would not easily be extinguished. Building upon the legacy of the New Deal years, Indian arts and crafts flourished in the postwar years. The Southwest particularly experienced an impressive outpouring of artistic expression. Kenneth Begay (silversmith, Navajo), Marie Chino (potter, Acoma), Lucy Lewis (potter, Acoma), Charles Loloma (silversmith, Hopi), and Daisy Tauglechee (weaver, Navajo), together with previously mentioned artists such as Allan Houser and Maria Martinez, gained heightened recognition and financial rewards from an expanding marketplace. Elsewhere a rediscovery of the beauty of traditional Native art set the stage for an imminent renaissance. For example, according to artist Bill Holm, exhibits of traditional Northwest Coast art in this era rekindled interest throughout the region, making it possible for extraordinary artists such as Robert Davidson (Haida) to prosper in the next generation.

Cattle ranching offered other opportunities for the reaffirmation of Indian identity and proved to be a livelihood that enabled individuals and families to remain on reservation lands. On San Carlos and Tohono O'odham in Arizona, Blackfeet and Northern Cheyenne in Montana, and other reservations throughout the West, Native ranchers attempted to improve the quality of their livestock and increase their returns from the industry. They were often frustrated by BIA officials with little sympathy for tribalism, but they persisted in their determination. At times they enjoyed clear success. "Famed Apache Cattle Raisers to Complete Peak Spring Sales," the headline in the (Phoenix) *Arizona Republic* declared on May 25, 1952. In 1955 Tohono O'odham cattle sales totaled $634,000. In Lakota country, the people of Pine Ridge even succeeded in imposing a tribal tax on non-Indian ranchers who leased Lakota land. The matter went to federal court in 1956, with the white ranchers' indignant lawyer complaining that the Indians were acting like a "foreign nation." However, U.S. District Court judge George T. Mickelson eventually ruled against the white ranchers, saying they had a choice: pay the tax or do not use the land. Mickelson affirmed that Indian tribes were "sovereign powers and as sovereign powers can levy taxes."

By the end of the 1950s it had become evident that the courts presented one of the key arenas in the evolving battle for Indian rights. The acquisition of legal counsel inspired tribes to test the judicial waters in trying to determine just when and where their rights could be affirmed or clarified. And larger tribes such as the Navajos began to develop their own court systems, in part as a response to the potential of assumed state jurisdiction over Native lands. The establishment of tribal courts, in turn, provided the possibility of greater self-determination. *Williams* v. *Lee* in 1959 illustrated the point. A non-Indian trader on the Navajo reservation sought payment for goods obtained on credit. He sued his delinquent Navajo customer in state court. The U.S. Supreme Court ultimately denied the trader's case, concluding that the Navajo courts offered proper venue for such action. Writing for the majority, Justice Hugo Black contended: "There can be no doubt that to allow the exercise of state jurisdiction here would undermine the authority of the tribal courts over Reservation affairs and hence would infringe on the right of the Indians to govern themselves."

That right now appeared more possible. Although the withdrawal of federal responsibility still would take its toll in Indian country, around the United States Native people realized that the overall movement toward termination had started to slow. In many quarters the talk turned to the need to work even more strenuously within tribes and across tribal boundaries in order to achieve a greater degree of control over Indian lands and Indian lives.

CHAPTER FIVE

The Struggle for Sovereignty, 1962–1980

Each night and each morning, as he always had, the old man prayed. Juan de Jesus Romero had reached ninety years of age and as the cacique, the spiritual leader of his community, he had been the quiet and largely unobserved force behind the struggle by Taos Pueblo to regain sacred ground. Now, in 1970, the climax of that long campaign had finally neared. If Blue Lake could be regained, he had reason to be optimistic about the Taos future. If Congress rejected the rationale for the return of Blue Lake, then the Taos future would be grim, indeed. Determined that Blue Lake would be officially and fully returned to his people by the U.S. government, he had fought for more than six decades to regain the spiritual center of Taos Pueblo life. Earlier in the twentieth century, the federal government had granted a fifty-year use permit for Blue Lake to the pueblo, but had maintained control of the lake as part of Carson National Forest. The multiple use philosophy of the Forest Service caused lands in Carson to be scarred by logging; the idea of religious privacy or sacred space for the Native people had not enjoyed a high priority. The influential senator from New Mexico,

Clinton Anderson, had resisted the idea of returning Blue Lake and significant acreage surrounding it to Taos Pueblo. So Juan Jesus de Romero had made the long journey to Washington, D.C., to add his voice to that of the tribe's attorney and other members of his community.

He emphasized that if Blue Lake and the land around it were not fully returned to Taos Pueblo then it would mean the end of his people's life. "Our people," he declared, "will scatter as the people of other nations have scattered. It is our religion that holds us together." Through the force of his presence and testimony, combined with the efforts of Paul Bernal and others from the village, Taos Pueblo eventually won its battle for sovereignty—and survival. H.R. bill 471, which returned Blue Lake and 48,000 acres to the pueblo, found its champions in the federal government among Democratic senators Fred Harris, Ted Kennedy, and George McGovern and Republican senator Barry Goldwater. On December 2, 1970, the U.S. Senate passed the bill by a vote of 70 to 12; on December 15, 1970, President Richard M. Nixon signed the bill into law.

Before the vote in the Senate, the cacique had chanted with Bernal, Pueblo Governor Querino Romero, and another veteran of the campaign, James Mirabal. They prayed and they waited. At the moment the vote was announced in the Senate, the people of Taos Pueblo who had assembled in the Senate gallery joined in the celebration. Juan de Jesus Romero rose to his feet. He held up three canes, which along with Blue Lake, symbolized the vitality, the past, and the future of Taos Pueblo sovereignty. Those present on that occasion will always remember that sight and that triumph.

The canes of Taos and other pueblos in the Southwest involved a long and significant story. The first cane dated from the era of early Spanish incursion in the region. Each pueblo governor received a cane crowned with silver from the Spanish government, according to Jemez Pueblo historian Joe Sando, as "symbols of justice and leadership." The cane was passed down from one governor to the next. After Mexico gained its independence from Spain in 1821, its new government presented a second group of silver crowned canes. These were passed down from one lieutenant governor to the next. Following the Treaty of Guadalupe Hidalgo in 1848, the United States then assumed jurisdiction in the region. In 1863 the United States formally continued the tradition of presenting a cane. President Abraham Lincoln gave the pueblo governors new canes, again crowned in silver, with the pueblo name, 1863, and "A. Lincoln" engraved on each. The Lincoln canes were transferred from one pueblo governor to the next. In the 1980s, the governor of New Mexico and the King of Spain presented additional canes to the pueblos.

Blue Lake, the pueblo cacique and the pueblo governor, and the canes offer important emblems of the evolving struggle for sovereignty by American Indians in the 1960s and 1970s. During this period, many different confrontations erupted over control and revolved around symbols. In another time, the assumption of power over Blue Lake by the Forest Service had aroused strong emotions and encouraged passionate protests. Yet the degree of significance and seriousness of this action went largely unnoticed by the non-Indian public. By the beginning of the 1960s modern forms of communication, especially television, had altered how Americans heard and learned about such matters. Juan de Jesus Romero was not only often quoted but also frequently photographed. The image of this small, old, dignified man provided additional power to the Taos Pueblo cause. The fight over Blue Lake, the clash between Taos leaders and Senator Anderson, and the canes themselves all served as reminders of the importance of history, place, tradition, and memory in the Indian world. They also spoke to the ongoing, complicated relationships between Indian peoples and those who came later to the Americas. They attested to different claims of authority and, at times, different expressions and understandings of sovereignty.

In the 1960s and 1970s those expressions came in varying guises and those understandings revealed varying degrees and forms of self-determination. Through demonstrations in the Pacific Northwest over fishing rights, the emergence of the American Indian Movement, the occupation of Alcatraz, the Trail of Broken Treaties, and the confrontations at Akwesasne and Wounded Knee, Native Americans dramatized and underscored their commitment to vital concerns. In Alaska, Maine, and elsewhere Indians sought to claim, regain, or reassert their rights to land. In the areas of tribal recognition, the welfare of children, religious freedom, and tribal membership, Native peoples wrestled with central matters relating to identity. Indians also attempted to gain more control over their water, their economies, and their education. In literature, art, and history, Indian perspectives had major effect. In the course of a generation, termination was overcome and a new route charted toward the Native future. The hereditary religious leader of Taos Pueblo, Juan de Jesus Romero, lived to see a great many transitions. He died on July 30, 1978, confident about the Taos future.

Restoration

As termination of trust status began to take full effect in the 1960s, the results belied the buoyant optimism of Arthur Watkins and other congressional proponents. The ending of federal protection quickly impoverished heretofore relatively self-sufficient Indian communities such as the Menominees, who had operated their own utility company and hospital and been one of three tribes to reimburse the federal government for its provision of community services. Termination transformed Menominee into Menominee County. The Menominees already had dissipated half of the tribal treasury of $10 million in order to pay for court costs to implement a process few had wanted. In addition, they had to spend much of their remaining budget to modernize the tribal sawmill, which had been neglected by the BIA. The small hospital and utility company could not meet the new state standards and soon closed. The lumber mill faced a declining market for its product and new business taxes. Families now had to pay state taxes on their lands. Some Menominees were compelled to sell their homes, and some now asked for welfare assistance as they confronted a downward economic spiral. Congress had wanted to reduce federal appropriations to Menominees, but the effects of its action now forced the federal government to pour much more money into the new county. Furthermore, Menominee students now faced long commutes to attend school in a neighboring county often facing racism when they got there.

Menominee determination to overturn termination encouraged the development of new organizations to fight for that objective. Members of the Citizens' Association for the Advancement of the Menominee People (CAAMP) helped inaugurate DRUMS (Determination of Rights and Unity for Menominee Shareholders). DRUMS revealed the connection between Indians living in the cities and those living on reservations or former reservations during this era. Menominees in Milwaukee and Chicago organized DRUMS to protest non-Indian influence in Menominee Enterprises Incorporated (MEI), the entity created to manage tribal assets after reservation status had been eliminated. MEI had initiated controversial economic development ventures, such as Legend Lake, to sell vacation home sites to outsiders. Menominees were furious about these developments. Protestors would lie down in roads leading toward realtors' offices, trying to block outsiders from purchasing Menominee land. DRUMS would eventually grow into a movement that united tribal members in an effort to restore reservation status. Ada Deer became a major spokesperson for restoration. Deer later remembered that initially supporters of restoration were regarded as "agitators and crazies." Undeterred, she gained valuable allies within Wisconsin, such as attorney Joseph Preloznik of Madison. Deer was aided by the efforts of many other resolute Menominee women, including her mother and her sister, as well as Joan Keshena Harte, Sylvia Wilbur, and Shirley Daly. In time the Menominees succeeded in overturning termination, although they could not erase all of its effects. Wisconsin senators Gaylord Nelson and William Proxmire introduced legislation to restore reservation status and, after the Congress voted its approval, President Nixon signed the Menominee Restoration Act on December 22, 1973.

The Menominees had not been alone, either in suffering ill effects from termination or in fighting to overturn it. The Klamath reservation also experienced severe economic, cultural, and social trauma from cessation of trust status. In 1986 the community regained its position as a reservation, but not until after major damage had been inflicted upon its land holdings and overall economy. Most of the other terminated Indian groups also gained restoration, yet the process took usually two decades or more to accomplish. Those communities today are still recuperating from the divisive, catastrophic impact of an ill-advised policy, but their very survival is additional testimony to Native resilience.

Restoration of reservations should be understood in the context of shifts in national politics and ongoing contradictions or paradoxes in regard to the status of Indians in American life. The director of the American Indian Law Center, P. Sam Deloria (Standing Rock Sioux) argued: "The transition of recent federal policy from termination to self-determination reflects only a tactical shift in the fundamental commitment of a society to bring Indians into the mainstream, not a movement toward a true recognition of a permanent tribal right to exist." Deloria concluded that a tension continued to exist between self-determination and federal trust responsibility. During the heyday of President Lyndon Johnson's Great Society, the desire to improve conditions on Indian reservations and elsewhere inspired the creation of a variety of programs through the Office of Economic Opportunity (OEO). Federal funds now came to Indian communities from sources other than the BIA. Although Indians increasingly assumed power within the bureau, it remained bureaucratic in its tendencies and chronically unable or unwilling to foster many plans that promised sudden or significant change. Thus Head Start, legal services, and other programs with important grass-roots consequences came to reservations from Washington but not from the BIA. Legal services programs gave individual Indians, as well as tribal governments access to legal counsel. This permitted Native people generally for the first time to confront more directly a host of concerns, ranging from sales contracts and wage claims to family-related issues. The California Indian Legal Services program started a project that grew into the Native American Rights Fund (NARF). A Ford Foundation grant in 1970 permitted NARF to open its doors in Boulder, Colorado. NARF quickly emerged as a major force in many different battles relating to tribal sovereignty and standing, including federal recognition, fishing and hunting rights, taxation, use of natural resources, water rights, religious freedom, education, and health care. David Getches served as the organization's founding director. Within three years, original staff attorney John Echohawk (Pawnee) became NARF's director, a position he still held in 1997. NARF also recruited other Natives who had recently completed law school, including Walter Echo-Hawk (Pawnee), Yvonne Knight (Ponca-Muscogee), Doug Nash (Nez Perce), Browning Pipestem (Otoe-Osage), and Leland Pond (Assiniboine).

Younger tribal members, many of them college-educated, seized upon varied new programs from the outside to promote community development, to foster their own political careers, or to work more aggressively for social, economic, or political change. This pattern, in turn, often encouraged more progressive tribal governments and also stiff resistance from established tribal leaders who feared a redistribution of both money and power. On many reservations, however, suspicion and uncertainty greeted the passage of the Economic Opportunity Act in 1964 as part of the "War on Poverty." These emotions gave way to more enthusiasm as funds became more generous and it became more evident that the communities themselves actually could control the community action programs. Programs like Head Start created opportunities for work and new career horizons. In the Salt River community in Arizona, for example, women gained a high percentage of positions in Head Start and youth programs, for they had more clerical skills and traditionally had more responsibility for care of children. Participation in such new endeavors encouraged the political as well as social empowerment of women. In the 1970s, women began to chair committees and boards dealing with industrial development and land management; in 1980 Alfretta Antone became the first woman vice president of the Salt River Pima-Maricopas. She served in this capacity until 1990, to be succeeded by Merna Lewis, whose career had begun as a teacher aide for Head Start.

At Salt River and throughout Indian America in the 1960s and 1970s one saw the rise of new leadership on reservations, in the cities, on college and university campuses, and in multitribal organizations. These leaders called upon Native peoples to regain control of their lives and lands, and to begin to realize more fully the kind of sovereignty that had once characterized Indian communities prior to European incursion. While still in his early twenties, Clyde Warrior (Ponca) became the leader of the National Indian

Youth Council. His speeches and essays articulated with angry eloquence the frustrations and urgency felt by his generation. In Washington state leaders like Joe DeLaCruz and Lucy Covington (Colville) spoke out for the rights of their people. In New Mexico, Zuni governor Robert Lewis started his tenacious quest for the return of sacred ground. In Mississippi, Philip Martin (Choctaw) began the first of three separate tribal chairmanships during which he would challenge BIA authority and eventually enjoy great success in building a viable local economy.

These initiatives sometimes were aided by federal funding and at other times were continued despite federal interference. Many observers perceived an inherent contradiction between true sovereignty and acceptance of federal funds or new programs conceived in Washington, D.C. Vine Deloria, Jr., retorted that while restoration of Indian tribes "to a status of quasi-international independence with the United States acting as their protector" might strike most Americans "as either radical or ridiculous," it was neither. The reality of the federal presence in Indian country did not mean Indians had to sacrifice principle, P. Sam Deloria concluded, but rather they had to make "realistic adaptation" to that fact. The federal government could accelerate or retard Indian control over Indian communities but could not achieve it altogether. Moreover, self-determination did not mean access to untold amounts of federal assistance with no accountability for that infusion. As for the new wave of publicity attending the push for self-determination, P. Sam Deloria contended: "Indians did not discover they were Indians in the early 1970s. We were not reborn; we were simply noticed."

Fishing Rights and the Growth of Activism

That notice accompanied a series of dramatic crusades to highlight inequity and injustice. These campaigns all had their roots in prior treaties, agreements, and judicial decisions. One of the first well-publicized attempts concerned Indian fishing rights in the Pacific Northwest. Washington territorial governor Isaac Stevens had negotiated five separate treaties in 1854 and 1855 with various Native groups. The tribes salvaged only small amounts of land from these deliberations, but all the treaties noted specifically that "The right of taking fish at usual and accustomed grounds and stations is further secured to said Indians in common with all citizens of the territory." The state of Washington over time, however, worked against the realization of these fishing rights by excluding Indians from traditional fishing sites and by favoring the interests of white sport fishers and the burgeoning salmon canneries of the region. The Yakamas and the Makahs in the 1940s began to take matters to court, and in 1954 Bob Satiacum (Puyallup) challenged state fish and game laws by gill-netting near Tacoma. He was arrested. Other "fish-ins" followed, inspired by both long simmering resentments against the restrictions of Indian fishing rights and the success of sit-ins in the national civil rights movement. The Survival of American Indians Association, founded in 1964, helped organize these protests. Janet McCloud (Tulalip) and Hank Adams were among its leaders. Film celebrities such as Marlon Brando and Jane Fonda began making their way to places like Frank's Landing to assert their support for the cause.

People like Brando and Fonda soon wandered off to other causes, but the confrontations continued. By the end of the decade, the federal government brought suit to insure that the states of Oregon and Washington would allow Indians an appropriate and fair share of the annual "harvest" of fish. The case in Washington had more serious overtones, as it involved a larger number of tribes and a more determined resistance from the state and the non-Indian sport and commercial fishing industry. Filed in 1970 and ruled upon in 1974 by U.S. District Court judge George Boldt, *United States* v. *Washington* sent shock waves through the waters of the Northwest. In what became commonly known as the "Boldt decision," the judge ruled that non-Indians could not take more than one-half of the salmon going through the "usual and accustomed" grounds of the treaty tribes. The state appealed, but lost; in 1979 the U.S. Supreme Court upheld the conclusions Boldt had reached.

The decision, according to attorney Alvin Ziontz, "proved to be a tremendous impetus for the revival of the Indian fishing economy. It not only affirmed the rights of Indians to have their harvest opportunity respected by the State, but left the Indians unrestricted as to the type of gear which could be used at any of their usual and accustomed grounds." More Indians began to fish and to add to their gear; more urban Indians returned home to their reservations. The percentage of the fish caught by Indians increased from an average of 5 percent in the four years prior to 1974 to 27.2 percent in 1980 to 49 percent in 1984. Heightened participation in the industry spawned related new industries on the reservations, including fish buying, fish processing, and the raising of fish through aquaculture programs. Tribes also built new fish hatcheries, started fisheries departments, and saw their governments grow in stature and influence. At the same time, questions arose over what constituted tribal membership, the amount of fish each tribe of the region should be allowed to harvest, and other related matters. The central importance of fishing in both the culture and the economy of the Northwest guaranteed that regardless of court decisions, fishing rights would remain a source of contention and disagreement.

The fight over fishing rights in the Northwest also offered early experience for a number of Indian activists who went on to participate in the early years of the American Indian Movement (AIM). Darrelle "Dino" Butler (Tolowa), Janet McCloud, Sid Mills (Yakama), Leonard Peltier (Anishinabe-Dakota), Bob Robideau (Anishinabe) and Jim Robideau (Anishinabe), and Joseph Stuntz Killsright (Coeur d'Alene) witnessed the effectiveness of the fish-ins as well as other protests and proceeded to appropriate lessons from them. Anishinabeg in Minneapolis, including Dennis Banks, Clyde and Vernon Bellecourt, and George Mitchell, started AIM in the summer and fall of 1968. Indian residents of the city had complained bitterly about their treatment by local police officers, so AIM first focused its attention on this issue. Soon AIM added to its ranks and to its agenda. Although the organization was not directly engaged in the occupation of Alcatraz Island in 1969, Banks had been involved in the overall protest. AIM moved over the next several years on a variety of fronts, applying the approach of highly publicized occupations and demonstrations. Paul Chaat Smith (Comanche) and Robert Warrior (Osage) later described

AIM as "less a political organization than a force of nature;" it enjoyed its greatest influence and success in the first decade after its founding. In the wake of the imprisonment of Leonard Peltier in 1977, federal infiltration and subsequent factionalism, and the deaths in 1979 from a suspicious house fire of AIM leader John Trudell's (Santee Dakota) wife, three children, and mother-in-law, it dissolved as a formal national association and continued in several locations through local efforts, with its most significant residual influence in the northern Plains. Not until the mid-1990s did the organization begin to attempt a national revitalization. The dissatisfaction of Indian women activists also contributed to AIM's decline. Janet McCloud and others had grown weary, as she phrased it, "of the sexist macho stuff we got from the men in AIM. We needed to do something for the women. We are the backbone of our communities—men are the jawbone." During the second half of the 1970s, McCloud and others established Women of All Red Nations. WARN addressed concerns ranging from involuntary sterilization and domestic violence to the revitalization of languages and cultures. By the late 1980s the Indigenous Women's Network (IWN) had become the primary Native women's organization, a place it continued to hold a decade later.

The occupation of Alcatraz represented an important landmark of this era. And, while the decision to take control of the infamous island erupted from local conditions, the choice also rested upon the legacy of the civil rights, women's, student and other movements of the 1960s. Most of the early protesters on Alcatraz were not initially from the San Francisco Bay area but had migrated there from all over the United States. Many of them were relocatees who had experienced poor housing, inadequate schooling, and other problems; they knew about the struggles over Kinzua Dam in New York and fishing rights in the Northwest. The creation of United Native Americans (UNA) in the area in the summer of 1968 provided another common bond. UNA encouraged recognition of common Indian concerns and expressions of unity across tribal boundaries.

Other developments also had an immediate influence on the decision to occupy Alcatraz. On the United States-Canada border,

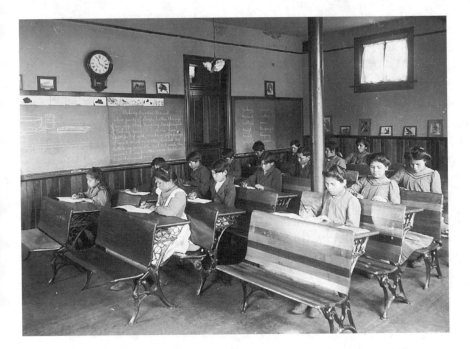

Above: Oneida students complete their assignments, with a recipe for baking powder biscuits on the blackboard. Oneida Indian School, Wisconsin, 1910. Courtesy of the State Historical Society of Wisconsin (WHi 20549)

Opposite top: Carlos Montezuma (Yavapai), M.D., started a newsletter, Wassaja, *to call for the abolition of the Bureau of Indian Affairs. From his home in Chicago, Montezuma sent the publication throughout the United States.* Courtesy of Arizona Collection, Arizona State University Libraries.

Opposite bottom: Gertrude Simmons Bonnin (Yankton Dakota), musician and writer, served as an officer in the Society of American Indians and later founded the National Council of American Indians. Courtesy of Institute of Indian Studies, University of South Dakota.

Vol. 2, No. 8   ISSUED MONTHLY   November, 1917

Opposite top: Apache students demonstrate an interest in baseball and cattle ranching. Lutheran mission school, San Carlos, Arizona, early 1920s. Courtesy of Arizona Collection, Arizona State University Libraries.

Opposite bottom: Navajo family prepares for a journey, 1930s. Photograph by Milton Snow. Courtesy of Arizona Collection, Arizona State University Libraries.

Above: Commissioner of Indian Affairs, John Collier, addresses a crowd at the Tohono O'odham rodeo, 1940. Standing next to Collier is Tohono O'odham leader Pete Blaine. Courtesy of the Arizona Historical Society, Tucson (AHS #8508).

Opposite top: D'Arcy McNickle (Salish-Kootenai) was an important writer, who also helped start the National Congress of American Indians, and later headed the Newberry Library's Center for American Indian History. Courtesy of the Newberry Library.

Opposite bottom: Taos Pueblo, New Mexico, was the site of an important campaign for the return of Blue Lake, a sacred place. Taos Pueblo regained Blue Lake in 1970. Courtesy of Arizona Collection, Arizona State University Libraries.

Below: The occupation of Alcatraz Island from November 1969 to June 1971 publicized the concerns of urban and reservation residents and encouraged subsequent protests and occupations. Courtesy of the Heard Museum, Phoenix.

Opposite top: Calvin Fast Wolf (Lakota) greets Stevie King (Oneida) at the D'Arcy McNickle Center for American Indian History booth during the 27th annual Chicago powwow, 1980 . Courtesy of The Newberry Library.

Opposite bottom: Northern Wisconsin witnessed confrontations in the 1980s and 1990s over the assertion of Indian fishing rights. Photograph by Amoose. Courtesy of Amoose, Ashland, Wisconsin.

Top: Rodeo became a significant tradition in many western Indian communities in the twentieth century. Breakaway roper Michelle Walking Bear (Crow), was also Miss Rodeo Crow Fair in 1994. Crow Agency, Montana. Photograph by Linda MacCannell. Courtesy of Linda MacCannell, Calgary, Alberta.

Bottom: Steer rider Ben Hart (Three Affiliated Tribes) of New Town, North Dakota, participated in 1994 in one of rodeo's most challenging events. Crow Nation Fair and Rodeo, Crow Agency, Montana. Photograph by Linda MacCannell. Courtesy of Linda MacCannell, Calgary, Alberta.

Mohawks protested the denial of their free access between the two countries. Citing the Jay Treaty of 1794, which specifically permitted Indians to take goods without customs payment and to travel without restriction between Canada and the United States, the Mohawks balked at tolls on the Cornwall International Bridge and fees demanded by customs agents. They blockaded the bridge in 1968 and by February, 1969, the Canadian government had given in to these demands. The controversy helped spark the start of a newspaper published on the Akwesasne reservation, *Akwesasne Notes,* and the founding of White Roots of Peace, a group of Mohawks dedicated to traditional tribal values who traveled throughout North America to speak. *Akwesasne Notes* immediately attracted thousands of readers across the continent. It brought news not only from Akwesasne but elsewhere in Indian country; it carried word of other protests, such as on the Pit River reservation in northern California. Finally, the occupation was encouraged by the involvement of many college students, who had become increasingly aware of the roles and results of organized protest. By the fall of 1969, the idea of occupying Alcatraz began to move from possibility to probability. A fire in October 1969 burned down the San Francisco Indian Center. In the aftermath of this event, Indian activists began to see in the occupation of Alcatraz a way to dramatize the need for such centers and the denial of Indian rights. Alcatraz had been a military prison before it became a federal penitentiary. Modocs and Hopis had been imprisoned there. But the memories of such incarcerations had dimmed and Alcatraz simply stood as a symbol of the federal presence.

The actual occupation of the island also had its antecedents. A brief protest had been waged there by five Lakota men on November 9, 1964. They claimed the island for " Indians of all tribes," left, returned for an overnight stay, then left again. The 20th of November found the occupying group back once again, their numbers swelled to eighty by the addition of seventy UCLA Native students recruited by Richard Oakes (Mohawk). Oakes, Adam Nordwall (Anishinabe), and others from the Bay Area shared a common objective in taking control of the island, but differed in regard to personality and the range of their goals. Even with internal disagreements, the Indians succeeded in holding the island until June 11, 1971, when remaining occupants were taken from Alcatraz by the U.S. Coast Guard. During this period, the "Indians of All Tribes" generated national and international publicity for grievances shared by a great many Native Americans. Permanent control of the island proved to be impossible. Many Native students returned to college in January, 1970. The twelve-year-old-stepdaughter of Richard Oakes fell down a stairwell in the former prison and died as a result of her injuries that same month; Oakes and his family departed the island following this tragedy. Other Indians arrived and disagreements arose over leadership. Through the period of occupation, nonetheless, Native Americans on "the Rock" brought the attention of the world to the general question of the status of urban and reservation Indians and the more particular needs of Indian students. In addition, as historian Troy Johnson has noted, the occupation played no small role in inspiring more than seventy other occupations of other sites in the years that immediately followed.

Two of the most significant of these occupations were those which occurred in Washington, D.C., and on the Pine Ridge reservation. In the fall of 1972 a Native protest group calling itself the Trail of Broken Treaties converged upon the capital. This procession publicized a number of grievances, both local and national, both new and of long-standing. But the main reason for the caravan stemmed from the treaties themselves and the failure of the federal government to live up to their part of the agreement. AIM and NIYC members helped carry out the protest. Robert Burnette (Sicangu Lakota), Reuben Snake (Ho-Chunk), Anita Collins (Paiute-Shoshone), and LaVonne Weller (Caddo) served as officers. After the caravan arrived in Washington, several hundred people proceeded to the BIA offices for initial discussions. BIA security guards demanded that the protesters leave. Resistance to this demand led to occupation of the building itself. The occupation of "The Native American Embassy," as the protesters labeled it, lasted a week. Opponents of this action charged that occupation of the building caused considerable damage to federal property and to the non-Indian view of Native peoples. Supporters of the action believed it highlighted BIA mismanagement through the release of previously confidential files and pressured the government to take the group's demands more seriously.

The occupation of Wounded Knee followed directly from the standoff in the national capital. Russell Means (Oglala Lakota), Banks, and others from AIM journeyed to Pine Ridge in South Dakota, where they joined with traditional Lakota leaders to try to unseat the new tribal chairman, Richard Wilson. Pine Ridge politics long had been characterized by severe factionalism, and under the Wilson administration things had reached a breaking point. Wilson did not permit disagreement and strong-armed those who dissented from his opinion. Efforts to impeach him failed. Just over the reservation border in Buffalo Gap, a Lakota man, Wesley Bad Heart Bull, was murdered and the non-Indian who killed him was charged only with second degree manslaughter. Some Indians who protested the watered-down charge made their way to the county courthouse in Custer, South Dakota, where they confronted local authorities and then set fire to the building.

Three weeks later, on February 27, 1973, AIM members and their allies took over the village of Wounded Knee on Pine Ridge. Angry about Wilson's unwillingness to meet with them, AIM members assembled on February 27 at a community center, Calico Hall, near the town of Pine Ridge. People from throughout the reservation expressed their fears and frustrations, often in a rush of Lakota, a language spoken by neither Dennis Banks nor Russell Means. Even if the men required English translations of the speeches, the emotions expressed were evident instantly to all. Gladys Bissonette and Ellen Moves Camp were among those giving eloquent pleas for action. Later that night, in a subsequent meeting held in the basement of the Holy Rosary Church, traditional leaders like Frank Fools Crow called upon Banks, Means, and other AIM members to go to Wounded Knee. And so they did, that very evening. Once they arrived, they were blocked from leaving by barriers set up around the community by BIA police and Wilson supporters. Then FBI agents and U.S. marshals quickly arrived on the scene, together with additional BIA police and units of the National Guard. The surrounded AIM group had commandeered food and weapons from the local trading post and began to dig in. The standoff began. As had been the case with Alcatraz, the activists understood the symbolic value of this particular location; if they had taken over Kyle or Wanblee, it would not have been the same. "Wounded Knee received more attention in its first week," conclude Paul Chaat Smith and Robert Warrior, "than the entire previous decade of Indian activism." Nonetheless, even if effective in the short run, the precipitous decision left the occupants vulnerable. They could not really expect to defend the village in the face of the military forces allied against them. The blockade proved porous; food and supplies continued to make their way into Wounded Knee. The defiant men and women who held Wounded Knee declared the enclave the Independent Oglala Nation. The rhetoric and the sniping escalated and during the protracted ordeal, Frank Clearwater (Eastern Cherokee) and Buddy Lamont (Oglala Lakota) were shot and killed. But as days turned into weeks and months, the American public began to lose interest in the details. Surrounded by heavily armed federal marshals and FBI agents, the protesters eventually called a halt to the occupation after seventy-one days. By the time the siege ended, much of the initial public relations advantage had evaporated.

Wounded Knee, as in the case of Alcatraz, again brought worldwide media attention to Native issues (at Pine Ridge) and to the goals of AIM leaders. But under the terms of the agreement that halted the occupation, the federal government promised to examine the conditions on Pine Ridge. But while Banks, Means, and other AIM members faced one trial after another on the basis of past incidents, the government did little to follow up on its promise, and in the aftermath Wilson and his cohorts, a group known widely as "the goon squad," had free reign to terrorize the reservation. The murder of Anna Mae Pictou Aquash (Micmac) symbolized the pervasive violence at Pine Ridge. In this atmosphere, two FBI agents, Jack Coler and Ronald Williams, and AIM member Joseph Stuntz Killsright were all killed on June 26, 1975, following an exchange of gunfire. Leonard Peltier of AIM was charged with the agents' deaths. His trial resulted in conviction and Peltier began to serve two consecutive life sentences. Books such as *In the Spirit of Crazy Horse* by noted writer Peter Matthiessen and *The Trial of Leonard Peltier* by Jim Messerschmidt raised considerable doubt about the government's actions and thus Peltier's status. Public officials like William Janklow had concluded that the ends justified the means. Years later the former attorney general for South Dakota had been asked how he could justify the methods he employed in prosecuting Peltier. Janklow replied that he believed Peltier was guilty, and he was going to convict him any way he could. Despite ongoing protests about Peltier's conviction, he remained imprisoned in 1997.

In the area of health care, Indians criticized the operation of the Indian Health Services branch of the Public Service. Until the medical draft ended in 1973, most Anglo doctors served Indian communities as an alternative to military service. Although there were men and women who defied the prevailing image, most of these physicians were perceived as too young, too inexperienced, and culturally insensitive. They resided in segregated housing and often were antagonistic toward traditional Native healers. A short-lived newspaper cartoon character, "SuperNavajo," nicely documented this image. In one episode, the heartless Dr. Meanie refused to treat a patient, using vicious dogs at his home to ward off the unwelcome intruder. In another, the injured rodeo cowboy, Yazzie Manykids, eventually gained treatment, but only after the doctor complained about being understaffed and overworked. Hospitals and clinics remained too distant from many Indian people and monolingual staffs could not communicate effectively with many of their patients. By the 1970s, more Indian men and women were finishing medical school, but they had not yet altered time-worn practices at most facilities. Without adequate Indian participation in the system nor adequate safeguards against abuses within it, some IHS employees proved guilty of scandalous practices. Although some physicians were sensitive to the needs of their patients, many other doctors believed they were empowered to make decisions for their patients without appropriate consultation and approval. The most appalling of all examples of malpractice occurred from 1973 to 1976, when thousands of American Indian women were involuntarily sterilized. These women were not informed about either the seriousness or the irrevocable nature of this decision that had been made for them. One of the few Native physicians of the era, Connie Uri (Cherokee), eventually helped reveal this horrifying procedure and bring about its cessation.

Lands and Recognition

Control and appropriate use of the land continued as a rallying cry throughout this generation. Alaska and Maine provided two major cases in point. The Alaska Native Claims Settlement Act (ANCSA) in 1971 had been hailed by many commentators for yielding a much better deal for the Native peoples of the region than American Indians had received in the past. Alaska Natives through ANCSA obtained title to 44 million acres of land and nearly a billion dollars in compensation. Twelve different regional Native corporations and more than 200 village corporations were established to manage these lands and to promote economic development. For an initial period of twenty years, only Alaska Natives would be eligible for membership and voting rights in these corporations.

After the initial self-congratulation had subsided, it soon became apparent that ANCSA bore more resemblance to the General Allotment Act of 1887 and termination than its proponents preferred to acknowledge. Natives worried over the 1991 date, after which individual shares could be alienated from the corporations. They agonized over the children born after 1971 who could not become shareholders. Discovery of oil in the Prudhoe Bay area in 1968 had necessitated the settlement of Native land claims. In their eagerness to expedite the construction of the Alaskan oil pipeline, federal lawmakers revealed that although termination had ceased, assimilation and economic progress remained higher priorities than maintenance of traditional Native subsistence or assertions of Native sovereignty. Therefore, at the same time that he opposed returning Blue Lake to Taos Pueblo, Senator Henry Jackson of Washington helped lead the fight for ANCSA's approval. As they had done so frequently in the "lower 48," newcomers to Indian country in Alaska underestimated the importance Natives gave to subsistence and disregarded the significance of sovereignty. Advisors to those who fashioned ANCSA concluded Alaskan Natives were poor because they lacked the comparable material comforts possessed by most other Americans. What the Natives needed, they decided, was access to more materialism rather than the means to continue their traditional ways of life. The chief economist for the field study, Douglas Jones, later admitted that he and others "probably misjudged" the "fierceness" Natives felt about the land and acknowledged that pleas for subsistence had been judged one-third legitimate and two-thirds politics. The desire to exploit natural resources overrode any nagging concerns that might have surfaced about the short- or long-term effects ANCSA might have upon Alaska's indigenous occupants.

Testimony presented by Native elders and younger political leaders at federal hearings held in 1968 and 1969 anticipated the kind of problems ANCSA brought. Over and over again members of the recently established Alaskan Federation of Natives and other Native persons underlined their desire to continue to use and occupy specific lands and their determination to realize continuity in cultural integrity. Herman Rexford, chief of the village of Kartovik, spoke about a different kind of ownership, one won "through battles" and that was "by tradition . . . the inheritance we received from our ancestors." It was, anthropologist Ann Fienup-Riordan added, "a relational" concept of ownership, "where a man has a right to, and in fact an obligation to, use a site because of his relationship to previous generations of people who had a definite relationship to the species taken at the same place." On Nelson Island, for example, "when a person lives like his grandparents from the land and the sea, he feels that those grandparents are still alive in him." And you could honor the old values of generosity and reciprocity because the animals would come back. But money was different. If all you had was money, you could not give the same gifts and you lacked "the social and spiritual bonds that make gift giving both necessary and possible." The Natives understood this point, in fact perceived it as a given that hardly needed to be articulated. For most non-Natives, it reflected a world they did not know and one they believed they did not need to understand.

ANCSA appeared to most Natives to have brought some marginal economic benefits; it contributed to improved health care, education, and housing. Yet it had not noticeably decreased major and ongoing social problems, including relatively high incidences of alcoholism and suicide. Alaskan Natives had hoped that implementation of the act might encourage greater independence and that it might somehow promote cultural integrity, but thus far they could not be encouraged by what they had witnessed. They became all the more determined to amend ANCSA and to combat more effectively the problems that remained.

In Maine, the Passamaquoddies, Penobscots, and the Houlton Band of Maliseets also reached agreement on a land claims settlement. This settlement appeared to have been more satisfactory to the Native communities concerned. On October 10, 1980, President Jimmy Carter signed the Maine Indian Settlement Act (Public Law 96-420), which appropriated $81.5 million for the Passamaquoddy Tribe, the Penobscot Nation, and the Houlton Band of Maliseets to purchase 300,000 acres of the 12 million acres of land taken from them through unratified treaties with the states of Maine and Massachusetts. The act also established a $27 million trust fund for economic development. The Native American Rights Fund declared the settlement "far and away the greatest Indian victory of its kind in the history of the United States."

The victory took decades to achieve, from the day in 1957 when a Passamaquoddy tribal elder, Louise Sockabesin, said to reservation governor John Stevens, "I have some old documents you should see." They had been stored in a cardboard box beneath her bed. In the box Stevens found original materials from long ago, including letters from George Washington and the treaty of 1794 that the Passamaquoddy had signed with Massachusetts (Maine did not become a separate state until 1820). The treaty made clear that the 17,000-acre Indian Township Passamaquoddy Reservation had once encompassed 6,000 additional acres. The Passamaquoddies tried for more than a decade to work out some kind of settlement with local and state authorities, who balked at any such arrangement. In 1971 Stevens turned to Tom Tureen, a young attorney in Calais, Maine, who soon joined the Native

American Rights Fund. After consulting with colleagues, Tureen concluded that the Passamaquoddy and the Penobscot peoples were entitled not to 6,000 acres but up to 12 million acres—two-thirds of the state of Maine—since the Indian Trade and Intercourse Act of 1790 had specified that any transfer of Native land without federal approval was null and void. The 1794 treaty and other treaties had never been ratified by the U.S. Congress. As one might expect, Maine politicians and land "owners" in the state disagreed. Nonetheless, the Indian communities prevailed in the legal battles that followed. Bolstered additionally by full federal recognition, they began to use the appropriations to purchase the additional acreage to which they had so long been entitled.

Other Native groups in the East, Midwest, and South also sought federal and state recognition. Historian Laurence Hauptman and anthropologist Jack Campisi traced the impetus for this effort to the Chicago conference of 1961. In helping to organize that conference, anthropologists Sol Tax and Nancy Lurie had worked against contemporary perspectives that assumed that other than the Iroquois and eastern Cherokees there were few Indians east of the Mississippi River. Tax's own association with the Mesquakie Settlement in Iowa had encouraged him to reconsider his own notion of Indian communities and, in concert with the Cherokee social scientist Robert K. Thomas and other associates, he began to map Indian populations generally omitted from BIA and other geographical delineations. Not all federally recognized tribes applauded this initiative, because they either doubted the legitimacy of these groups or questioned whether already limited federal funding would be increased to cover more Native communities. Tax's map, displayed at the Chicago conference, included the Haliwas (North Carolina), Houmas (Louisiana), Lumbees (North Carolina), Mashpee Wampanoags (Massachusetts), Mohegans (Connecticut), Narragansetts (Rhode Island), Pequots (Connecticut), and Tunica-Biloxis (Louisiana). William Rickard (Tuscarora) and Lucy W. Maynor (Lumbee) helped plan the conference and Pembroke State College hosted one of the regional meetings prior to Chicago. Many Indians from the eastern half of the country came to Chicago, and participation in this gathering encouraged individuals from unrecognized to strive all the more to alter their status.

Recognition had always been important for such groups, but the Indian Claims Commission, the Chicago conference, the new Office of Economic Opportunity programs, and the *Passamaquoddy* v. *Morton* case all contributed to a heightened sense that recognition needed to be achieved. In the 1970s the ground-swell for such acknowledgment reached a point where it could no longer be set aside or ignored. In 1979 the federal government established the Federal Acknowledgment Branch in the Department of the Interior. Tribes were supposed to apply to this branch, providing documentation of their existence and operation from the past to the present. Within five years seventy groups had begun this process.

Education and Economies

All Indian communities of this era faced common questions. Tribes sought to reverse the process of urban migration through revitalization of local economies and improvements in such crucial areas as education. If terms such as "self-determination" and "sovereignty" were going to have more than rhetorical meaning, then significant headway had to be accomplished in gaining greater control over education and achieving more vital economies.

Although termination of trust status had been renounced, the drive to terminate federal schooling for Indian children continued. The BIA still wanted to move children from federal boarding and day schools into public schools. By 1980 about 80 percent of all Native children attended public schools. With the continuing migration off of the reservations and the growth of the public junior high and high school network on the reservations, many of the old off-reservation boarding junior high/high schools began to close in the 1970s. Chilocco in Oklahoma had enrolled more than 1,000 students in 1935, but by 1972 it claimed less than 500. It closed its doors by the end of the 1970s. Phoenix Indian School built new classroom buildings and new athletic facilities in the mid-1960s. School officials hoped that the school would continue to improve academically and that the Braves and Bravettes would continue to enjoy success in athletic competition. However, by the 1970s the student body at Phoenix and other remaining off-reservation schools attracted a steadily higher percentage of students who had serious problems. Although Phoenix Indian School continued into the 1980s, its days were numbered.

During this era Native individuals and communities fought to establish and maintain control of schools they increasingly defined as their own. Enhanced funding of public schools on reservations, the development of community or contract schools, the founding of tribally operated community colleges, and the growth of enrollment and graduation of Indian college students were all hallmarks of the period. This transition was also hastened by the report in 1969 of the U.S. Senate Special Subcommittee on Indian Education. The so-called Kennedy report, so named because the subcommittee had been chaired by Robert Kennedy and then Ted Kennedy, labeled national Indian education policy "a failure of major proportions." This document did more to dramatize shortcomings than reveal solutions, but it did offer a useful mandate for significant and prompt alteration.

From the mid-1960s through the 1970s Congress passed more legislation relating to Indian education that it had approved during the prior two centuries. Passage of the Elementary and Secondary Education Act in 1965 represented a useful step. Title I of the act specifically encouraged greater community involvement and the act itself was designed to assist children from families with limited incomes. In the 1970s, three new laws promised additional help: the Indian Education Act of 1972 (P.L. 92-318), the Indian Self-Determination and Education Assistance Act of 1975 (P.L. 95-638), and Title XI of the Education Amendments of 1978 (P.L. 95-561). The first included Title IV, which dealt with programs under the U.S. Office of Education. It provided funding to programs reaching new constituencies ignored by the BIA, including urban and rural non-reservation groups as well as communities that had been terminated or had not received federal recognition. The second encouraged contracting the management of schools to Indian tribes and groups as well as needed changes to Johnson-O'Malley. The third offered additional revisions to how public schools gained funding to help Indian children and yielded other stipulations to promote parental involvement. Such legislation seemed positive, if dependent upon the whims of future congresses and presidential administrations

Deliberations over such legislation and the contents of the laws themselves contributed to the realization of greater Indian control of Indian education. At the local level, exciting initiatives began to alter permanently the future course of schooling for Native young people and adults. Rough Rock Demonstration School on the Navajo Nation furnished the inaugural example of a contract school. Begun in 1966, Rough Rock was financed by the BIA and the OEO. The community contracted with the federal government to run its own school; the school board emphasized the importance of having the children obtain a bilingual, bicultural education. Other pioneering contract schools included the Ramah Navajo High School and the Busby School on Northern Cheyenne. In addition, in the 1960s Indian voters, many of them recently registered, began to transform the composition of public school boards for schools enrolling a significant number of Native children. By the beginning of the 1970s, seventy-eight public school districts had boards in which Indian members formed the majority. Given the power of such boards to hire and fire personnel, make contracts, and revise curriculum, this new level of participation often led to sweeping changes in the curriculum, and opened the door to more Native superintendents, principals, and teachers. Not all Native school board members shared the same perspective about priorities and possibilities. But in school districts where Indians served in larger numbers on such boards, there resulted a more positive assessment of Native cultures and more vigorous recruitment of Indian employees.

Why did this transition matter? In 1997 journalist Betty Reid (Navajo) supplied her own answer in a searching and poignant remembrance published by her employer, the *Arizona Republic*. At the age of seven, in the mid-1960s, she had enrolled in the Tuba City Boarding School. That action, Reid wrote, "would change my life in ways that I still struggle to understand." She no longer accompanied her parents to the Blessingway and other curing ceremonies; the school required her to attend Christian church services. Reid spoke no English at first, but dormitory aides punished her for speaking the Navajo language; for this infraction she scrubbed toilets with a toothbrush. During the night she heard "little girls sniffle in the dark for their far-away parents or grand-parents." "My heart ached too," Reid added, "for my parents, my home, my lambs and my rock toys left behind near a sheep camp called Pillow Hill. Tears streamed down my cheeks as I tried hard to imagine myself chasing pet goats through the grass at a place where the Rabbits Run Up a Butte. . . ." Reid recalled: "I adjusted to the school as the years passed. I played basketball, participated in the student council, published a school newspaper, and took several trips to Disneyland." She left Tuba City to attend high school in Massachusetts, then earned a journalism degree at the University of Colorado. Although she liked certain dimensions of her life in Phoenix, she mourned her loss of fluency in the Navajo language and revealed that sometimes when she visited her family in Tuba City, she felt "like a misfit—like a tourist looking at what used to be my life." In 1997 she began her day in the city by greet-ing the Dawn People and saying prayers to the Holy People. Some day, she vowed, she will live again near "The Place Among the Sagebrush. . . ."

The establishment of tribal colleges also represented an im-portant achievement. Founded in 1968, Navajo Community Col-lege began offering courses in the spring of 1969. It shared facili-ties with a new BIA boarding high school in Many Farms, Arizona, until its own campus could be constructed in Tsaile in 1973. Passage of the Navajo Community College Act in 1971 (P.L. 92-189) assured a continuing funding base, together with financial contributions from the Navajo Nation and private foundations. The college was governed by its own board of regents who encouraged a central place for the study of Navajo history, language, and cul-ture in the overall curriculum. In 1997 the board voted to change the name of the institution to Diné College, in order to incorp-orate the people's name for themselves and to prepare for the in-stitution's transition to a four-year curriculum. Two other tribal colleges, Oglala Lakota College and Sinte Gleska College (later University) followed on the Pine Ridge and Rosebud reservations of South Dakota. Both because of their early founding in the late 1960s and early 1970s and the size of their constituencies, these three institutions became the largest and most ambitious of the reservation-based Native colleges.

All of the colleges faced continuing challenges, including the perennial problem of funding. Faculty and staff accepted comparatively low salaries in order to contribute their efforts; students experienced not only financial difficulties but often conflicting emotions about their obligations to their families as well as, in some instances, the limits of their academic preparation at the secondary level. Increased emphasis on the recruitment of promising Native American students to regional public universities as well as national private colleges and universities drained away many of the most able young high school graduates. The tribal colleges offered a second chance for adult re-entry students and for others who could not have started college away from home. They also generally reaffirmed the importance of traditional knowledge, teachings, and values.

The colleges symbolized the aspirations of Native peoples for new opportunities and new futures. Most of these institutions were established on reservations, but others developed for off-reservation populations. The most prominent, Deganawidah-Quetzalcoatl University, began in 1970 after an extended effort by Jack Forbes (Powhatan-Lenape) and other Indian scholars and leaders in California to establish an Indian university. Such an institution, Forbes argued as early as 1961, "would train Indians to control their own destinies in today's complex society." As its name indicates, the university sought to offer instruction to both Indian and Chicano students. Occupying a former federal communications center near Davis, California, the school struggled against not only a lack of adequate federal funding but hostility from Department of Health, Education, and Welfare officials who had wanted the center to be transferred to the University of California at Davis. Passage of the Tribally Controlled Community College Act (P.L. 95-471) in 1978 offered potential assistance to DQ-U, as the school was popularly known, if it redefined itself as an urban tribal college. DQ-U chose to take that action, and the Chicano board members resigned their positions. After a first decade noted for perseverance as well as turmoil, DQ-U hoped for a more stable future.

In 1972 DQ-U joined Navajo Community College, Oglala Lakota College, Sinte Gleska College, Turtle Mountain Community College (North Dakota) and Standing Rock Community College—recently renamed Sitting Bull College (North Dakota)—to form the American Indian Higher Education Consortium (AIHEC). Three BIA institutions, Haskell Junior College (later Haskell Indian Nations University) in Lawrence, Kansas; the Institute of American Indian Arts in Santa Fe, New Mexico; and Southwest Indian Polytechnic Institute in Albuquerque, New Mexico, participated in the first discussions and later joined the consortium. AIHEC proved invaluable in assisting tribal colleges, especially newer and smaller ones established in the 1970s, and in securing the Tribally Controlled Community College Assistance Act in 1978. By that year fifteen additional schools had been founded, of which only four failed to survive, due primarily to insufficient financing and internal political disagreements. Seven served Native communities in Montana: Blackfeet Community College, Dull Knife Memorial College (Northern Cheyenne), Fort Belknap College, Fort Peck Community College, Little Bighorn College (Crow), Salish Kootenai College, and Stone Child Community College (Rocky Boy). Four others started in the Dakotas: Cheyenne River Community College, Fort Berthold Community College, Little Hoop Community College (Spirit Lake), and Sisseton-Wahpeton Community College.

Many of the tribal college students later transferred to other colleges and universities; still other Native American students began and completed their collegiate work at non-Indian schools. Establishment of student support services, Indian clubs, pow-wows, and other means of assisting Native students slowly started to provide more successful experiences for a progressively larger number of people. The dropout rate of Indians enrolled at large public universities remained too high. Nonetheless, public universities in that region as well as private institutions, including Brigham Young, Cornell, Dartmouth, and Stanford, started to increase their commitment to and improve the success rate of Native students. Beginning in the late 1960s, some universities started to plan and to develop Indian studies programs. These fledgling academic enterprises faced considerable opposition from faculty members in traditional departments and generally received limited funding and few staff or faculty positions. But even if their promise remained largely unfulfilled in their first years, the very existence of American Indian Studies at the University of Minnesota and other institutions comprised a necessary first step toward the eventual development of more substantial and successful programs in the next generation. Efforts to increase the number of Native attorneys, on the other hand, realized more immediate results. The pre-law summer institute at the American Indian Law Center played a central role in achieving this objective. This program, started in 1967 by the University of New Mexico Law School, and headed since 1977 by P. Sam Deloria, became an independent entity, but remained situated at the university. The number of Indian attorneys rose from only twenty-five in the late 1960s to over 1000 by the early 1990s. More Native teachers, engineers, and other professionals also began to appear by the end of the 1970s.

The increased Native enrollment in colleges and universities encouraged reconsideration of the use of Indian names for mascots for athletic teams. Most Indian students detested the employment of tribal names like the "Seminoles" for college teams, as well as similar uses of such terms as "braves," "warriors," "redmen," "redskins," and "Indians." Conservative students and alumni members of many institutions frequently resisted Native Americans' attempts to alter "tradition" by calling for name changes. Public schools generally delayed or altogether refused to change the names of their teams, but some private institutions took the lead in doing so in the early 1970s, despite considerable opposition within their ranks. Stanford and Dartmouth teams no longer would be called "Indians," but, rather "Cardinal" and "Big Green." However, followers of the Big Green continued for years to give "scalp 'em" cheers at football games, and two students in 1979 even appeared in mock Indian attire at a hockey game, skated across the ice, and departed to applause. The Dartmouth hockey team went on to enjoy a banner year, reaching the national championships, where it lost to the University of North Dakota Fighting Sioux.

Native communities had achieved considerable headway in the area of education, but the record in the realm of economic development appeared more mixed. The 1960s saw the number of Native college students double and the percentage of Indians twenty-five years of age and older who had completed high school increase in the decade from less than one-fifth to one-third. By contrast the 1970 census reported the median income of Indian families as $5,832, compared to the national median of $9,590. Nearly 40 percent of the Indian population lived below the federal poverty level in 1969, about three times the percentage of the entire population. On most reservations unemployment remained high, thus contributing to a continuing migration of residents to uncertain futures in off-reservation towns and cities.

At the beginning of this period, federal officials had anticipated a different outcome. The Johnson and Nixon administrations chose to invest heavily in Indian country through measures and agencies designed to reduce poverty across the United States. However, as applied to Native communities the approach still emphasized industrialization and corporate models. The government wanted to increase investment in factories or assembly plants by major outside companies, while prompting tribes to establish their own enterprises. Public works projects on and for Native communities also benefited from a substantial amount of federal funds. During the 1960s on some reservations these efforts seemed to produce some positive results.

However, most of the advances proved short lived. Much of the investment on reservations had been made either by marginal companies or established companies confronting a changing economy; when military spending began to decline in the 1970s, more than a few of the new reservation factories dependent on defense-related production went out of business. Introduction of the Comprehensive Employment and Training Act (CETA) in 1973 provided jobs in areas such as construction and craft production for over 100,000 Native Americans. When CETA became politically expendable during the Reagan years, unemployment rose precipitously. Aided by Small Business Administration loans and monopoly status, tribal enterprises occasionally enjoyed significant success. But, again, these developments were fragile. For many reservation-run businesses, managerial changes usually accompanied the arrival of a new tribal administration. Enterprises based on use of natural resources, such as timber, often prospered, but, like all such businesses, remained vulnerable to a sudden decline in the market for a particular commodity.

Tourism offered a market with great potential. A number of communities built facilities, such as Kah-nee-ta at Warm Springs in Oregon, Inn of the Mountain Gods at Mescalero in New Mexico, Sunrise Ski Resort at White Mountain Apache in Arizona, and Bottle Hollow on the Uintah and Ouray in Utah. The first three resorts succeeded; Bottle Hollow did not. Location, amenities, management, and local tribal politics all figured into the scenario. Tourists from the United States and western Europe flocked to the scenic and cultural splendors of Indian communities, but few of the dollars they spent in the process wound up in Native wallets. The monies were more likely to flow off the reservation to bordertown communities which boasted the familiar motel and fast-food franchises as well as other services. What happened with tourists, of course, also happened with reservation residents. Most of the money they spent on food, clothing, transportation, and other goods went to those same bordertowns.

The economic picture, nonetheless, was not entirely bleak. Indian communities attempted to take control over more of the functions historically carried out by the federal government. Passage of the Indian Self-Determination and Educational Assistance Act in 1975 expedited this process. Members of various reservations became increasingly likely to occupy local federal positions and to assume new responsibilities for social and health services. Tribal mineral resources had brought substantial profits to outside companies in the past; during the 1970s, energy-rich tribes started to try to obtain a larger percentage of those returns for themselves.

In 1975 twenty-five Indian tribes thus founded the Council of Energy Resources Tribes (CERT). Navajo tribal chairman Peter MacDonald, a key figure in CERT's early years, labeled the Navajos "an emerging nation." He contended: "Like other underdeveloped countries with rich but exhaustible supplies of fuel and minerals, we realize we must use our natural resources to create jobs for our people and put us on the road to self-sufficiency." In a much publicized move obviously designed to embarrass federal officials, CERT asked the counsel of OPEC nations about possible strategies and approaches. Federal officials expressed their displeasure but also accelerated their grants to the new organization. CERT furnished badly needed technical and legal assistance to its members, and the agreements they reached for additional development appeared to be far more lucrative than ones reached in the previous generation. Back then, energy companies had taken advantage of the lack of Native leadership on the matter to craft long-term leases with limited returns to the people whose lands and lives were being disrupted by the extraction of the resources.

That disruption inspired protests in the 1970s and revealed considerable misgivings on the part of many Native peoples about the desirability of this kind of economic development. On Black Mesa in northern Arizona, on Crow and Cheyenne lands in southeastern Montana, and elsewhere, Indians worried about damage to the earth itself and agonized over the impact of mining on traditional subsistence. In places where mining had taken place for a period of time new objections surfaced over the effect of the industry upon the health of Natives living nearby the operations. Evidence mounted that the uranium miners in the southwestern states were experiencing far higher rates of cancer because of their exposure to radiation; hundreds of these miners were Navajos, who labored in the Kerr-McGee mines near Cove, Arizona, and Red Rock, New Mexico, from 1952 to 1963. As Harry Tome, the Red Rock representative on the Navajo Tribal Council put it in 1979, "No one ever told us of the danger in it. . . . It was the only employment that was ever brought to our part of the reservation." The jobs, he observed, brought in "quite a lot of income. Then the mines closed. They went away. Now the people are dying." The development of natural resources on Native land continued in the late 1970s but leases no longer were automatically renewed, for the tribes concerned were far more knowledgeable and skeptical than they had been in the recent past.

Recognition of their water rights loomed as another key to Indian economic development in the 1960s and 1970s. Even after the *Winters* decision, Indian water rights had existed primarily on paper rather than in acre feet (the amount of water needed to cover an acre of ground with an inch of water, or 326,000 gallons). The decision of the U.S. Supreme Court in 1963 in *Arizona* v. *California,* indicated the future might hold more promise for the realization of those rights. In *Arizona* the Court concluded that Indian reservations on the lower Colorado River should receive almost 1 million acre feet of water each year. In arriving at this total, the Court ascertained the "practicably irrigable acreage" the Indians possessed. The decision eventually expedited the delivery of water not only to these particular Native groups but potentially to other groups in the Southwest as well, but it took years of lobbying and negotiation before that delivery became a reality. In the meantime, once prosperous farming operations languished for lack of water.

Rights and Restrictions

The Indian Civil Rights Act of 1968 reflected the desire of congressional representatives to restrict the power tribal governments could exercise over their members. It reaffirmed the applicability of much of the Bill of Rights to those persons, including free speech. However, the interpretation of the act opened the door to a flood of lawsuits against different tribes, contesting tribal authority and sovereignty in a variety of realms. The case of *Dodge* v. *Nakai* in 1968 confirmed the suspicions of those who feared the repercussions of the act. Ted Mitchell, a non-Indian attorney who headed the legal services program on the Navajo Nation, had an angry confrontation with Annie Wauneka, a prominent member of the tribal council. Mitchell had laughed scornfully after Wauneka had answered a question during a tribal council advisory meeting in the council chambers. Furious at Mitchell's behavior, she sought him out the following day in the chambers, slapped him and ordered him to leave the room. The advisory committee then voted to banish Mitchell from the reservation. Under the terms of the Civil Rights Act, Mitchell was able to sue successfully in federal court to return to the Navajo Nation and to obtain financial compensation. *Dodge* v. *Nakai* thus prompted the federal courts to assume general jurisdiction in matters involving suits against the tribe. This assumption clearly constituted a major setback to the assertion of greater tribal sovereignty and undermined the workings of tribal governments, including the tribal courts.

In the decade following *Dodge,* the Supreme Court began to delineate some of the possibilities and limits of contemporary sovereignty. In *McClanahan* v. *Arizona State Tax Commission* in 1973 the Court ruled that an Indian employee did not have to pay state taxes on a salary she had earned working on the reservation. On the other hand, as *Dodge* had made evident, the Court wished to curb the efforts of tribes to expand their jurisdiction over non-Indians in certain areas. *Oliphant* v. *Suquamish Indian Tribe* (1978) restricted the ability of Indian communities to exercise control over nonmembers in regard to criminal matters. *Santa Clara* v. *Martinez* (1978), however, reaffirmed the right of an Indian community to decide who was entitled to membership within it. But the particular details of the case gave pause to many observers. A woman from the Santa Clara Pueblo had married a Navajo man. They lived at Santa Clara and brought up their children there. The pueblo government decided that the children of Julia and Myles Martinez could not be enrolled as members at Santa Clara. Many at Santa Clara disagreed with this decision, but the Supreme Court determined that the pueblo had the power to determine its own membership on its own terms. This decision served another function. It turned back the tide of lawsuits against the tribes. It returned authority to tribal governments, including tribal court systems, and affirmed sovereign immunity for the tribes from suit under the terms of the Indian Civil Rights Act.

The American Indian Religious Freedom Act (AIRFA) of 1978 and the Indian Child Welfare Act (ICWA) of 1978 also confronted issues of major concern to Native Americans. AIRFA reaffirmed the "inherent right of freedom" for Indians "to believe, express, and exercise the traditional religions." They thus should have full access to sacred sites as well as the ability to practice traditional ceremonies without hindrance. Such legislation promised to limit harassment of the Native American Church and to allow Indians in prisons the right to sweat lodges. The ICWA attempted "to promote the stability of Indian tribes and families by the establishment of minimum Federal standards for the removal of Indian children from their families." As with AIRFA, this act mirrored sentiment rather than compelled compliance, but it emphasized the existence of an important dilemma. One study concluded that almost 25 percent of all Native children under the age of one were being adopted in the early 1970s. During this time many non-Indian social workers consistently misunderstood different cultural practices, including comfort with silence and the role of the extended family in child rearing, and thus often recommended children be taken from Indian parents without due justification. Churches, particularly the Church of Jesus Christ of Latter-day Saints, had seen in adoption a means to "save" Indian children. As in the past, modern boarding schools and placement programs increased the chances for Indian children to be removed to non-Indian homes. Passage of the ICWA by no means eliminated such practices but may have constrained them. The act also emboldened tribes to take more vigorous actions through their own court systems and agencies to protect the rights of Indian parents and children.

In this matter, and in so many others throughout these two decades, Native Americans kept asserting their need and their ability to define themselves, to reaffirm their identities, and to articulate their determination to continue. In nonfiction and fiction, in paintings and other forms of art, Indians expressed contemporary Native life in all of its complexity and richness. Just as the events, rulings, and decisions of the era helped underline for all Americans that Indians were a force to contend with, the voices and imaginations of Native writers, musicians, artists, and historians attested to that continuing presence.

Writers, Musicians, and Artists

In nonfiction, Vine Deloria, Jr.'s *Custer Died For Your Sins* (1969) had a particularly profound impact. This "Indian Manifesto" showed no mercy to those who had created the problems and entanglements of the present. Deloria's sardonic assessment of anthropologists and missionaries, his dissection of termination, and his call for a redefinition of Indian affairs not only gained him applause from throughout Indian country but made clear to the non-Indian public issues of paramount importance. His subsequent publications, ranging from *God is Red* to *We Talk, You Listen* reinforced his own importance in helping to "write the final chapter of the American Indian upon this continent."

N. Scott Momaday (Kiowa) won the Pulitzer prize for fiction in 1968 for *House Made of Dawn*. Momaday and Leslie Marmon Silko (Laguna Pueblo), the author of *Ceremony* (1977), introduced characters who were Army veterans, struggling with life on the reservation and in the city, yet finding harmony through the power of the land and the cultural traditions of their communities. Both Momaday and Silko also received critical acclaim for their poetry. So, too did Gros Ventre-Blackfeet author James Welch for *Riding the Earthboy 40*. In this collection and in his first two novels, *Winter in the Blood* (1975) and *The Death of Jim Loney* (1979), Welch etched the Native world of northern Montana. Momaday penned an elegant tribute to his Kiowa heritage through the montage of *The Way to Rainy Mountain* (1969), a work accompanied by illustrations completed by his uncle, Al Momaday. With *Wordarrows* (1978) Gerald Vizenor (Anishinabe) combined fiction and nonfiction in distinctive fashion. Simon Ortiz (Acoma Pueblo) became well regarded for his poetry and short stories, which spoke to historical memory, the pain of contemporary life, and the resilience of Indian people.

More than in previous generations, contemporary Indian musicians established national audiences for an eclectic range of styles, from folk to rock. Buffy Sainte-Marie (Cree) lent her remarkable voice to a variety of songs, including "Now That The Buffalo's Gone." Floyd Westerman (Lakota) employed some of the main themes from *Custer Died For Your Sins* in a very successful album. Rock bands Redbone and XIT engaged the loyalties of fans across the country.

Indian painters explored connections between the traditional and contemporary arts. Two of the most compelling artists were

Fritz Scholder (Luiseno) and T. C. Cannon (Kiowa-Caddo), who used irony and humor in their forceful portrayals of Native and non-Native men and women. Scholder opened new doors for other artists through his pathbreaking work, such as "Super Kachina" and "Three Indian Dancers." Cannon died in a car accident while still a young man. Lloyd Kiva New (Cherokee) emphasized that Cannon "broke through the barriers of confusion and unnecessary prevailing constraints that had become an impediment to progressive creativity in Indian art." "Collector #5," "Indian Princess Waiting for Bus in Anadarko," and "Grandmother Gestating Father and the Washita Runs Ribbon-Like" exemplified Cannon's extraordinary talent and vision. Pablita Velarde's daughter, Helen Hardin (Santa Clara Pueblo), died of cancer in 1984. Her paintings and etchings earned her considerable critical and popular appeal; "Looking at Myself I Am Many Parts" spoke to her own complicated life and career. Among many other significant artists of the era whose first-rate work continued in the 1980s and 1990s, one should mention George Longfish (Seneca-Tuscarora), a professor of Native American studies at the University of California, Davis, whose early work included "You Can't Roller Skate in a Buffalo Herd Even If You Have All the Medicine;" Jaune Quick-to-See-Smith (Salish-Kootenai-Cree-Shoshone) who painted "Horse Constellation with Jack Rabbit;" and the traditional Wintu singer and dancer (as well as professor of Native American Studies at California State University, Sacramento) Frank La Pena, whose "Deer Rattle, Deer Dancer" is one of the most striking examples of contemporary Indian art.

Two important forums promoted the writing of Indian history. The American Indian Historical Society, established in 1964, was headed by Rupert Costo and Jeannette Henry Costo (Eastern Cherokee). The society sponsored convocations for Native scholars, published from 1972 to 1984 a national newspaper, *Wassaja,* and, from 1964 to 1982, a journal, *The Indian Historian.* In addition, through its Indian Historian Press, the society published over fifty books. The first, *Textbooks and the American Indian,* written by Jeannette Henry Costo, skewered publishers for their inadequate treatment of American Indians in American history. The Indian Historian Press opened new areas of inquiry and published the work of Native authors.

In addition, D'Arcy McNickle devoted the final portion of his life to the creation and maturation of the Center for American Indian History at the Newberry Library in Chicago, which now bears his name. At the McNickle center, founded in the fall of 1972, young and senior Indian and non-Indian scholars, traditional Indian historians, community archivists, and others discovered a meeting ground through which they could learn from each other and take advantage of the Newberry's impressive collections. Alfonso Ortiz assumed the crucial role of chairman of the national advisory board, a task that he carried on for most of the center's first quarter-century until his death early in 1997. In time, the center increasingly realized McNickle's vision as a place that encouraged Native history to be understood and written in a new way. McNickle's words provide an appropriate summary of Native peoples in the 1960s and 1970s: "People are like Grass. . . . They toss and sway and even seem to flow before the forces that make for change, . . . but when the rude force moves on, people are found still rooted in the soil of the past."

CHAPTER SIX

"We Are All Indians," 1981–1997

A young Shoshone-Bannock man glanced through the old newspapers. Reading through the pages of *Tevope* (or paper, in the Shoshone language) from Fort Hall, Idaho, he encountered the words of editor Ralph Dixey, published in 1939: "Friends, we are all Indians no matter how white or dark you are. It does not make any difference where you are, what you are doing, or how much money you are making. We are all Indians. . . . Our chiefs call us half-breeds and no good and we call them darn fools. Now, who is right? We are both wrong," Dixey concluded. "We are all Indians." For Mark Trahant, a "mixed blood" enrolled member of Fort Hall, the words had particular meaning. He thought about who he was and who he might become; he began to realize that being an Indian today, as it always had, included the incorporation of change. He started to understand more fully, as he later wrote, that Indian peoples had "always made alliances, intermarried, and borrowed ideas and technology from other people." "Indian history didn't end in the 1800s," Trahant added. "Indian cultures aren't some sort of museum piece, that are frozen in time, preserved under glass. They evolve, grow, and continually try to renew themselves."

In 1996 Trahant accepted a new position as publisher of the *Moscow-Pullman Daily News,* newspaper for the neighboring towns of Pullman, Washington, and Moscow, Idaho. Today one of the leading American Indian journalists in the country, Trahant came of age in a time when being Native American appeared less bounded by narrow definition in blood quantum or physical location. He spent years in Navajo country, served as editor of the *Navajo Times* and publisher of *The Navajo Nation Today,* and married a Diné woman; he worked for newspapers in Phoenix and Salt Lake City, held a prestigious fellowship at Vanderbilt University in Nashville, Tennessee, and joined the national advisory board for the D'Arcy McNickle Center of the Newberry Library in Chicago. His own life testified to the possibilities of evolution, growth, and renewal.

American Indians faced recurring problems at century's end. Alcoholism and diabetes plagued the lives of countless people; AIDS now claimed Indian victims. Unemployment remained too high on most reservations. The dropout rate from high schools, college, and universities continued to be excessive. Youth gangs appeared for the first time on some reservations. Even if more Americans seemed somewhat more informed about Indians, all too many people within the United States still embraced ignorance and bigotry. Yet even with an unflinching recognition of such dilemmas, one sensed, on balance, a cautious optimism in Indian country as the twentieth century entered its final few years. Five hundred years after Columbus, one hundred years after Wounded Knee, American Indians had not disappeared. Unlike a century ago, there could be no doubt about their permanent place in the future of this nation. Thomas Jefferson Morgan had been proven incorrect; "the great body of Indians" had not "become merged in the indistinguishable mass of our population."

Contemporary Identity

Data from the most recent censuses attested to that place. The American Indian population had reached its nadir early in this century, with less than a quarter million people counted. By 1930, the census began to record an increase in that population; by 1960, slightly more than half a million (523,591) were enumerated. Since 1960, there has been a rapid statistical expansion: 792,370 in 1970, 1.37 million in 1980, and 1.9 million in 1990. Some of that demographic explosion can be explained through a change in how the census was compiled, whereby individuals could identify themselves as Indians or as Indians of multiple ancestry or people of Indian descent. Although the last category appeared largely irrelevant in regard to cultural identification, the middle category encompassed persons who might not be enrolled as members of particular tribes, but who perceived themselves as Indians. In addition, the growth of the percentage of Indians who lived away from reservations meant they were simply more likely to be reached by the census takers.

Moreover, most observers suggest that efforts by previously unrecognized Indian communities to gain federal recognition and the more positive image enjoyed by American Indians in the United States may well have bolstered these numbers. However, the increases also mirrored better health care and thus longer life expectancy and a recent upswing in birthrates.

Regardless of how they were counted precisely, there could be no question about an increasing Native American population. One-fourth of this population were American Indians who resided on the 278 reservations (including the pueblos of the Southwest and the rancherias of California). Still others lived in Alaskan Native villages. While less than one-half of 1 percent of American Indians resided in urban areas in 1900, by 1950 this percentage had increased to 13.4 and by 1990 to a little over 50. New York City, Oklahoma City, Phoenix, Tulsa, Los Angeles, Minneapolis–St. Paul, Anchorage, and Albuquerque contained especially sizable Indian populations in 1990, but many other cities included a significant number of Native persons. About 53 percent of the Indian population were enrolled in a particular tribe. Those Indians who were not enrolled include those of more than one tribal heritage or of primarily Indian ancestry who did not meet the particular standards of a particular Native community (as the *Martinez* case illustrated) and those of mixed ancestry who claimed affiliation without being eligible for enrollment (for example, two-thirds of the 308,132 Cherokees counted in 1990). Many enrolled Indians as well were of mixed ancestry and had spent part, most, or all of their lives away from their "home" communities.

Such patterns affected crucial dimensions of traditional tribal cultures. Among nearly all groups, the percentage of people who spoke a Native language as a first language continued to decline. In addition, the percentage of children who did not speak a Native language at all escalated markedly. Even in the Navajo Nation, which had shown little decrease prior to the present generation, a significant number of children grew up in the 1980s and 1990s as non-Native-language speakers. Television, of course, was far more pervasive by this time, but it could not be blamed entirely for this transition. Increased intermarriage with non-Indians, for example, had also been an important contributing factor. Through the efforts of community members, teachers, and scholars, many Indian nations attempted to alter this trend. Noted Native poets like Ofelia Zepeda (Tohono O'odham) and Rex Lee Jim (Navajo) wrote most of their work in their tribal languages. However, the outlook here remained uncertain, at best.

Intermarriage could not be equated with assimilation, even if it had affected language. A student of the subject of intermarriage, anthropologist Brenda Kay Manuelito (Navajo), noted that "intermarried families and mixed-blood children construct their identities within particular historical and cultural context" and that "individuals move back and forth between social and cultural milieus." These generalizations can be applied to the lives of all Indians, regardless of heritage. The world of the 1980s and 1990s permitted, often demanded, a considerable degree of flexibility in terms of the construction of culture. Affiliation with a particular Indian community did not preclude common participation in pow-wows or the Native American Church. The work of Indian writers, artists, and musicians transcended tribal boundaries. Although engaged specifically at the local level, certain issues or questions involved Indians across America. These included repatriation, gaming, and land and water rights. Successes achieved in particular locales encouraged or inspired renewed efforts in other places. In sum, as the twentieth century drew to a close Indian communities sought, often in unprecedented ways, to reclaim their pasts and re-define the possibilities of their futures.

During this era the powwow became all the more established as a national Indian institution and as a prevailing symbol of In-dian identity. As W. Richard West, Jr. (Southern Cheyenne) re-marked, "Dance is the very embodiment of indigenous values and represents the response of Native Americans to complex and sometimes difficult historical experiences. . . . The dance of native peoples is thus both a vital means of surviving culturally and a powerful expression of that survival." Whether it involved one community or many tribes, the powwow provided the opportunity not only to compete, but to pay homage to past and present through particular dances, honoring songs, the giving of gifts, and the selection of head singers, dancers, and other ceremonial lead-ers. It also afforded the opportunity to eat. Frybread, roasted ears of corn, beans, soups, stews, and other choices awaited one and all. From its customary beginning of grand entry, flag song, and invocation, until its close, dancer and spectator alike were joined in common observance of continuity and change in Native Ameri-can life. The flag song spoke to identity as an Indian and as Ameri-can, as in the instance of the Lakota National Anthem, where a soldier says:

Tunkasilayapi tawapaha kin oihanke sni najin ktelo
lyohlate oyate kin wicicagin;
ktaca, lecamon.
(The flag of the United States will fly forever
Under it the people will grow and prosper;
Therefore I have done this (fought for my country).

The powwow was not identical from one region to another and must be understood as an evolving institution, incorporating new categories or elements. For example, men used to be the only participants in fancy dancing, but in recent years women have competed in fancy-shawl and jingle dress dances.

Given the evolving nature of the powwow, it was fitting that the event called "The World Championship of Powwow" would be held not somewhere on the plains but in Connecticut. Schemitzun

("Feast of the Green Corn and Dance" in the Pequot language), re-newed an old traditional feast in autumn for the Pequots of Mash-antucket. The fifth annual gathering held on September 14–17, 1996, included fifty invited drum groups and dancers from throughout North America who vied for the three quarters of a million dollars in prize money.

In 1996 powwows took place all over Indian America, com-mencing with the New Years annual powwow at the Lac Courte Oreilles tribal grounds in Hayward, Wisconsin. The Grand Village of Natchez Indians in Mississippi hosted the Natchez annual pow-wow on March 22–24. A week later the 24th annual Ann Arbor Dance for Mother Earth Contest Powwow began in Michigan. The largest of the powwows held on university campuses, the Gather-ing of Nations, took place on April 25–27 at the University of New Mexico in Albuquerque. On the last weekend in May, one could choose between the Cherokee Memorial Day Powwow in Chero-kee, North Carolina, and the Delaware Annual Powwow in Copan, Oklahoma. June 7–9 featured at least eleven powwows, including the gigantic Red Earth Powwow in Oklahoma City, but also the Cheyenne Homecoming Powwow in Lame Deer, Montana; the Native American Educational Services College Powwow in Chi-cago, and the Honoring Our Veterans Powwow at Bay Mills Com-munity College in Brimley, Michigan. On through the summer newly founded and time-honored gatherings occurred, from Ore-gon's Coquille Restoration Powwow in Brandon, and the Po-Ume-Sha Powwow & Treaty Days at Warm Springs to the annual pow-wow of the Ho-Chunk Nation in Nebraska and the Comanche Homecoming Powwow near Walters, Oklahoma. Autumn brought the Eastern band of Shawnee powwow in Seneca, Missouri, and the 29th annual Louisiana Indian Heritage Association fall pow-wow in Folsom.

Indian communities shared common determinations to con-tinue as Indian entities. The most recent period featured a revital-ization of smaller communities, which found new ways to reassert their uniqueness. The Nanticoke people in Delaware experienced many difficulties and the Nanticoke Indian Association had been dormant for a generation before its revival in 1975, with the elec-tion of another Clark, Kenneth Clark, as chief. A subsequent Nanticoke Indian Heritage project placed nine buildings on the National Register of Historic Places; an annual powwow the first weekend of September and an annual homecoming the second Sunday in October provided important times to gather and to celebrate continuation. A Nanticoke museum opened in 1985. Like so many other eastern groups, the Nanticoke community had refused to disappear. The people remained on the land.

Throughout Indian America one could not disregard the importance of the land itself. "Wisdom sits in places," remarked Dudley Patterson, a Western Apache man from the White Mountain community of Cibecue. "Wisdom—or 'igoya'i—," wrote anthropologist Keith Basso, "consists in a heightened mental capacity that facilitates the avoidance of harmful events by detecting threatening circumstances when none are apparent. This capacity for prescient thinking," he continued, "is produced and sustained by three mental conditions, described in Apache as bíni' godilkǫǫh (smoothness of mind), bíni' goniɬ'iz (resilience of mind), and bíni; gonɬdzil (steadiness of mind.)" When one comes to know the cultural significance of a particular place, one begins a long journey toward wisdom, a quality that helps sustains life, that is, above all, "an instrument of survival." Even if reduced in size or splintered through the legacy of allotment, the land bases had been vital to the maintenance of distinct Native communities. Specific sites remained sacred or offered teachings and lessons from the stories and lives of one's ancestors and, as Betty Reid's story illumines, from one's own life. The natural landscape still yielded cultural meaning and significance.

For a steadily growing number of American Indians, the Native American Church also constituted a kind of instrument of survival. Participants found spiritual and social meaning in its ritual and its fellowship; the church remained a bulwark against the abuse of alcohol. NAC members often took part as well in the traditional ceremonies of Christian churches, depending on their needs and the customs of their families. An incident in Oregon furnished ample evidence that Indian religious freedom remained a fragile entity. Alfred Smith and Galen Black of Portland had been employed by a drug rehabilitation group but were dismissed for their use of peyote. The state of Oregon denied unemployment benefits to the NAC members, based on its conclusion that Smith and Black had been guilty of misconduct. The resulting case, *Employment Division, Department of Human Resources of Oregon et al.* v. *Alfred Smith et al.* (1990) made its way on appeal to the U.S. Supreme Court. There the Court majority agreed with Justice Antonin Scalia's determination that Oregon was entitled to prohibit peyote because a state had the power to control drug use. Other states have not followed Oregon's lead, but the Court's decision offered a disturbing legal precedent. A congressional amendment in 1994 to the Native American Religious Freedom Act of 1978, however, reaffirmed the right of an Indian "who uses peyote in a traditional manner for bona fide ceremonial purposes in conjunction with the practice of a traditional Indian religion" to use, possess, or transport peyote without penalty.

New Voices, New Images

The 1980s and 1990s witnessed a great variety of achievements in a variety of fields, accomplishments that often became sources of family, community, or more general Indian pride. Louise Erdrich (Turtle Mountain Anishinabe), whose *Love Medicine* (1984) became the best selling novel ever written by a Native American, was but one of many Indian writers to earn critical acclaim and popular recognition. In *Love Medicine, The Beet Queen* (1986), *Tracks* (1988), and *Bingo Palace* (1994), Erdrich explored the challenges faced in her native North Dakota by Indian people of mixed ancestry. Another Anishinabe writer, Gerald Vizenor, enjoyed heightened acclaim; Vizenor employed crossblood (to employ his term) characters to reveal dimensions of the Indian world, especially in urban settings. His satire and trickster figures enhance his many novels, including *Griever: An American Monkey King in China* (1987), *The Trickster of Liberty* (1988), and *The Heirs of Columbus* (1991). Chickasaw poet and novelist Linda Hogan wrote *Mean Spirit* (1990), a brilliant, dark depiction of an Indian community preyed upon because of its oil resources. Thomas King (Cherokee) provided memorable characters and scenes from Blackfeet country in *Medicine River* (1990) and *Green*

Grass, Running Water (1993). Michael Dorris (Modoc) presented three generations of women in his highly regarded *A Yellow Raft in Blue Water* (1987) and also published a compelling account of fetal alcohol syndrome in *The Broken Cord* (1989).

Younger writers also made major contributions, with many focusing on contemporary off-reservation life and the questions faced by characters of mixed-blood heritage. Sherman Alexie (Coeur d'Alene) gained a large following for his poignant characters from the Northwest, introduced in *Lone Ranger and Tonto Fistfight in Heaven* (1993) and *Reservation Blues* (1995). In Alexie's *Indian Killer* (1996), set in Seattle, John Smith (a Native American who has been adopted by a white couple) confronts a world in which "White people no longer feared Indians" and "Indians had become invisible, docile." "John wanted to change that," Alexie wrote. "He wanted to see fear in every pair of blue eyes." In *Grand Avenue* (1994), Greg Sarris (Pomo-Miwok) offered contemporary urban vignettes of Indian people in Santa Rosa, California. Adopted as a child by Anglo-American parents, Sarris only learned as an adult that his biological mother was Jewish, his biological father Filipino, Miwok, and Pomo. Growing up near the people he would incorporate into *Grand Avenue,* Sarris, now chairman of the Coastal Miwoks, remembered being "an orphaned coyote at the edge of camp where everyone else is eating."

Kimberly Blaeser (Anishinabe), Joy Harjo (Muscogee), Roberta Hill (Oneida), Luci Tapahonso (Navajo), and Ray Young Bear (Mesquakie) numbered among many outstanding Indian poets of the era. Readers welcomed their words, to quote from Blaeser's "Rituals, Yours—and Mine," ". . . as if i haven't enough of my own/ever/to make them stretch/that long distance/from home to here/from then to now. . . ." They recognized Tapahonso's Navajo cowboys "with raisin eyes" who "were just bad news" and they smiled at the way she portrayed her uncle drinking Hills Brothers coffee. Many shared Roberta Hill's disavowal of the "tyranny of the marketplace and of the heart" and her unflinching awareness that "unemployment and alcoholism continue to kill us on our reservations, radiation poisoning and acid rain kill our means of life, sky and earth wounded again and again." They seconded Hill in her belief that "it is the artisan's responsibility to overcome such dreadful tyranny. It is the artisan's responsibility to sing the sky clear so that we can walk across the earth, in a place fit for flowers."

Within colleges and universities Indian scholars began to obtain more positions in the traditional liberal arts departments as well as in fields such as education, where they previously had gained some representation. At the same time, they often accepted or developed joint appointments in Indian studies programs. As their numbers increased, the influence of Native professors also expanded within their home institutions and in regard to their work within their disciplines. American Indian scholars Duane Champagne (Turtle Mountain Anishinabe), Vine Deloria, Jr., Jennie Joe, Beatrice Medicine (Sihasapa Band of Lakota), Alfonso Ortiz, C. Matthew Snipp (Cherokee-Choctaw), Robert Thomas, Russell Thornton (Cherokee), and David Wilkins (Lumbee) authored important analyses of Native societies and communities. Indian historians such as Blue Clark (Muscogee), Stephen Crum (Western Shoshone), R. David Edmunds (Cherokee), Donald Fixico (Muscogee, Seminole, Sac and Fox, Shawnee), Jack Forbes, Clara Sue Kidwell (Choctaw-Anishinabe), Jean O'Brien (White Earth Anishinabe), James Riding In (Pawnee), Charles Roberts (Choctaw), Clifford Trafzer (Wyandot), and Terry Wilson (Potawatomi) contributed valuable studies. Brenda Child (Red Lake Anishinabe), Devon Mihesuah (Choctaw), Grayson Noley (Choctaw), Tsianina Lomawaima, and Karen Swisher (Standing Rock Sioux) were significant students of the history and practice of Native American education. In addition, in the late 1990s a large number of Indian graduate students in the social sciences and humanities were completing their studies and preparing to play leadership roles in the academic world of the twenty-first century.

Native artists presented an ever-expanding creative constellation. Many offered more familiar, realistic representations, while others through more symbolic and abstract work probed new terrain. David P. Bradley (White Earth Anishinabe), Harry Fonseca (Maidu), Bob Haozous (Chiricahua Apache-Navajo), Hachivi Edgar

Heap-of-Birds (Cheyenne-Arapaho), Peter Jemison (Seneca), Jean LaMarr (Paiute-Pit River), Nora Naranjo-Morse (Santa Clara Pueblo), Diego Romero (Cochiti Pueblo), Susan Stewart (Crow-Blackfeet), Kay Walkingstick (Cherokee), Emmi Whitehorse (Navajo)—to name but a few—were among the major artists of this era. From Naranjo-Morse's inimitable character of Pearlene to Heaps-of-Birds' "Smile for Racism," which protested the symbol utilized by the Cleveland Indians baseball team, the creations of Native artists reflected a diversity of inspirations and agendas. In addition, the impressive work of Indian photographers became increasingly visible. Hulleah J. Tsinhnahjinnie produced a series of magnificent portraits of Native American and Hawaiian women for the Bread and Roses Cultural Project. The photographs of Kenny Blackbird (Assiniboine-Sioux), Larry McNeil (Tlingit/Nisga'a), Victor Masayesva, Jr. (Hopi), Monty Roessel (Navajo), and many others were displayed in major exhibits and featured in a wide variety of publications.

Graham Greene (Oneida) and Gary Farmer (Cayuga) were among the Indian actors whose work in film earned praise and recognition. Greene became familiar to the world through his performance in Kevin Costner's *Dances with Wolves*, and he tackled a wonderful array of roles in films that ranged from *Ishi: The Last of the Yahi* to *Thunderheart*. Farmer was a memorable figure in *Pow-Wow Highway*, driving an ancient used car—which he dubbed his war pony—from Northern Cheyenne country via Bear Butte to Santa Fe. The American Indian Theater Company, the Native American Theater Ensemble, the Red Earth Performing Arts Company, and the Spiderwoman Theater Company provided opportunities for Native actors and Native playwrights. Significant playwrights included Hanay Geiogamah (Kiowa-Delaware) and Tomson Highway (Cree). Indian producers such as Sandy Johnson Osawa (Makah) and Chris Spotted Eagle (Houma) also completed noteworthy film documentaries.

Canyon Records of Phoenix figured as a leading force in the recording and distributing of Native American music. In some instances, the company launched the careers of musicians, such as R. Carlos Nakai (Navajo-Ute), whose flute has now been heard by audiences around the world. From waila (chicken scratch) to pow-wow music to peyote songs, Canyon Records helped make available this vital medium. Joanne Shenandoah (Oneida) and other singers enjoyed national followings. Indian musicians broke new ground through jazz, reggae, and other contemporary forms. Red Thunder, a rock band of Apache, Pueblo, and Mayan musicians, enjoyed considerable popularity, as did the band, Poetic Justice—featuring saxophonist Joy Harjo, attorney Susan M. Williams (Sisseton-Wahpeton Dakota) on drums, judge Willie Bluehouse Johnson (Isleta Pueblo-Navajo) on guitar, John Williams (Sisseton-Wahpeton Dakota) on bass, and Frank Poocha (Hopi-Pima) on keyboards. Brent Michael Davids (Stockbridge-Munsee) earned praise for his compositions. His pieces were commissioned by such internationally recognized groups as the Joffrey Ballet and the Kronos Quartet.

Residents of the Southwest also heard the unmistakable voice of Vincent Craig (Navajo). In one of Craig's western songs he tells the story of hearing a strange noise outside of his home and going out to investigate: ". . . . There were my boys just ropin' on a ropin' dummy, wearin' those Wranglers and those beat up old Bailey hats . . . I said, what do you want to be when you grow up. . . . and they said, 'we've got our own heroes here on the Navajo Nation.'" His sons wanted "to ride a bull like Stanley Young or ride like Herm McCray, throw a rope like Felix Gilbert and old James Begay. . . ."

Indian artists in various media often focused their attention on the hopes developed and accomplishments realized in competitive athletics. In Indian country just as much as elsewhere, sports could encompass individual, family, and community aspirations. The Wyoming Indian High School boys basketball team won one state championship after another in the 1980s and 1990s. When Ryneldi Becenti (Navajo) competed at the intercollegiate level in basketball, her relatives and other community members drove hundreds of miles to watch her play point guard for Arizona State University. Young men and women in cross-country and track-and-field dreamed of duplicating the achievement of Billy Mills (Oglala Lakota), who had won the 10,000-meter run in the 1964 Olympics. Sports offered the chance not only for family achievement from one generation to the next, but also another kind of continuation. Howard Hunter of Pine Ridge allowed that rodeo presented the opportunity to gain the upper hand in the small bit of rivalry that persisted between the Lakotas and the Crows. Athletic competition also could encourage boundaries to be transcended. Justin Giles, (Muscogee), may have been from Oklahoma, but he played well for the eighteen-and-under squad of the Iroquois National Lacrosse Team. An eager participant in Denver's Blue Pony League, Jesse Holder (Tlingit-Navajo-Lakota) may follow in Giles's footsteps, just as anthropologist Brenda Kay Manuelito would have predicted. Whether in time-honored sports such as Lacrosse or in sports like basketball and rodeo that had become traditional, Indians found additional means to foster competition, achievement, and community.

Museums and Repatriation

In tribal museums and visitor centers, Indians determined the means and the manner through which their histories and cultures would be presented. These facilities gave Native architects, such as Dennis Sun Rhodes (Northern Arapaho) and Dennis Numkena (Hopi), and non-Indian architects sympathetic to Native design, the opportunity to create imaginative and culturally appropriate structures. The Warms Springs community in Oregon, for example, built an impressive new museum, which allowed for tribal artifacts to be displayed appropriately and provided a place to sell fine examples of beadwork and basketry. By the late 1990s more than 200 such museums and centers had been completed. At the Seneca-Iroquois museum in upstate New York, the Makah Tribal Museum on the Olympic Peninsula, the Pamunkey Indian Museum and Cultural Center in Virginia, and elsewhere one saw not only valuable depictions of tribal life but also key examples of Indian self-determination.

The Mashantucket Pequot Museum and Research Center, scheduled to open on June 1, 1998, will combine a public museum devoted to the story of the tribe with a research facility focused on Indian histories and cultures. This extraordinary facility, designed by Polshek and Partners, will include 85,000 square feet of permanent exhibits, a 5,000-foot temporary exhibit space, a 420-seat auditorium, a large research and children's library, state-of-the-art research and conservation laboratories, collections storage area, print and electronic archives, a restaurant, and a retail store.

Another crucial step occurred on October 30, 1994, when the George Gustav Heye Center of the National Museum of the American Indian/Smithsonian opened in New York City, as the first component of the National Museum of the American Indian. The Cultural Resources Center in Suitland, Maryland, and the National Museum on the National Mall in Washington, D.C., will follow. In addition, as Founding Director W. Richard West, Jr., declared, a "fourth museum" will use "satellite link-ups, interactive media, and other high technology forms" to share the resources of the National Museum "with schools, libraries, tribal museums, and other institutions throughout the nation." "Ours will be a museum," West promised, "that integrates a strong first-person voice into its presentation of the hundreds of diverse Indian cultures throughout the Western Hemisphere."

Museums illustrated the different perspective a century had brought. In the late 1800s and early 1900s federal, public, and private museums had sponsored expeditions to collect artifacts and objects from Indian communities. One hundred years later, repatriation of funerary objects, sacred objects, and items of cultural patrimony stored in museums had become an issue of paramount importance. First at the New York State Museum in Albany and then at the Heard Museum in Phoenix, administrator Martin Sullivan demonstrated that a skilled cultural broker could facilitate and expedite the process whereby Indian nations could reclaim certain objects of cultural significance. The Heard and many other museums in this era became more sensitive to Native concerns. At the same time they explored a wider range of subjects, including such important topics as the impact of tourism and of boarding schools. Passage of the National Museum of the American Indian Act of 1989 and the Native American Graves Protection and Repatriation Act (NAGPRA) in 1990 hastened the repatriation of material items and the return of the hundreds of thousands of skeletal remains still possessed by historical societies, universities, and various public and private museums. NAGPRA affected not only federal museums but all agencies receiving federal support. The process of repatriation was made more complicated by the objections of private collectors and many archaeologists who, respectively, defended the retention of Native sacred objects and skeletal remains. Bureaucratic inertia, vested interest, and cultural insensitivity also created obstacles. For example, in the 1980s the director of the Nebraska State Historical Society, James Hanson, tried to deny the Pawnees the repatriation of the remains of their relatives as well as funerary objects; Hanson went so far as to contend that the Pawnees really did not have a religion and that his institution somehow was not a state agency. Following an extended controversy, Hanson eventually resigned.

Through their writings, presentations, and research, James Riding In, Roger Echo-Hawk (Pawnee), and a host of other Native scholars kept pushing for continued progress in regard to repatriation. As Riding In noted, this effort addressed "a pressing need to disestablish racial, institutional, and societal barriers that impede this country's movement toward a place that celebrates cultural diversity as a cherished and indispensable component of its social, political, and economic fabric." Riding In concluded progress had been possible because more Americans, including "a growing number of sympathetic archaeologists and museum curators," had "recognized that Indians are not disappearing, and that Indians are entitled to burial rights and religious freedom."

Even with such headway, significant problems persisted. Many Native people argued the case of an independent origin of Native peoples in the Americas, as opposed to the widely accepted theory that the ancestors of American Indians migrated across the Bering Strait from the Asian continent. Contending that Indian accounts of their own origins were as well founded as the judgments of archaeologists, these individuals rejected the utility of additional archaeological work to study past Native cultures. They believed that archaeologists had had ample time to do their research and often had exceeded their authority in conducting their investigations. Vine Deloria, Jr., articulated this perspective in *Red Earth,*

White Lies: Native Americans and the Myth of Scientific Fact, published in 1996. During the 1990s many tribes employed NAGPRA to demand the return of ancient skeletal remains found near their ancestral lands. The case of the so-called Kennewick man illustrated that controversies would continue. In this instance, the Army Corps of Engineers had turned over a recently discovered skeleton, perhaps as old as 9,000 years, to the Confederated Tribes of the Umatilla reservation. The Native people were determined to rebury these remains; some archaeologists argued against reburial, claiming the skeleton held potentially significant clues to human origins in North America. This specific disagreement had not been resolved by the summer of 1997.

Gaming

If repatriation indicated a new attitude about the Indian past, gaming emboldened a new outlook concerning the Native future. The U.S. Supreme Court decision of *California* v. *Cabazon Band of Mission Indians* in 1987 had opened the door to expanded gaming activities on Indian reservations. The court had ruled that California regulatory laws in regard to gambling could not be applied on Indian lands. The Indian Gaming Regulatory Act, passed by Congress in the following year allowed certain forms of gaming to take place on reservations even if these activities were illegal elsewhere in particular states. Many Indians harbored misgivings about starting bingo parlors and, later, casinos, on their lands, but they argued that ongoing economic difficulties had left them little choice other than to seek new economic alternatives. Some laid part of the blame for their most recent difficulties on the "new federalism" of Ronald Reagan. As president, Reagan charged federal paternalism as the cause for the economic ills besetting the people of most reservations. He slashed a billion dollars from the $3.5 billion budgeted for Indian affairs and gained congressional approval for the reduction. Secretary of the Interior James Watt embodied this philosophy; Watt suggested that "If you want an example of the failures of socialism, don't go to Russia. Come to America and go to the Indian reservations." He also charged the political leaders of reservations with purposely keeping tribal members poor in order to hold on to their positions.

The Reagan budget cuts hit hardest in the areas where Indians could least afford them. Job-training programs were dismantled and funds for new housing were erased. Elimination of the Concentrated Training and Employment Act program cost 18,000 Indians their jobs and placed 6,000 Indian families on welfare. The Indian Health Service, already woefully underfunded, found itself a target for reduced expenditures. But surveys in the early 1980s concluded that the IHS needed more rather than less; more than 800 additional doctors and 3,000 more nurses were required for IHS care to be brought up to an average national standard. Clearly the IHS should have constructed more hospitals and clinics and remodeled or abandoned old and obsolete facilities. Instead the Reagan administration cut expenditures, especially in regard to the provision of health care to urban Indians.

Around the same time, gaming seemed to offer Indian communities the chance to provide new jobs and new housing and thus enable more of their residents to remain on the land. Casinos reversed the economic fortunes of many Indian nations, including Pojoaque Pueblo in northern New Mexico, a community seemingly on the verge of disappearance earlier in the century. There the Cities of Gold casino offered tangible proof of a new status.

Operating gaming parlors could be justified on the basis of financial need, but many also suggested that gambling always had been a part of tribal cultures. Offering a benediction at the groundbreaking ceremony for the 45,000-square-foot casino at Toppenish, Washington, Yakama religious leader Frederick Ike, Sr., said, "Gambling is a traditional way of life for our Indian people. This is nothing new to us. . . ." Contentions of tradition notwithstanding, the hard economic realities of the day were undeniably compelling. The presence of this new source of tribal revenue and employment made it possible for people like Victrietta Hensley (Oneida) to move home to the place where her parents were born and raised. Her parents had moved away in search of employment, and Hensley had lived in Michigan and Ohio, but never on the Oneida reservation, eight miles west of Green Bay,

Wisconsin. But in 1976, the initiative of two members of the tribe, Sandra Ninham and Alma Webster, began to change Oneida fortunes. They searched for a way to pay the tribal civic center's utility bills. Ninham and Webster finally settled on the option of holding Sunday afternoon bingo. From this modest foundation, the Oneidas proceeded to develop a multimillion-dollar casino gaming industry. By 1993 the tribe employed over 2,000 people, including Victrietta Hensley and her husband, Harvey.

The Oneida experience has not proved typical. A Government Accounting Office report in June 1997 revealed that just eight casinos brought in 40 percent of the $4.5 billion in total revenue of Native gaming in 1996 (compared to a total of about $100 million in 1988). The profits of many of the smaller operations are marginal at best, and some Indian casinos have failed to make money. And, even if they are somewhat profitable, casinos do not necessarily transform conditions on the reservations. The $1 million earned at Pine Ridge in 1996, for example, did not seem to have much effect on that community, whose splintered land base reflected the terrible legacy of the allotment era. In 1996 unemployment remained at 75 percent on Pine Ridge and hovered at an average of 50 percent on all reservations. So gambling could not be considered a panacea, even though it had produced unprecedented revenues and helped significantly to reduce unemployment and boost the economy of many tribes.

Gaming could also cause or exacerbate divisions within or between Indian nations. In November 1996, a traditionalist, Michael Schindler, became president of the Cattaraugus Seneca Nation in part because of his opposition to casinos as socially destructive forces. In May 1997, Menominee tribal chairman Apesanahkwat sent an open letter to Deborah Doxtator, chairperson of the Oneida Nation in Wisconsin, noting the "great disparity among the eleven tribes insofar as gaming profits are concerned" and contending that "gaming has separated all tribes into Haves and Have Nots." In this letter, published in a full-page display in the newspaper, *News From Indian Country,* Apesanahkwat severely criticized the Oneidas for their opposition to an off-reservation casino site being considered by the Menominees.

Where casinos proved profitable, Indian nations had been able to regenerate their treasuries and reimagine their futures. Although some tribes chose to divide the proceeds on a per capita basis, many others used the proceeds from their gaming operations to build child care centers, schools, clinics, housing, nursing homes, cultural centers, and other similar institutions designed to benefit their members. The funds also could transform the workings of tribal government. Doxtator stated the revenue had facilitated self-determination, by allowing the Oneidas to prove "we can conduct our government, and we can regulate ourselves." "With gaming," she added, "Oneida and other tribes have been able to start healing the wounds of poverty, joblessness, and isolation." Nowhere had this optimistic scenario been more striking than in the Pequot community of Mashantucket, Connecticut.

At the turn of the century this community appeared to outsiders to be on its way to extinction. Less than twenty tribal members resided at Mashantucket in 1900, and by 1930 there were less than ten. Elizabeth George Plouffe and Martha Langevin Ellal served as tribal leaders until their deaths in the early 1970s. Through their determined efforts the small group persisted. Then Plouffe's grandson, Richard "Skip" Hayward became chairman. Under his leadership the small community started to push for federal recognition and for the return of lands stolen in the 1800s. By 1983 the Mashantucket Pequots had gained federal recognition. With a $900,000 land claims settlement they started to buy back land and develop their economy. Under the terms of the Indian Gaming Regulatory Act (IGRA) of 1988, they negotiated in 1992 a compact with Connecticut governor Lowell Weicker to build Fox-woods Casino. The Mashantucket Pequots agreed to give a minimum of $1 million a year to the state of Connecticut for use in assisting economically depressed towns and cities. Given the overwhelming success of the casino, this annual donation has not been difficult to make. By 1994 tribal membership had increased to three hundred persons. Although the exact amount of revenue generated by Foxwoods has not been made public, it has been estimated that it produces at least not $1 million but $1 billion a year. Much of this sum is diverted directly to Connecticut under the terms of the compact. The Pequots have purchased additional land, contributed generously to the Native American Rights Fund, sponsored their powwow and traditional feast, Schemitzun, and are completing a world-class museum.

The IGRA permitted tribes across America to work out deals with the states in which they operated gaming establishments, but it could not forestall collisions over economic empowerment and sovereignty. Opponents to Indian gaming would not accept the concept of sovereignty. They perceived Native gaming as a kind of bone thrown to a group designated as deserving. They rejected any assertion of sovereignty as a joke not worthy of attention. From the moment the Florida Seminoles initiated high-stakes bingo games in the late 1970s, states and elected federal representatives voiced objections. Even though Indian gaming constituted less than 10 percent of the gambling activity in the United States, the presence in the country of 281 gaming facilities being run by 184 tribal communities sparked a great deal of animosity. State officials not only were frustrated by their inability to tax tribal proceeds from gaming and their inability to exert as much control as they wanted over the casino and bingo operations, but they also faced pressure from other interests within their borders who opposed Indian gaming. These interests included horse and dog track owners who saw their base reduced, conservative constituents who opposed gambling, and hotel owners and others involved in the hospitality industry who also perceived their clients as being lured away to greener pastures.

When the Wisconsin Dells Greyhound Park closed, its officials blamed the nearby casino owned by the Ho-Chunk. In contrast, the Pokagon Band of Potawatomi, the Little Traverse Band of Odawa, and the Little River Band of Ottawa sued the state of Michigan for rejecting compacts they had negotiated with Governor John Engler. In New Mexico in 1996 the state supreme court ruled that the compacts signed by the tribes with Governor Gary E. Johnson were illegal, and yet the state hesitated to close down an industry that employed about 4,000 people and generated $200 million a year. U.S. District Attorney General John Kelly persisted, with the Mescalero Apache casino forced to close and others operating while the ruling was appealed. A poll by the *Albu-*

querque Journal indicated that a clear majority of non-Indians within the state favored giving Indians the opportunity to operate gaming enterprises, either because they enjoyed gambling or because they believed that Indians had not been treated fairly by American society and deserved this chance to develop their economies. Early in 1997 the New Mexico legislature on a 35–34 vote passed a bill permitting the continuation of Indian gaming, but imposing a 16 percent assessment for the state from casino profits. The tribes promised to take this latest legislative initiative to court.

In Arizona Governor Fife Symington refused to negotiate a gaming compact with the Salt River Pima-Maricopa community, as he had with other Indian tribes. Salt River, which bordered the upscale city of Scottsdale, obtained enough signatures on referendum petitions to force a statewide vote on the matter in November 1996. Arizona voters overwhelmingly supported the right of the Salt River community to a compact comparable to those previously signed with other Indian tribes. Symington signed into law provisions to allow two casinos at Salt River, but then tried to block the specific plans of the Salt River community to locate casinos close to Scottsdale, so the matter remained undecided.

In another instance, attorneys representing the state of Minnesota and county governments appealed the Federal District Court decision in 1994 that upheld the hunting, fishing, and gathering rights an 1837 treaty had reserved in east central Minnesota for the Mille Lacs Band of Anishinabe. The people of Mille Lacs did not need any longer their "special" hunting, fishing, and gathering "privileges," these lawyers contended in Circuit Court in 1997, because, due to gaming revenue, the average personal income at Mille Lacs now exceeded that of non-Indians in the region. For generations Indians had been condemned by other Americans who perceived Native peoples as being too lazy and too poor. Now it appeared Indians were being castigated by others for being too ambitious and too rich.

By-mid decade, some congressional representatives began to target Native American gambling income for taxation. In June 1997, Bill Archer, the chair of the House Ways and Means Committee, proposed a 34 percent income tax on revenue from tribal casinos and other Indian businesses. Archer argued that Indian gaming enterprises had an unfair advantage over other casinos and businesses that were taxed. Indian leaders quickly opposed this attempt to deal with tribes as businesses or charities rather than as sovereign governments. Colorado Senator Ben Nighthorse Campbell (Northern Cheyenne) also fought against this measure and anti-Indian initiatives sponsored by Senator Slade Gorton of Washington.

Native American leaders understood that even the small percentage they controlled of the overall amount Americans spent on gambling was subject to shrinkage. They saw the current period as a window in time that in all likelihood would not last beyond the early years of the next century. Thus they encouraged the development of reservation economies based upon other means, employing casino profits to start new businesses. In addition, other commercial enterprises reconsidered Native land as a more plausible possibility for new developments. Some important success stories could be related.

Communities

In a period of twenty years the unemployment rate among the Mississippi Band of Choctaw had been reduced from over 80 to 4 percent. The community employed nearly 3,000 people in 1996, including about 1,000 non-Indians from the surrounding area. Chief Philip Martin presided over this transition. Martin first became chairman of the tribal council in 1959 and, other than for a term in the late 1970s, remained at the helm. The Choctaw industrial park became home to a host of businesses, beginning with General Motors's Packard Electric Division, with most of them now tribally owned. In 1994 the Silver Star Casino opened, with 1,550 slot machines, 71 table games (including blackjack, craps, poker, and roulette), and a fine restaurant called Philip M's. It brought $50 million into the community in 1995.

When the Ak-Chin Indian Community held the ground-breaking ceremony for its new eco-museum on November 17, 1990, it marked another in a long series of steps that marked the revitalization of this reservation. Situated adjacent to the small farming town of Maricopa, Arizona, the 21,000-acre Ak-Chin reservation was blessed with good farmland. But until the early 1960s non-Indian leasing of the land had prevailed. Brothers Wayne and Richard Carlyle led the battle in the 1960s against renewing leases to outsiders. Then the Carlyles helped create Ak-Chin Farms, a tribal operation. By 1968, Ak-Chin Farms cleared $1 million and the tribe had regained control of half of its land. However, the excessive pumping of water by non-Indian farmers in the area had extracted a toll from the water table and by the 1970s Ak-Chin farming was imperiled. The community had realized a less than 2 percent unemployment rate, but it all seemed for naught unless a new source of water could be provided. Passage of Public Law 95-328 in 1978 guaranteed delivery of water to the tribe; Public Law 98-350 in 1984 determined the water would come from the Central Arizona Project (CAP). In 1988 the CAP water actually arrived. In 1989 the unemployment rate at Ak-Chin stood at 3.8 per cent, or 10 people out of a labor force of 260. By decade's end the community received almost no money from the federal government. Revenues from the farm and, over the past few years, from Harrah's Ak-Chin Casino are funneled into housing, care for the elderly and other projects rather than divided on a per capita basis. Leona Kakar, Delia Antone, and others provided the necessary leadership that enabled members of the Ak-Chin community to possess an optimistic view of its future. One of Ak-Chin's proudest achievements was its museum, a unique blending of building and surrounding environment that, its staff declared, "attempts to serve the community that owns it and to share the spirit of the community with the museum visitor."

The Turtle Mountain Anishinabe of North Dakota ran a multi-million-dollar business. This tribally owned data-entry firm, Uniband, employed 875 full-time people nationwide, with an annual payroll of $18 million. Founded in 1987, the corporation was purchased by Turtle Mountain in 1990. The key to its expansion came with its status as a minority firm, which allowed it to bid successfully on federal contracts. Its chief executive officer was Bernardine Martin-Lufking (Navajo).

The ability of the Barona community in the San Diego area to open and operate a casino had dramatically changed its status. When this small community opened a new gas station thanks to proceeds from the Barona Casino, tribal chairman Clifford La Chappa asserted, "A few years ago no one would have dreamed that we would have the resources to open a successful tribal-owned business." He added, "With revenues from Barona Casino, we have been able to become self-sufficient, eliminate unemployment on the reservation and give more than one and a half million dollars to San Diego charitable organizations."

Community identity fueled drives for federal recognition waged by many Indian groups. Attorneys from the Native American Rights Fund often played an important role in this process. Between 1980 and 1994, the Grand Traverse Band of Ottawa and Chippewa in Michigan, the Jamestown Klallam Tribe in Washington, the Tunica-Biloxi Tribe of Louisiana, the Death Valley Timbi-Sha Shoshone Band of California, the Narragansett Indian Tribe of Rhode Island, the Poarch Band of Creeks of Alabama, the Wampanoag Tribe of Gay Head in Massachusetts, the San Juan Southern Paiute Tribe in Arizona, the Snoqualmie Tribe in Washington, and the Mohegan Tribe of Connecticut were among those to gain recognition through the Department of the Interior's branch of acknowledgment. In addition, between 1978 and 1991, Congress extended federal recognition to the Pascua Yaqui of Arizona, the Ysleta del Sur Pueblo in Texas, the Texas Band of Traditional Kickapoos, the Cow Creek Band of Umpqua Indians in Oregon, the Confederated Tribes of Coos, Lower Umpqua, and Siuslaw Indians in Oregon, the Lac Vieux Desert Band of Lake Superior Chippewa in Michigan, and the Aroostook Micmac Tribe of Maine. As with the recently recognized Mashantucket Pequots, these additional examples, together with the dozens of other communities still fighting for recognition, spoke to the determination of Native peoples to resist a disappearance that once seemed inevitable and to position themselves to achieve new development in the century to come. In Vermont, where the census takers had counted five Indians in 1900, the 1990 census total had increased to 1,696.

Tribal Membership and Indian Rights

Tribal membership persisted as a dilemma within many Indian nations. Most people agreed with political scientist David Wilkins, who wrote to the *Wall Street Journal* in 1995 in regard to this issue within his own tribe. "Who is a Lumbee," Wilkins declared, "is the business of the Lumbee people to decide." The Lumbees of North Carolina had not yet achieved federal recognition, and the long battle to gain it had taken its toll. Several segments had chosen to seek separate political recognition; the Lumbee Tribal Council and the Board of Directors of the Lumbee Regional Development Association were at odds. Such internal strife, Wilkins suggested, did "not mean that the tribe is unclear about its core identity. This has never been disputed or questioned."

In Santa Clara Pueblo of New Mexico, the issue of membership had not evaporated. Robert Montoya, a life-long resident of Santa Clara, raised his four children in the community. Although his mother was from Santa Clara, his father was from Isleta Pueblo. As a result, Montoya has been denied membership and voting rights in tribal elections, his property ownership at Santa Clara may be challenged, and his children and grandchildren may not be eligible for enrollment in Santa Clara school programs or for village scholarships. However, the pueblo may be ready to alter its customary stance based upon a growing number of residents whose profiles are similar to those of the Montoya family.

Other groups continued to fight for federal recognition. The Miami Nation in Indiana had not reached that objective, but its approximately 6,000 members did have the satisfaction in April 1997 of observing unprecedented attention being paid to their history: the Eiteljorg Museum of American Indians and Western Art in Indianapolis had opened the largest exhibit it had ever attempted. "In the Presence of the Past: The Miami Indians of Indiana," was completed with the assistance of a Miami advisory panel, and included consideration of Miami efforts to persevere in their home country of north central Indiana.

The past two decades witnessed some clear victories in regard to Indian rights, but, as always, particular dimensions of Native sovereignty and jurisdiction became the subjects of litigation. The Supreme Court supported the ability of Indian tribes to tax and regulate Indians and non-Indians in decisions such as *Merrion* v. *Jicarilla Apache Tribe* (1982) and *Kerr-McGee Corp.* v. *Navajo Tribe* (1985). According to legal scholar Robert N. Clinton, in these decisions "the Supreme Court ruled that the inherent sovereignty possessed by Indian tribes permitted the tribes to impose mineral and oil and gas severance taxes and possessory interest taxes on natural resources extracted by non-Indian companies from leased Indian lands." In addition, *New Mexico v. Mescalero Apache Tribe* (1983) supported the right of the Mescaleros rather than the state to regulate non-Indian hunting and fishing on their reservation.

However, other rights remained in question. Because of treaties or agreements and their status as aboriginal occupants of the land, Indians believed they were entitled to particular rights in regard to water and land use. In addition, they often confronted difficult issues relating to their legal status. In Wisconsin the different Anishinabe bands had signed treaties in 1837, 1842, and 1854, that had reserved the right for their people to spear fish in off-reservation waters. The state and throngs of non-Indians in Wisconsin bitterly contested that right. Such opponents carried signs that expressed such sentiments as "Save a walleye, spear an Indian." The protests persisted, even though in the late 1980s the Anishinabeg were taking about 1 percent of the walleyes. The courts eventually ruled that the Anishinabeg were entitled to spear for walleye and to take half of the harvest. Bad River Band member Patty Loew concluded the successful struggle yielded several key results, including a mandate from the Wisconsin state legislature that all public schools must teach about Indian cultures, histories, and sovereignty. But, she added: "Perhaps the most important legacy … is the spiritual revolution it produced within the Anishinabe Nation" creating a cultural renaissance. As had been true throughout the twentieth century, conflict and harassment had produced a heightened rather than reduced sense of Indian identity.

In the western United States, the issue of water rights provoked countless lawsuits during this period. The issues at stake included quantification of the amount of water to which a particular Indian community was entitled, the kinds of uses tribes could have for this water, whether the tribes could sell or lease water reserved to them to other parties, and the kind of authority tribes could have in regard to managing their own water resources or the water use by non-Indian successors to allottees. As the example of Ak-Chin indicated, some tribes ultimately chose to negotiate for a specific amount of guaranteed water. Others remained in court, fighting long, costly, and extremely complex legal battles. Control over groundwater and underground water represented two areas of contemporary legal battles. Zuni Pueblo had already won two cases against the United States in regard to land claims and environmental damages. In a third case, this time with the assistance of the United States, they won access to Kolhu/wala:wa ("Zuni Heaven"), a sacred site in Arizona, to which they made a pilgrimage every four years. The Zuni religion taught that it was to this place that all Zunis go after death, historian E. Richard Hart explained, "and where the supernatural Kokko reside under a sacred lake fed by the waters from a precious spring." On their trek, the Zunis "make offerings, say prayers, gather sacred paint pigments, and eventually reach Kolhu.wala:wa, where their religious activities and prayers are aimed at bringing peace, order, and prosperity, not only to the Zunis but also to the entire world." An Anglo rancher did not care what the Zunis were doing or how long they had followed the trail. He would not grant an easement to these intruders who dared to trespass on his land. In 1990, the presiding judge eventually ruled in favor of Zuni. As had been true with Blue Lake and Taos, a way of life had been at stake, and the people had triumphed.

For the Native peoples in Alaska who placed their highest priority on carrying on traditional subsistence activities, the money received from the Alaska Native Claims Settlement Act seemed unimportant. Antoinnette Helmer of Craig explained, "Profit to non-Natives means money. Profit to Natives means a good life derived from the land and sea." "The land we hold in trust is our wealth," she added. "It is the only wealth we could possibly pass on to our children. . . . Without our homelands we become true paupers." Federal acknowledgment of that priority had been halting, but in 1993 Assistant Secretary of the Interior for Indian Affairs (the altered title and status of the former Commissioner of Indian Affairs) Ada Deer included Alaskan Native communities as federally recognized groups.

When Canadian jurist Thomas Berger traveled through Alaska from 1983 to 1985 to assess ANCSA for the Alaska Native Review Commission, a body sponsored by the Inuit Circumpolar Conference and the World Council of Indigenous Peoples, he concluded ANCSA had failed. Berger predicted the regional corporations were likely to bring "minimal" benefit to Alaska Natives. He termed ANCSA a misguided attempt "to recreate Main Street on the tundra." A decade later, the jury remained out on the future of the twelve regional corporations and the 220 smaller village companies. Some of the corporations had fared better than they had initially and better than most had anticipated, given the different world they represented. There had been understandable hesitation about diversification of corporate investments, particularly in regard to investments in the lower forty-eight states. Some regional corporations, particularly Cook Inlet Region and Sealaska, fared well in the 1990s while others lagged behind.

Some of the worst fears regarding the settlement had not been realized. Amendments to ANCSA passed by Congress in 1987 now permitted shareholders in the different corporations to vote to allow children born after 1971 to enroll and to provide special assistance to elders. The restrictions on stock ownership, due originally to expire in 1991, had been extended. However ANCSA, even in its amended form, left unresolved the future of traditional subsistence activities and the status of individual Native communities in Alaska.

As the issue of gaming had revealed, Alaska was not alone in its attempts to block realization of sovereignty for Native Americans. In New York, for example, Indians clashed with state authorities over the proposed collection of state taxes on tobacco and gasoline. The sale of such products at lower prices had created lucrative Native businesses throughout the United States. However, after the U.S. Supreme Court concluded in 1994 that New York could collect such taxes on reservation sales to non-Indians, New York governor George Pataki decided to pursue such a course of action. Some Indian nations in New York tentatively agreed to raise the price of cigarettes, but much remained to be decided. On the Cattaraugus Seneca Nation, there were continuing confrontations both with the state of New York and within Cattaraugus itself. Senecas stayed protests by blocking highways through their lands. State troopers clashed with protesters, resulting in injuries and arrests. The heightened efforts of state and local governments to assume expanded jurisdiction on Indian lands thus had emerged during this period as an especially vital concern.

Economies and Education

If the state or the federal government could pose obstacles to Indian economic development, so too could two other forces: outside private interests and internal conflicts. Indian economies had always relied considerably on the use of natural resources. Mineral, timber, farming and ranching, and other activities remained significant components of some tribes' overall economic strategies. In 1989, for example, 75 percent of all reservation land was used for farming and ranching, although on most reservations farming and ranching yielded a shrinking percentage of overall tribal and individual income. Native communities still struggled against private individual and corporate interests that sought to appropriate indigenous resources for their own benefit. The presence of the Native American Rights Fund, the Council of Energy Resource Tribes, and generally improved legal counsel improved the odds that tribes would gain better returns from such resources. However, except when gaming or some other windfall provided a considerable influx of money, Indian nations usually lacked the capital needed to launch major enterprises. In the case of energy resources, the tribes with oil, gas, and other minerals leased rather than owned those extractive companies. Passage of the Indian Mineral Development Act of 1982 allowed for joint ventures, but a changing market discouraged such possibilities. In addition, federal agencies mismanaged royalties and contractors stole oil and gas from tribal sources. Even though these tribes did not receive what they should have, those who could invest some of their royalties over time reaped considerable dividends. The Jicarilla Apaches in the 1970s and 1980s invested 15 percent of their royalties from oil and gas and by 1991 had amassed a portfolio worth over $200 million. But whether it was large-scale or small-scale business, internal hurdles also posed problems. The allotment era, especially in the northern Plains, had left a legacy of a quilted real estate, wherein individual Indian and non-Indian interests could stymie group designs. On many reservations, tribal councils meddled in the operation of tribally sponsored commercial enterprises to the detriment of these concerns. Native economic development potentially benefiting the group often had to be weighed against the particular rights or vested interests of an individual family or local area. Although by this time there were more Indian professional people, specific individual communities frequently lacked particular expertise.

However, there were some promising signs that the training and education of these professionals had entered a new stage. Despite their ongoing financial difficulties, the thirty members of the American Indian Higher Education Consortium played a vital role in this process. A few new tribal colleges had joined the consortium, and all those institutions in existence at the beginning of the 1980s remained in operation. Together they allowed a steadily larger number of Native students to attend college, with several institutions offering or about to offer bachelor's and master's degree programs. Public and private colleges and universities were making a greater and more successful effort to recruit and graduate Indian students. As Anne N. Medicine (Mohawk), Director of Native American Recruitment and Retention at Stanford University, stated in 1993, "to successfully recruit and retain American Indians and Alaskan Natives as under graduate and graduate students, a program of support must be in place as well as a strong institutional commitment." Dartmouth College, for example, graduated over 350 Indian students from 1970 to 1995. Between 1989 and 1997, 58 Indian students graduated with bachelor's degrees through the Evergreen State College's "Tribal Reservation-Based, Community Determined" program. The college offered classes in Makah, Quinault, Port Gamble S'Klallam, and Skokomish reservation communities on the Olympic Peninsula. The Navajo Nation entered into an agreement with Arizona State University in August 1995 to prepare Navajo teachers who already had bachelor's degrees to become administrators. On May 16, 1997, nine of the first Navajo Fellows received their master's degrees in educational leadership. They and others in the program will be striving to in-corporate the Diné philosophy of education in Navajo schools. One of the fellows, Debbie Jackson Dennison, explained that this philosophy of education encompassed spirituality, intellect, planning, and life skills. The schools should be informed, she said, by the "very beautiful, meaningful, and respectful principles that have allowed for a history of survival through great catastrophes for our people."

New and continuing programs offered essential assistance. The American Indian Science and Engineering Society, under the leadership of Norbert S. Hill, Jr. (Oneida), strove to increase the number of Indian scientists and engineers and to encourage future Native leaders to be more informed about contemporary technology. During the first two decades of its existence, this private, non-profit organization awarded well over $1 million in scholarships and developed chapters at colleges and universities throughout North America. In 1994, funding from the National Science Foundation permitted the creation of the All Nations Alliance for Minority Participation, consisting of twenty-four tribal colleges and thirty-one state and private universities in Kansas, Nebraska, Michigan, Minnesota, Montana, North Dakota, South Dakota, Washington, and Wisconsin, with the headquarters of the consortium at Salish Kootenai College. Through this program, students were encouraged to seek degrees in science, beginning with summer bridge projects for high school graduates. The W. K. Kellogg Foundation implemented in the late 1990s another major initiative to bolster tribal colleges.

"We Are Still Here"

There remained, to be sure, other battles to be fought over the status of Indians in their native land. Native peoples continued to protest the appropriation of Indian persons and symbols for a variety of non-Indian projects and products. Condemning sculptor Korzcak Ziolkowski's monument of Crazy Horse in the Black Hills of South Dakota, Dakota writer Elizabeth Cook-Lynn observed how Crazy Horse had been treated: "He has become a steak house in California and his name is used profanely to sell everything from beer to poetry magazines and third rate novels. And now they blow up a mountain to invent his image in the stone that he knew as sacred." The G. Heileman Brewing Company advertised Crazy Horse Malt Liquor as coming from the "land where wailful words whisper of Sitting Bull, Crazy Horse, and Custer . . ." Companies profited from Indian imagery by concocting everything from Eskimo Pies and Sue Bee Honey to Big Chief tablets and Heap Good Potatoes. The Atlanta Braves and Florida State Seminoles maintained their mascots; the boosters of these teams still delivered "tomahawk chops." One understood why Thom Little Moon caricatured such appropriation in his "advertisement" in *Indian Country Today* for Custer Bourbon: "Makes you feel strong ... Makes you feel powerful ...Makes you feel like slaughtering women and children...." "In every shot of Custer Bourbon," Little Moon pledged, "you'll hear the sounds of hoof beats, the yells of soldiers and the cries of the wounded the day the warriors came out to fight...."

There remained much about which to be angry. Yet even with ongoing indignities and injustices, Native Americans looked to the year 2000 and beyond with far different perspectives than could have been mustered 100 years before. Edward Curtis and James Earle Fraser had missed the mark. Indians were here to stay. New leaders were emerging. In many communities, women were assuming new responsibilities. At Menominee in 1997 Beth Moses served as the county sheriff, Karen Neconish-Gardner as tribal chief of police, and Pam Gignon as county highway commissioner. Together with many other women from other tribes, Susan Crispen Shaffer of the Cow Creek Band of Umpqua, Deborah Doxtator of the Oneida Nation of Wisconsin, and Wilma Mankiller of the Cherokee Nation of Oklahoma had been elected as political leaders of their communities. Mankiller had grown up in San Francisco, a member of a family who had participated in the relocation program. She participated in the Alcatraz occupation, eventually moved back to eastern Oklahoma in the mid-1970s, and served as Principal Chief of the Cherokee Nation of Oklahoma from 1985 to 1995. Her autobiography, *Mankiller,* commanded a considerable readership and her example inspired countless members of the next generation.

Indian women also tackled crucial tasks as educational leaders. In Shiprock, New Mexico, Glojean Todacheene (Navajo) moved from her teaching position at the high school to take on the challenges presented to any principal of Mesa School. Janine Pease Pretty on Top (Crow) assumed the presidency of her tribe's institution of higher education, Little Bighorn College, and remained at the helm more than a decade later. A MacArthur fellowship provided one form of recognition for her ability. After holding administrative posts at the University of California, Berkeley, and the National Museum of the American Indian, Clara Sue Kidwell returned home to build the Native American Studies program at the University of Oklahoma.

At the local, regional, and national level, new strategies were being formulated. For example, technology, old and new, offered the promise of unprecedented opportunities for Indian individuals and institutions to express their own perspectives and to create their own images. In the northern Plains, KILI-FM radio, "The Voice of the Lakota Nation" could be heard over the 100,000-watt stations; in the Southwest, the 50,000-watt KTNN of the Navajo Nation reached an untold number of listeners. Beginning in 1986, "National Native News" on the Alaska Public Radio Network provided daily coverage of important matters affecting Native peoples. Radio Station WOJB from Lac Courte Oreilles won many awards and garnered considerable financial support from non-Indian as well as Native listeners. From its base in Lincoln, Nebraska, Native American Public Telecommunications since 1977 has produced and distributed programs. Through the Vision Maker Video Collection, American Indian Radio on Satellite (including the "Native American Calling" program), the Tribal Infrastructure Information Highway Project, and other endeavors, it took advantage of computer, telephone, and broadcast technologies to deliver information, education, and entertainment. In the late 1990s Native American web sites began to offer a tremendous amount of information to all who had access to a computer.

For American Indians in the late 1990s, knowledge gleaned from web sites could be combined with wisdom imparted from the elders. Familiarity with urban centers could be merged with strength drawn from the old landmarks on tribal terrain. There were lessons to be learned from the traditional stories and from the tales of new storytellers. Just as they always had, Indians combined components of a new era with more established elements incorporated through the years. If life meant struggle in this day and age, the young people were reminded that it had never been easy, that it always had been difficult—and that, somehow, Native peoples persevered. Polly Koutchak (Inupiat) of Unalakleet, Alaska, expressed a common understanding: "How firm we stand and plant our feet upon our land determines the strength of our children's heartbeats." Twelve-year-old Daniel Archuleta (San Juan Pueblo) understood the connection between generations. His Tewa name, O'kuu Taa, means striped turtle. "It came from my dad," he said, "who was born right when they start dancing the Turtle Dance. They wanted me to carry on his name. I think my name is about power. It's like something hit me and striped my shell. . . . I have the power to take whatever hits me."

"It is through the stories of my grandmother's grandmother, and my grandmother's grandmother's grandmother and their lives," concluded Angela Cavender Wilson, "that I learned what it means to be a Dakota woman, and the responsibility, pain, and pride associated with such a title. . . . my connection to land and place is solidified with each telling of the story." "The line where my grandmother ends and I begin is no line at all," wrote Linda Hogan. "I am a child that once lived inside her, that was carried inside the builders of the mounds, the cells of mourners along the Trail of Tears. From them I still remember to honor life, mystery, and this incomparable, ongoing creation."

In the final years of the nineteenth century most Americans assumed that Indians were about to disappear. However, the twentieth century has reflected, instead, another chapter of an ongoing story. The continuation of Native America had to be acknowledged. "We're always there," Onondaga-Micmac poet Gail Tremblay reiterated in "Indian Singing in 20th Century America," "singing round dance/songs, remembering what supports/our life—impossible to ignore." Wilma Mankiller observed that the past 500 years had brought "utter devastation among our people. But as we approach the 21st century," she added, "we are very hopeful. . . . despite everything we survive. . . ." "Five hundred years from now," she declared, a person like herself would proclaim the continuation of Native languages and ceremonies.

Upon that occasion, as that person considers the approach of the twenty-sixth century, she will say again: "We are still here."

The Memorial Ride

The Lakotas neared the conclusion of their long journey. They had ridden their horses for days through the bitter cold. As they approached their destination in late December 1990 they thought about a particular day a century before and they thought about the future of their children's children. And then they arrived at Wounded Knee.

In the traditional way, they had prepared four times for their journey. Beginning in 1986, they had traveled each year a distance of 250 miles, retracing the route taken by Big Foot and his people. It had been said that seven generations of suffering and hardship would have to pass after so many wisdom keepers had died and so much sacred knowledge had been lost. Now, these men and women had decided, it was time to end this period of mourning.

Although it had been called a memorial ride, they emphasized they were not commemorating what had happened one hundred years before. "A heinous crime was committed," one of the riders said, "and this doesn't mean we forget." Instead the ride constituted an integral part of a traditional Lakota ceremony called

Washigila: "Wiping the Tears." As one man explained, "It signaled to all our people the end of seven generations of mourning." Washigila offered healing to the participants and to all the families who had lost loved ones.

The ceremony also emphasized the need to celebrate the forthcoming resurgence of Lakota spirituality and culture. One person observed that future generations would continue to maintain "what the true identity of the Lakota is all about." Another said, "Our people have a hope for a better tomorrow." "Our children will grow up to be Lakota," he added. "They will know the rituals and the ceremonies."

The memory of what happened a century ago would never disappear. But neither would the people. At a place where so much had been lost, a period of mourning came to an end. The people could now look forward to the generations yet to come.

American Indian Communities

What follows is, admittedly, a less than comprehensive listing of American Indian communities within the United States. All the communities mentioned in this book are listed below. I have also included some additional groups in order to indicate more fully the range of Native peoples in this country. In some instances I have included alternative names by which tribes or groups are known. The list includes names of tribes and bands and names of specific reservation and non-reservation communities. I have not attempted to enumerate off-reservation urban communities, because they generally comprise people from a great many different groups. Many members of a particular Indian community now live away from traditional locales, but often are able to maintain ties with relatives and friends who reside in these areas.

Abenaki: Significant presence in Canada, but with communities also in Maine, New Hampshire, and Vermont
Acoma: Pueblo community between Grants and Albuquerque, New Mexico
Agua Caliente: Reservation near Palm Springs in southern California
Ahtna: Southeastern Alaskan group with villages in the Copper River valley area
Ak-Chin: Reservation community southwest of Phoenix, Arizona; members are of Pima and Tohono O'odham heritage

Akwesasne (St. Regis): Mohawk reservation in northern New York

Alabama-Coushatta: Divided into three groups in Louisiana (Coushatta), Oklahoma (Alabama-Quassarte), and Texas (Alabama-Coushatta)

Aleut: *See* Unangan

Allegany: Seneca reservation in western New York

Alutiq (formerly Eskimo): western Alaskan communities of the lower Kenai peninsula, Kodiak Island, and Prince William Sound

Anishinabe (also Chippewa or Ojibwa): In addition to a significant population in Canada, the Anishinabe reside on reservations in Michigan (Bay Mills, Burt Lake Band, Grand Traverse Band, Keweenaw Bay, Lac Vieux Desert, Saginaw, Sault Sainte Marie); Minnesota (Bois Forte, Fond du Lac, Grand Portage, Leech Lake, Mille Lacs, White Earth); North Dakota (Turtle Mountain); and Wisconsin (Bad River, Lac Courte Oreilles, Lac du Flambeau, Red Cliff, Sokaogon, St. Croix). Residents of the Rocky Boy reservation are Chippewa-Cree

Apache: Reservations in Arizona (San Carlos, White Mountain); New Mexico (Jicarilla, Mescalero); and communities in Oklahoma (Apache Tribe of Oklahoma, Fort Sill)

Arapaho: The southern Arapahos reside in western Oklahoma, with tribal offices in Concho, while the Northern Arapahos live on the Wind River reservation in central Wyoming.

Arikara: Part of the Three Affiliated Tribes (Arikara, Hidatsa, Mandan), who live on the Fort Berthold reservation in west central North Dakota

Aroostook Band of Micmacs: Community in northern Maine (federal recognition: 1991)

Assiniboine: Tribal population resides in Canada and in Montana (Fort Berthold and Fort Peck).

Bad River: Anishinabe reservation in northern Wisconsin

Battle Mountain: Western Shoshone reservation in Nevada

Big Cyprus: Seminole reservation in southern Florida

Blackfeet: In addition to the Blackfeet reservation in northern Montana, there are Blackfeet communities in Canada.

Brighton: Seminole reservation in southern Florida

Brothertown: Tribal members live primarily in Fond du Lac, the Fox River valley, and Gresham in central Wisconsin.

Caddo: The Caddo Tribe of Oklahoma has its offices in Binger, in the southern part of the state.

Cahuilla: Tribal members reside on the Agua Caliente, Augustine, Cabazon, Cahuilla, Los Coyotes, Morongo, Ramona, Santa Rosa, and Torres-Martinez reservations in southern California.

Catawba: Tribal members reside on a state-recognized reservation in South Carolina.

Cattaraugus: Seneca reservation of western New York

Cayuga: One of the Six Nations of the Iroquois. Members now reside primarily on the predominantly Seneca reservations in New York and in the Seneca-Cayuga community in Oklahoma.

Chehalis: Part of the Confederated Tribes of the Chehalis reservation in southwestern Washington

Chemehuevi: Southern Paiute peoples who reside on two reservations bordering the Colorado River: Chemehuevi in California and Colorado River in Arizona

Cherokee: One of the Five Tribes. Tribal members live in eastern Oklahoma (the Cherokee Nation of Oklahoma and the United Keetowah Band both have tribal offices in Tahlequah) and western North Carolina (Eastern Band of Cherokee).

Cheyenne: The Southern Cheyennes reside in communities in western Oklahoma, while the Northern Cheyenne occupy the Northern Cheyenne reservation in southeastern Montana. The Southern Cheyenne tribal offices are in Concho.

Cheyenne River: One of the western Lakota reservations, situated in central South Dakota

Chippewa: *See* Anishinabe

Chickahominy: State recognized tribe, whose members reside primarily in the area of Charles City, Virginia

Chickasaw: One of the Five Tribes. Tribal members live in southern Oklahoma communities; tribal offices are in Ada.

Chiricahua: One of the Apache bands, represented at Fort Sill and Mescalero.

Chitimacha: Reservation community in St. Mary Parish of southern Louisiana

Choctaw: One of the Five Tribes. Tribal members live in central Mississippi (Mississippi Band of Choctaws) and eastern Oklahoma (Choctaw Nation of Oklahoma)

Cochiti: One of the Pueblo communities located along the Rio Grande in north central New Mexico

Cocopah: Tribal members live in several reservation enclaves in Yuma County in southwestern Arizona.

Coeur d'Alene: Tribal members live primarily on the Couer d'Alene reservation in northern Idaho.

Coharie: Members of the tribe live in Sampson and Hartnet counties of North Carolina.

Colorado River: Reservation community bordering the river in southwestern Arizona, comprised of Mojave, Chemehuevi, Hopi, and Navajo

Colville: Reservation in northeastern Washington; the home of the Confederated Tribes of the Colville

Comanche: Tribal members live in communities in southwestern Oklahoma (tribal offices are in Lawton).

Coos: Part of the Confederated Tribes of Coos, Lower Umpqua and Siuslaw, with a land base in southwestern Oregon (federal recognition: 1984)

Coquille: Tribal members reside in the Coos Bay area of west central Oregon

Cow Creek Band of Umpqua: Tribal members possess a new land base at Canyonville in southern Oregon (federal recognition: 1982)

Cree: Group primarily residing in Canada, but represented as well in the Chippewa-Cree community on the Rocky Boy reservation in Montana and the landless Little Shell Band in Montana

Creek: *See* Muscogee

Crow (Absaroka): Tribal members live on the Crow reservation in southeastern Montana

Crow Creek: Yanktonai reservation in South Dakota

Cupeno: Represented on the Pala reservation in southern California

Dakota (Santee or Eastern Sioux): The four bands of Mdwekanton, Wahpekute, Sisseton, and Wahpeton are included in the Dakota. Dakotas live on reservations in Minnesota, Montana, and South Dakota. The Yankton and Yanktonai are generally considered Dakota, although some scholars consider them as a separate "Nakota" group.

Delaware (Lenape): The main population is in Canada, but tribal members also reside in western and eastern Oklahoma (tribal offices in Anadarko and near Copan)

Diné: *See* Navajo

Duck Valley: Western Shoshone and Northern Paiute reservation on the Nevada-Idaho border

Duckwater: Western Shoshone reservation in Nevada

Duwamish: Community in Puget Sound area of Washington

Edisto: Tribal members live in Colleton and Dorchester counties of South Carolina

Elko: Western Shoshone colony in Nevada

Esselen: Tribal members reside in Monterey County, California

Flathead: Reservation in northwestern Montana, home of the Confederated Salish and Kootenai

Fort Belknap: Reservation in northern Montana, home of the Assiniboines and Gros Ventres

Fort Berthold: Reservation of the Three Affiliated Tribes in west central North Dakota

Fort McDowell: Yavapai reservation north of Phoenix, Arizona

Fox: *See* Mesquakie, Sac and Fox

Gila River: Reservation community of Pima and Maricopa in southern Arizona

Goshute: Division of western Shoshones, with community members living on the Goshute reservation in eastern Nevada and western Utah and the Skull Valley reservation in western Utah

Grand Ronde: Reservation in northwestern Oregon for the five Indian tribes comprising the Confederated Tribes of the Grand Ronde

Gros Ventre: One of the two tribes occupying the Fort Belknap reservation in northern Montana

Haida: Primarily residing in Canada, but also living in the Hydaburg community of southeastern Alaska

Haliwa-Saponi: Tribal base is in Halifax and Warren counties of northeastern North Carolina

Havasupai: Tribal members live on the Havasupai reservation, which borders the Grand Canyon in northern Arizona

Hidatsa: One of the Three Affiliated Tribes of Fort Berthold in west central North
    Dakota
Ho-Chunk (Winnebago): Tribal members live in two reservation communities, one
    in eastern Nebraska and the other in western Wisconsin
Hollywood: Seminole reservation in southern Florida
Hoopa Valley: Reservation of the Hupa people in northern California
Hopi: Tribal members live on the Hopi reservation in northeastern Arizona
Houlton Band of Maliseet: Community in northern Maine (federal recognition:
    1980)
Houma: Tribal members reside in Terrrebonne and Lafourche parishes of
    southeastern Louisiana
Hualapai (Walapai): Tribal members live on the Hualapai reservation in northwest-
    ern Arizona
Hunkpapa: One of the divisions of the Lakotas
Hupa: Tribal members live on the Hoopa Valley reservation in northern California

Ingalik: West central Alaskan community whose members live in the Yukon and
    Kuskokwim river basins
Inuit: *See* Alutiiq, Inupiat, and Yup'ik
Inupiat (formerly Eskimo): communities of northwestern and northern Alaska; also
    centered in Canada and Greenland
Iowa (Ioway): Divided into the Iowa Tribe of Kansas and Nebraska, situated in
    northeastern Kansas; and the Iowa Tribe, located in central Oklahoma
Iroquois: The Iroquois nations are located in Canada and upstate New York.
    The six nations are the Cayuga, Mohawk, Oneida, Onondaga, Seneca, and
    Tuscarora
Isleta: Pueblo community in Rio Grande area of northern New Mexico
Itapzico (Sans Arc): One of the divisions of the Lakotas

Jamestown Klallam: Klallam community in Washington (federal recognition:
    1981)
Jemez: Pueblo community in Rio Grande area of northern New Mexico
Jicarilla: A division of the Apaches, with tribal members living on the Jicarilla
    reservation in northern New Mexico

Kalispel: Reservation in eastern Washington; the people are also included in the
    Confederated Salish and Kootenai on the Flathead reservation
Karuk: Tribal members live in northern California
Kaw: The Kaw Nation is situated in the Kaw City area of central Oklahoma
Keweenaw Bay: Anishinabe reservation in the upper peninsula of Michigan
Kickapoo: Divided into three communities: the Kickapoo Tribe of Kansas, north of
    Topeka; the Kickapoo Tribe of Oklahoma, in the center of that state; and the
    Kickapoo Traditional Tribe of Texas (federal recognition: 1985), in the Eagle
    Pass area. The Texas group is also linked to Kickapoos residing in Mexico.

Kiowa: Tribal members live in communities in southwestern Oklahoma, with tribal offices in Carnegie.

Klallam: Three reservation communities (Jamestown, Lower Elwho, and Port Gamble) in bordering the Straits of Juan de Fuca in northern Washington

Klamath: A community of southern Oregon, terminated but now restored to recognized status without its former land base

Kootenai: Part of the Confederate Salish and Kootenai Tribes on the Flathead reservation in Montana. See also Kutenai.

Kumeyaay: Residing in San Diego area reservations of Santa Ysabel, Barona, Campo, Mesa Grande, and San Pascual

Kutchin: Residing primarily in Canada with additional settlements in northeastern Alaska

Kutenai: One of the Kootenai bands, with a community today in northern Idaho near Bonners Ferry. *See also* Kootenai

Lac Courte Oreilles: Anishinabe reservation in northwestern Wisconsin

Lac Vieux Desert: Anishinabe reservation in the upper peninsula of Michigan (federal recognition for the Lac Vieux Desert Band: 1984)

Laguna: Pueblo community between Grants and Albuquerque, New Mexico

Lakota (Western or Teton Sioux): Divided into seven bands: Hunkpapa, Itapzico (Sans Arc), Mnikowoju (Minneconjou), Oglala, Oohenunpa (Two Kettles), Sicangu (Brulé), and Sihasapa (Blackfeet). Lakotas reside on the Standing Rock reservation bordering North Dakota and South Dakota and on Cheyenne River, Crow Creek, Lower Brule, Pine Ridge, and Rosebud in South Dakota.

Lenape: *See* Delaware

Lower Brule: Lakota reservation in South Dakota

Lower Umpqua: Part of the Confederated Tribes of the Coos, Lower Umpqua, and Siuslaw of southern Oregon (federal recognition: 1984)

Luiseno: Southern California people who reside on the La Jolla, Pala, Pauma-Yuima, Pechanga, and Rincon reservations

Lumbee: Tribal members live primarily in Robeson County, North Carolina

Lummi: Tribal members live on the Lummi reservation near Bellingham in northern Washington

Maidu: Peoples of northern California, including Maidu, Konkow, and Nisenan (Southern Maidu)

Makah: Tribal members live on the Neah Bay reservation bordering the Straits of Juan de Fuca in northern Washington

Maliseet: Primarily residing in Canada, but also including the Houlton Band of Maliseet in northern Maine

Mandan: Part of the Three Affiliated Tribes of Fort Berthold in west central North Dakota

Maricopa: Represented on the Gila River and Salt River reservations in Arizona

Mashantucket Pequot: Community in Connecticut (federal recognition: 1983)

Mashpee: A Wampanoag community on Cape Cod in Massachusetts

Mattaponi: State reservation in King William County of Virginia

Mdewakanton: One of the divisions of the Dakotas

Menominee: Tribal members live on the restored Menominee reservation in north central Wisconsin.

Mescalero: Division of the Apaches, whose members live today on the Mescalero reservation in southeastern New Mexico

Mesquakie (Fox, Sac and Fox): A tribally owned settlement near Tama, Iowa

Miami: Divided into the Miami Nation of Indiana, whose members live in the north central part of the state, and the Miami Tribe of Oklahoma, in northeastern Oklahoma

Miccosukee: Tribe in south Florida, separate from the Seminoles; tribal offices are 25 miles west of Miami

Micmac: Residing primarily in Canada, but including the Arostook Band of Micmacs in northern Maine

Mille Lacs: An Anishinabe reservation located in north central Minnesota

Miwok: Peoples of north central California, including the Coast Miwok, north of San Francisco; and the Lake Miwok and Sierra Miwuk of the Sierra Nevada foothills

Mnikowoju (Minneconjou): One of the divisions of the Lakotas

Modoc: Divided between the Oregon-California border country and the Modoc Tribe of Oklahoma in eastern Oklahoma

Mohawk: One of the Six Nations of the Iroquois. Community members reside in Canada and on the Akwesasne (St. Regis) reservation in northern New York

Mohegan: Tribal members live in New London County, Connecticut (federal recognition: 1994)

Mojave: Tribal members reside on the Colorado River and Fort Mohave reservations, both bordering the Colorado River in Arizona

Monacan: State recognized community in Amherst County, Virginia

Mono: Situated in the Central Valley of California on the Cold Springs rancheria and the now terminated rancherias of North Fork and Big Sandy

Muckleshoot: Tribal members live on the Muckleshoot reservation in the Puget Sound area of Washington

Muscogee: One of the Five Tribes. Tribal members live in Okmulgee County and surrounding counties in Oklahoma.

Nambe: Pueblo community of the Rio Grande area of northern New Mexico

Nansemond: State recognized community in Chesapeake, Virginia

Nanticoke: Tribal members live near Millsboro, Delaware

Narragansett: Tribal members reside in the Charlestown and Waverly areas of Rhode Island (federal recognition: 1983)

Navajo (Diné): The largest of the U.S. reservations, the Navajo Nation is situated in northern Arizona, northwestern New Mexico, and southeastern Utah

Nez Perce: Tribal members live on the Nez Perce reservation on northern Idaho, with others residing on the Colville reservation in eastern Washington

Nisenan: *See* Maidu

Nisqually: Tribal members live on the Nisqually reservation in Thurston County of western Washington

Nooksack: Tribal members reside on the Nooksack reservation, near Bellingham in northern Washington

Northern Cheyenne: Reservation home for the Northern Cheyenne people, located in southeastern Montana

Oglala: One of the divisions of the Lakotas

Ojibwa: *See* Anishinabe

Omaha: Tribal members live on the Omaha reservation in eastern Nebraska

Oneida: One of the Six Nations of the Iroquois. Tribal members live in Canada, the Oneida Nation of central Wisconsin and the Oneida reservation in upstate New York.

Onondaga: One of the Six Nations of the Iroquois. Community members reside on the Onondaga reservation, near Syracuse, New York.

Oohenunpa (Two Kettles): One of the divisions of the Lakotas

Osage: Tribal members live in Osage County in north central Oklahoma; mineral resources held in trust in an "underground reservation"

Otoe-Missouria: Tribal members live in Noble County of north central Oklahoma

Ottawa (Odawa): In addition to Canada, tribal members reside in Michigan (Burt Lake, Grand River, Grand Traverse, Little River, Little Traverse Bay) and in northeastern Oklahoma (Oklahoma Ottawa).

Owens Valley: *See* Paiute

Paiute: Generally divided among Northern, Owens Valley, and Southern. Northern Paiute communities include Bridgeport and Fort Bidwell in California; Fallon, Fort McDermott, Lovelock, Pyramid Lake, Reno-Sparks, Summit Lake, Walker River, Winnemucca, and Yerington in Nevada; and Burns and Warm Springs in Oregon. Owens Valley Paiute communities in California include Bishop, Big Pine, Lone Pine, Fort Independence, and Benton. Southern Paiute communities include Kaibab and San Juan in northern Arizona; Moapa, Las Vegas and Pahrump in Nevada; the Paiute Tribe of Utah, Shivwits Band, Indian Peaks Band, Cedar Band, Koosharem Band, Kanosh Band, and San Juan in Utah.

Pamunkey: State reservation community in King Williams County, Virginia.

Papago: *See* Tohono O'odham

Passamaquoddy: Tribal members live on the Pleasant Point and Indian Township reservations in Maine

Pawnee: Tribal members reside in the area of Pawnee in north central Oklahoma

Penobscot: Tribal members live on the Indian Island reservation near Old Town in central Maine

Peoria: Community members live in the Miami area of northeastern Oklahoma

Pequot: Two communities in Connecticut: the Mashantucket and the Paucatuck

Picuris: Pueblo community in the Rio Grande area of northern New Mexico

Pima (Akimel O'odham): Community members live on the Gila River and Salt River reservations in Arizona.

Pine Ridge: Oglala Lakota reservation in western South Dakota

Pit River (Achumawi and Atsugewi): Northern California people who reside on the Pit River rancheria

Poarch Band of Creeks: Community in southern Alabama (federal recognition: 1984)

Pojoaque: Pueblo community in the Rio Grande area of northern New Mexico

Pomo: Includes the various geographical divisions, centered in Lake, Mendocino, and Sonoma counties of northern California

Ponca: Divided into the Northern Ponca and Southern Ponca. The Northern Ponca Tribe of Nebraska is centered in Knox County in eastern Nebraska; the Ponca Tribe of Oklahoma is situated in north central Oklahoma, with tribal offices in White Eagle.

Potawatomi: Divided into the Prairie Band of Potawatomi in Kansas (west of Mayetta); the Hannahville Potawatomi (upper peninsula), Huron Potawatomi (south central) and Pokagon Potawatomi (southwest) of Michigan; the Citizen Band Potawatomi of Oklahoma (Shawnee); and the Forest County Potawatomi of Wisconsin

Puyallup: Tribal members reside on the Puyallup reservation near Tacoma, Washington

Quapaw: Tribal members live in northeastern Oklahoma, in the community of Quapaw

Quechan (Yuma): Tribal members reside on the Fort Yuma reservation, primarily in California, but also in Arizona

Quileute: Tribal members live in La Push on the western Olympic peninsula in Washington, but also are included in the Quinault reservation

Quinault: Tribal members reside on the Quinault reservation of the Olympic peninsula in Washington

Rappahonnock: State recognized tribe in Virginia

Red Lake: Anishinabe reservation in northern Minnesota

Rocky Boy: Chippewa-Cree reservation in northern Montana

Rosebud: Sincangu Lakota reservation in western South Dakota

Sac and Fox (Sauk, Mesquakie): Divided into the Mesquakie Settlement near Tama, Iowa, and the Sac and Fox Nation in central Oklahoma (tribal offices south of Stroud)

Salish: Included in the Confederated Salish and Kootenai Tribes on the Flathead reservation in northwestern Montana

San Carlos: Western Apache reservation in central Arizona

San Felipe: Pueblo community in Rio Grande area of northern New Mexico

San Ildefonso: Pueblo community in Rio Grande area of northern New Mexico

San Juan: Pueblo community in Rio Grande area of northern New Mexico

Sandia: Pueblo community in Rio Grande area of northern New Mexico

Santa Ana: Pueblo community in Rio Grande area of northern New Mexico

Santa Clara: Pueblo community in Rio Grande area of northern New Mexico

Santa Ysabel: Reservation community in southern California

Santee: *See* Dakota. The Santee Sioux reservation is in northeastern Nebraska.

Santo Domingo: Pueblo community in Rio Grande area of northern New Mexico

Seminole: One of the Five Tribes. Tribal members live on the Big Cyprus, Brighton, Hollywood, and Tampa reservations in Florida and in Seminole County in eastern Oklahoma

Seneca: One of the Six Nations of the Iroquois. Its members live in Canada, on the Allegany, Cattaraugus, and Tonawanda reservations in New York, and in the Seneca-Cayuga community of Oklahoma

Seneca-Cayuga: The Seneca-Cayuga Tribe is located in Ottawa County, Oklahoma

Serrano: Tribal members live on the San Manuel and Morongo reservations in southern California

Shawnee: Divided into three groups in Oklahoma (Absentee Shawnee, Eastern Shawnee, and Loyal or Cherokee Shawnee) and one in Ohio (Shawnee Nation United Remnant Band). The Eastern Shawnee of Oklahoma tribal headquarters is in Seneca, Missouri.

Shinnecock: Tribal members live on the Shinnecock reservation on eastern Long Island in New York

Shoalwater: Tribal members live on the Shoalwater reservation south of Aberdeen in western Washington

Shoshone: The Eastern Shoshones live on the Wind River reservation in central Wyoming; the Western Shoshones (Newe) are located in Duck Valley (bordering Idaho and Nevada) and in the additional Nevada colonies and reservations of Battle Mountain, Elko, Ruby Valley, South Fork, Wells, Timbisha, Yomba, Duckwater, Ely, and Te-Moak

Shoshone-Bannock: Group members reside on the Fort Hall reservation in southeastern Idaho

Sihasapa (Blackfeet): A division of the Lakotas

Siletz: Terminated community, now restored as the Confederated Tribes of Siletz, with a land base near Newport, on the north central coast of Oregon

Sioux: *See* Dakota, Lakota, Yankton, and Yanktonai

Sisseton: A division of the Dakotas

Siuslaw: Part of the Confederated Tribes of Coos, Lower Umpqua, and Siuslaw in Oregon (federal recognition: 1984)

Skokomish: The Skokomish Indian Tribe is situated on the Skokomish reservation in the lower Puget Sound area of Washington.

Snohomish: Tribal members live on the Tulalip reservation of the Puget Sound area of Washington.

Snoqualmie: Tribal members live in Richmond, Washington (federal recognition: 1993).

South Fork: Western Shoshone reservation in Nevada

Spirit Lake (formerly Devils Lake): Dakota reservation in east central North Dakota

Spokan: Tribe situated on the Spokane reservation of eastern Washington

Squaxin Island: Reservation community near Shelton, Washington

Standing Rock: Lakota reservation community bordering North and South Dakota

Stockbridge-Munsee: A band of the Mohicans, now living in a reservation community in north central Wisconsin

Suquamish: Tribal members live on the Port Madison reservation on the Kitsap peninsula in Washington.

Swinomish: Tribal members reside on the Swinomish reservation near LaConner, Washington.

Tanaina: Southwestern Alaskan community in the Cook Inlet area

Tanana: Eastern Alaskan community in the Tanana River area

Taos: Pueblo community in Rio Grande area of northern New Mexico

Te Tsu Geh (Tesuque): Pueblo community in Rio Grande area of northern New Mexico

Teton Sioux: *See* Lakota

Three Affiliated Tribes: The Arikaras, Hidatsas, and Mandans form the Three Affiliated Tribes on Fort Berthold in west central North Dakota

Timbi-Sha: Western Shoshone community in Death Valley, California (federal recognition: 1983)

Tlingit: Tribal members live in southeastern Alaska

Tohono O'odham (Papago): Tribal members live on the Gila Bend, San Xavier, and Tohono O'odham reservations in southern Arizona

Tolowa: Tribal members live on the Smith River rancheria in northern California

Tonkawa: Community members live in the area of Tonkawa in Kay County, Oklahoma

Tsimshian: Primarily in Canada, but including the Tsimshian of Metlakla, situated on the Annette Island reservation south of Ketchikan

Tulalip: The Tulalip reservation in Washington is the home for several tribes who now call themselves the Tulalip

Tunica-Biloxi: Tribal members live on a reservation in Avoyelles Parish in southern Louisiana (federal recognition: 1981)

Turtle Mountain: Anishinabe reservation in North Dakota

Tuscarora: Part of the Iroquois Confederacy. Community members live in Canada and on the Tuscarora reservation in upstate New York

Uintah and Ouray: Northern Ute reservation in Utah

Umatilla: The Cayuse, Umatilla, and Walla Walla form the Confederated Tribes of Umatilla on the Umatilla reservation in eastern Oregon

Umpqua: Included in the Confederated Tribes of Coos, Lower Umpqua, and Siuslaw in Oregon (federal recognition: 1984). *See also* Cow Creek Band of Umpqua.

Unangan (Aleut); Community members live on the Aleutian, Pribilof, and Shumagin islands of Alaska and the western Alaskan peninsula

Unkechaug: Tribal members live on the state recognized reservation of Poosepatuck on Long Island in New York

Upper Skagit: Tribal members live in the Skagit Valley of northern Washington

Ute: Divided into three communities: the Northern Ute in Utah and the Southern Ute and Ute Mountain in southwestern Colorado

Waccamaw: State recognized tribe in Bladen and Columbus counties of southern North Carolina

Wahpekute: A division of the Dakotas

Wahpeton: A division of the Dakotas

Wailiki: Community members live on the Round Valley reservation of northern California

Wampanoag: Tribal members live in the community of Gay Head (federal recognition: 1987) and the community of Mashpee in Massachusetts

Warm Springs: Reservation for the Confederated Tribes of Warm Springs (Warm Springs, Wasco, and Northern Paiute)

Washoe: Communities in the Lake Tahoe area of California (Woodfords) and Nevada (Carson, Dresslerville, and Stewart)

White Earth: Anishinabe reservation in northern Minnesota

White Mountain (Fort Apache): Western Apache reservation in central Arizona

Wichita: Tribal members live in western Oklahoma, with tribal offices in Anadarko.

Wind River: The Eastern Shoshone and Northern Arapaho occupy the Wind River reservation in central Wyoming

Winnebago: *See* Ho-Chunk

Wintu: Community members live in northern California

Wiyot: Community members reside in the Blue Lake, Rohnerville, and Table Bluff rancherias of northern California

Wyandot (Wyandotte): The Wyandotte Tribe is situated in northeastern Oklahoma (tribal offices in Wyandotte)

Yahi: Northern California tribe to which Ishi belonged

Yakama (Yakima): The Yakama Nation is situated in central Washington

Yankton: Part of the Dakota or Eastern Sioux. Group members live on the Yankton reservation in eastern South Dakota

Yanktonai: Part of the Dakota or eastern Sioux. Group members live on the Crow Creek reservation in central South Dakota, on the Spirit Lake (Devils Lake) reservation in North Dakota, and the Fort Peck reservation of northern Montana

Yaqui: Primarily residing in Mexico, but also present in Arizona, mainly on the Pascua Yaqui reservation near Tucson and the Guadalupe community near Phoenix

Yavapai: Tribe divided into the reservation communities of Camp Verde, Fort McDowell, and Yavapai-Prescott in Arizona

Yokuts: Tribal members live on three federally recognized rancherias (Picayune, Santa Rosa, and Table Mountain) and one federal reservation (Tule River) in northern California

Yomba: Western Shoshone reservation in Nevada

Ysleta del Sur: Pueblo community near El Paso, Texas (federal recognition: 1987)

Yuchi: Associated historically with the Muscogees, but separate today, with community members living in Creek County, Oklahoma

Yuki: Tribal members reside on the Round Valley reservation of northern California

Yuma: *See* Quechan

Yup'ik (formerly Eskimo): Community members live in the Yukon and Kuskokwim deltas of Alaska

Yurok: Tribal members reside on the Big Lagoon, Trinidad, and Yurok reservations of northern California

Zia: Pueblo community of the Rio Grande area of northern New Mexico

Zuni: Pueblo community south of Gallup in western New Mexico; "Zuni Heaven" or Kolhu/wala:wa is in eastern Arizona

BIBLIOGRAPHICAL ESSAY

This essay offers a brief overview of some of the most important publications in the rapidly expanding field of twentieth-century American Indian history. For reasons of space, other than a listing of journals and newspapers, this consideration is limited to books.

Bibliographies and General References

From 1976 to 1984, the D'Arcy McNickle Center for American Indian History of the Newberry Library in Chicago produced thirty bibliographies on selected topics. The final volume in this series, W. R. Swagerty, editor, *Scholars and the American Indian Experience* (Bloomington, 1984), provides a critical review of recent work; four chapters of this volume include material on Indians in the twentieth century. Two volumes of a second series have been published by the center in conjunction with the University of Oklahoma Press: Colin G. Calloway, editor, *New Directions in American Indian History* (Norman, 1990), and Jay Miller, Colin G. Calloway, and Richard A. Sattler, editors, *Writings in American Indian History, 1985–1990* (Norman, 1995). Initiated in 1980, the

Scarecrow Press bibliographical series currently numbers seventeen volumes and offers extremely thorough listings of materials relating to Native groups, areas, and other topics. Frederick E. Hoxie and Harvey Markowitz, *Native Americans: An Annotated Bibliography* (New York, 1991) is also very useful. An essential source on Indian women is Gretchen M. Bataille and Kathleen M. Sands, compilers, *American Indian Women: A Guide to Research* (New York, 1991). Three general references containing a wealth of information are Duane Champagne, editor, *Native America: Portrait of the Peoples* (Detroit, 1994); Mary Davis, editor, *Native America in the Twentieth Century* (New York, 1994); and Frederick E. Hoxie, editor, *Encyclopedia of North American Indians: Native American History, Culture, and Life From Paleo-Indians to the Present* (Boston, 1996). The Smithsonian Institution's *Handbook of North American Indians* includes published volumes on the Arctic, California, the Great Basin, Indian-White relations, Native languages, the Northwest Coast, the Southwest, and the Subarctic. Two pioneering volumes by Francis Paul Prucha on Indian-White relations remain indispensable: *A Bibliographical Guide to the History of Indian-White Relations in the United States* (Chicago, 1977) and *Indian-White Relations in the United States: A Bibliography of Works Published, 1975–1980* (Lincoln, 1982).

General Overviews

Frederick E. Hoxie and Peter Iverson have edited a volume on Indians in U.S. history: *Indians in American History: An Introduction* (2nd ed., Wheeling, Ill., 1998), while Albert L. Hurtado and Peter Iverson have edited a collection of essays and documents, *Major Problems in American Indian History* (Lexington, 1994). Peter Nabokov offers a carefully selected sampling of Native voices in *Native American Testimony: A Chronicle of Indian-White Relations From Prophecy to the Present, 1492–1992* (New York, 1992). Alvin M. Josephy, Jr., links past and present in *Now That The Buffalo's Gone: A Study of Today's American Indians* (New York, 1984). *Native Americans in the Twentieth Century*

(Provo, 1984) by James S. Olson and Raymond Wilson is an earlier synthesis of its subject, with a greater emphasis on federal policy. Donald L. Parman, *Indians and the American West in the Twentieth Century* (Bloomington, 1994) is regional in its focus and is primarily concerned with the impact of federal policies. A more wide-ranging study, limited to the era after the World War II, has been authored by James J. Rawls, *Chief Red Fox Is Dead: A History of Native Americans Since 1945* (Fort Worth, 1996). C. Matthew Snipp, *American Indians: The First of This Land* (New York, 1989) uses 1980 census data to analyze contemporary Indian populations, housing, family and household structures, languages and education, labor force participation, occupations, income, and migration.

Journals and Newspapers

Among the leading scholarly journals that regularly publish significant articles relating to American Indians in the twentieth century are *American Indian Culture and Research Journal, American Indian Quarterly, Ethnohistory, Pacific Historical Review,* and *Western Historical Quarterly.* Law journals, such as the *American Indian Law Review,* also provide important analyses of Indian rights, sovereignty, and economic development. *Native Peoples,* a handsome, illustrated quarterly magazine devoted to "the arts and lifeways of native peoples of the Americas," is published in affiliation with The National Museum of the American Indian and eleven other museums, centers, and associations. Lakota journalist Tim Giago publishes in Rapid City, South Dakota, the leading contemporary Indian newspaper, *Indian Country Today.* Another major newspaper is *News From Indian Country,* based in Hayward, Wisconsin. From 1972 to 1984, *Wassaja,* a newspaper, and from 1964 to 1982, *The Indian Historian,* were published by Rupert Costo and Jeannette Henry Costo of the American Indian Historical Society. Tribal newspapers such as the *Char-Koosta News,* the *Navajo Times,* the *Tribal Tribune,* and the *Ute Bulletin* are also important sources for news about contemporary developments. *Tribal College: Journal of American Indian Higher Educa-*

tion, published by the consortium of Indian colleges and universities, discusses subjects related to education and the future of Native communities.

Tribal Histories

The usual tribal histories produced by academic historians emphasized exclusively group experiences prior to the twentieth century. Using oral histories, tribal records, and other data, some historians have joined anthropologists to survey the less familiar terrain of the twentieth century. A new study of the Crows by Frederick E. Hoxie, *Parading Through History: The Making of the Crow Nation in America, 1805–1935* (New York, 1995), demonstrates the possibilities of these studies. Among the other examples of recent work completed by historians and anthropologists are Richard O. Clemmer, *Roads in the Sky: The Hopi Indians in a Century of Change* (Boulder, 1995); Steven J. Crum, *Po'i Pentum Tammen Kimmappeh: The Road On Which We Came: A History of the Western Shoshone* (Salt Lake City, 1994); John R. Finger, *Cherokee Americans: The Eastern Band of Cherokees in the Twentieth Century* (Lincoln, 1991); Morris W. Foster, *Being Comanche: A Social History of an American Indian Community* (Tucson, 1991); Loretta Fowler, *Arapahoe Politics, 1851–1978: Symbols in Crises of Authority* (Lincoln, 1982); Loretta Fowler, *Shared Symbols, Contested Meanings: Gros Ventre Culture and History, 1778–1984* (Ithaca, 1987); Peter Iverson, *The Navajo Nation* (Albuquerque, 1983); Harry A. Kersey, Jr., *An Assumption of Sovereignty: Social and Political Transformation among the Florida Seminoles, 1954–1979* (Lincoln, 1996); Melissa L. Meyer, *The White Earth Tragedy: Ethnicity and Dispossession at a Minnesota Anishinaabe Reservation, 1889–1920* (Lincoln, 1994); Joe S. Sando, *Nee Hemish: A History of Jemez Pueblo* (Albuquerque, 1982); Gerald M. Sider, *Lumbee Indian Histories: Race, Ethnicity, and Indian Identity in the Southern United States* (New York, 1993); Edward H. Spicer, *The Yaquis: A Cultural History* (Tucson, 1980); Veronica Velarde Tiller, *The Jicarilla Apache Tribe: A History, 1846–1970* (Lincoln, 1983); and C. A. Weslager, *The Nanticoke Indians—Past and Present* (Newark, 1983).

Histories of Confederacies, Groups, and Regions

Historians also have examined confederacies such as the Iroquois, groups such as the Pueblo Indians, and other Native peoples of distinct geographical areas. Laurence M. Hauptman's analyses of the Iroquois, *The Iroquois and the New Deal* (Syracuse, 1981) and *The Iroquois Struggle for Survival: World War II to Red Power* (Syracuse, 1986), are noteworthy for their use of oral history. Among the other pertinent volumes are Edmund Jefferson Danziger, Jr., *The Chippewas of Lake Superior* (Norman, 1979); Angie Debo, *And Still the Waters Run: The Betrayal of the Five Civilized Tribes* (Princeton, reprint, 1972); Elizabeth Ebbott, *Indians in Minnesota* (Minneapolis, 1985); Donald L. Fixico, editor, *An Anthology of Western Great Lakes Indian History* (Milwaukee, 1987); Joseph B. Herring, *The Enduring Indians of Kansas: A Century and a Half of Acculturation* (Lawrence, 1990); Peter Iverson, editor, *The Plains Indians of the Twentieth Century* (Norman, 1985); J. Anthony Paredes, editor, *Indians of the Southeastern United States in the Late Twentieth Century* (Tuscaloosa, 1992); Joe Sando, *Pueblo Nations: Eight Centuries of Pueblo Indian History* (Santa Fe, 1992); Rennard Strickland, *The Indians in Oklahoma* (Norman, 1980); Stephen Trimble, *The People: Indians of the American Southwest* (Santa Fe, 1993); Gerald Vizenor, *The People Named the Chippewa: Narrative Histories* (Minneapolis, 1984); and Walter L. Williams, editor, *Southeastern Indians Since the Removal Era* (Athens, 1979).

Biographies, Autobiographies, and Life Histories

Biographies, autobiographies, and life histories can make vital contributions to our understanding of Indians in this century, but these genres remain underutilized. There are a great many biographies of Indian military leaders of the 1800s and relatively few studies of leaders in the 1900s. The best works on twentieth-century subjects reveal something about personal values and priorities and provide a context in which to better understand an individual's significance. William T. Hagan, *Quanah Parker, Comanche Chief* (Norman, 1993) is a case in point. Other recent biographies include Peter Iverson, *Carlos Montezuma and the Changing World of American Indians* (Albuquerque, 1982); Dorothy R. Parker, *Singing an Indian Song: A Biography of D'Arcy McNickle* (Lincoln, 1992); Greg Sarris, *Mabel McKay: Weaving the Dream* (Berkeley, 1994); Michael F. Stoltenkamp, *Black Elk: Holy Man of the Oglala* (Norman, 1993); and Raymond Wilson, *Ohiyesa: Charles Eastman, Santee Sioux* (Urbana, 1983). Four collections of biographical essays that include portraits of Indian men and women of the twentieth century are Margaret Connell Szasz, editor, *Between Indian and White Worlds: The Cultural Broker* (Norman, 1994); R. David Edmunds, editor, *American Indian Leaders: Studies in Diversity* (Lincoln, 1980); Margot Liberty, editor, *American Indian Intellectuals* (St. Paul, 1978); and L. G. Moses and Raymond Wilson, editors, *Indian Lives: Essays on Nineteenth- and Twentieth-Century Native American Leaders* (Albuquerque, 1985). Most Indian autobiographies may be called more properly life histories, in that they are usually initiated by another person who assists in asking questions, recording oral accounts, and organizing the material. Two widely praised life histories are Madonna Swan, "as told through" Mark St. Pierre, *Madonna Swan: A Lakota Woman's Story* (Norman, 1991) and Margaret B. Blackman, *Sadie Brower Neakok: An Inupiaq Woman* (Seattle, 1989). Other examples of autobiographies or life histories that cover different time periods, communities, and experiences are Peter Blaine (edited by Michael Adams), *Papagos and Politics* (Tucson, 1981); Charles A. Eastman: *From the Deep Woods to Civilization: Chapters in the Autobiography of an Indian* (Lincoln, reprint, 1977); Janet Campbell Hale, *Bloodlines: Odyssey of a Native Daughter* (New York, 1993); John G. Westover, editor, *Papago Traveler: The Memories of James McCarthy* (Tucson, 1985); Frank Mitchell (edited by Charlotte J. Frisbie and David P. McAllester), *Navajo Blessingway Singer: The Autobiography of Frank Mitchell, 1881–1967* (Tucson, 1978); Wilma Mankiller and Michael Wallis, *Mankiller: A Chief and Her People* (New York, 1993); Anna Moore Shaw, *A Pima Past* (Tucson, 1974); and Fred W. Voget, *They Call Me Agnes: A Crow Narrative Based on the life of Agnes Yellowtail Deernose* (Norman, 1995).

Identity

Amidst the rapid pace of cultural, social, and economic change of the twentieth century, Indians and students of their histories have examined the question of identity. Gender, a culturally constructed category, generally is a central element in this examination. The issues of language, residence, and mixed ancestry are also often crucial concerns. Of course the biographies, autobiographies, and life histories listed above are helpful sources. N. Scott Momaday's portrait of his family, *The Names* (New York, 1976) is revealing. Leslie Marmon Silko mixes in stories about her relatives in *Storyteller* (New York, 1980). John Gattuso, editor, *A Circle of Nations: Voices and Visions of American Indians* (Hillsboro, Oregon, 1993) presents poignant personal essays by Paula Gunn Allen, Joy Harjo, Linda Hogan, Gabriel Horn, Simon Ortiz, Mark Trahant, Elizabeth Woody, and Deborah Calling Thunder, and the work of twenty-two gifted photographers, including Kenny Blackbird and Monty Roessel. A pioneering study, with some material on the twentieth century, is Patricia Albers and Beatrice Medicine, editors, *The Hidden Half: Studies of Plains Indian Women* (Lanham, Maryland, 1983). Nancy Shoemaker, editor, *Negotiators of Change: Historical Perspectives on Native American Women* (New York, 1995) offers several relevant chapters. *Reinventing the Enemy's Language: Contemporary Native Women's Writings of North America* (New York, 1997), edited by Joy Harjo and Gloria Bird, is a pathbreaking anthology of poetry, fiction, personal narratives, prayers, and testimonials. Also significant are Paula Gunn Allen, *The Sacred Hoop: Recovering the Feminine in American Indian Traditions* (Boston, 1986); Laura F. Klein and Lillian A. Ackerman, editors, *Women and Power in Native North America* (Norman, 1995); and Marla Powers, *Oglala Women: Myth, Ritual, and Reality* (Chicago, 1986). Cultural traditions are presented with particular understanding in Keith H. Basso, *Wisdom Sits in Places: Landscape and Language Among the Western Apache* (Albuquerque, 1996) and Ann Fienup-Riordan, *Boundaries and Passages: Rule and Ritual in Yup'ik Eskimo Oral Tradition* (Norman, 1994). Tom Holm reviews the experiences of Indian soldiers in

Strong Hearts, Wounded Souls: Native American Veterans of the Vietnam War (Austin, 1996). An imaginative and perceptive reinterpretation is L. G. Moses, *Wild West Shows and the Images of American Indians, 1883–1933* (Albuquerque, 1996). For an example of photography as a means to portray Indian identity, see Jim Hubbard, editor, *Shooting Back From the Reservation: A Photographic View of Life by Native American Youth* (New York, 1994).

Policy Histories and Indian-White Relations

Francis Paul Prucha, *The Great Father: The United States Government and the American Indian* (Lincoln, 1984) is the central study of federal policy; volume two analyzes the period from 1880 to 1980. Other standard accounts include Alison R. Bernstein, *American Indians and World War II: Toward a New Era in Indian Affairs* (Nor-man, 1991); Vine Deloria, Jr., editor, *American Indian Policy in the Twentieth Century* (Norman, 1985); Donald L. Fixico, *Termination and Relocation: Federal Indian Policy, 1945–1960* (Albuquerque, 1986); Frederick E. Hoxie, *A Final Promise: The Campaign to Assimilate the Indians, 1880–1920* (Lincoln, 1984); Lawrence C. Kelly, *The Assault on Assimilation: John Collier and the Origins of Indian Policy Reform* (Albuquerque, 1983); Janet A. McDonnell, *The Dispossession of the American Indian, 1887–1934* (Bloomington, 1991); Lewis Meriam, et al., *The Problem of Indian Administration* (Baltimore, 1928); Kenneth R. Philp, *John Collier's Crusade for Indian Reform, 1920–1954* (Tucson, 1977); and Kenneth R. Philp, editor, *Indian Self Rule: First Hand Accounts of Indian-White Relations From Roosevelt to Reagan* (Salt Lake City, 1986).

Legal Status and Questions of Sovereignty

Many authors have examined the nature of Native American rights. The powers of tribal government, tribal recognition, and tribal membership are three of many key concerns. John R. Wunder has contributed *"Retained by the People": A History of*

American Indians and the Bill of Rights (New York, 1994), which contains an extended discussion about Indian rights in the twentieth century. Francis Paul Prucha, *American Indian Treaties: The History of a Political Anomaly* (Berkeley, 1994) devotes three chapters to this century. Other valuable considerations are Jack Campisi, *The Mashpee Indians: Tribe on Trial* (Syracuse, 1991); Stephen Cornell, *The Return of the Native: American Indian Political Resurgence* (New York, 1988); Vine Deloria, Jr., *Behind the Trail of Broken Treaties: An Indian Declaration of Independence* (New York, 1974); Vine Deloria, Jr., and Clifford Lytle, *American Indians, American Justice* (Austin, 1983); Vine Deloria, Jr., and Clifford Lytle, *The Nations Within: The Past and Future of American Indian Sovereignty* (New York, 1984); Troy R. Johnson, *The Occupation of Alcatraz Island: Indian Self-Determination and the Rise of Indian Activism* (Urbana, 1996); Sharon O'Brien, *American Indian Tribal Governments* (Norman, 1989); Frank Pommersheim, *Braid of Feathers: American Indian Law and Contemporary Tribal Life* (Berkeley, 1995); Paul Chaat Smith and Robert Allen Warrior, *Like a Hurricane: The Indian Movement From Alcatraz to Wounded Knee* (New York, 1996); and Charles Wilkinson, *American Indians, Time, and the Law: Native Societies in a Modern Constitutional Democracy* (New Haven, 1987). Native land claims are weighed in Thomas R. Berger, *Village Journey: The Report of the Alaska Native Review Commission* (New York, 1985); Paul Brodeur, *Restitution: The Land Claims of the Mashpee, Passamaquoddy, and Penobscot Indians of New England* (Boston, 1985); R. C. Gordon-McCutchan, *The Taos Indians and the Battle for Blue Lake* (Santa Fe, 1991); E. Richard Hart, editor, *Zunis and the Courts: A Struggle for Sovereign Land Rights* (Lawrence, 1995); Imre Sutton, editor, *Irredeemable America: The Indians' Estate and Land Claims* (Albuquerque, 1985); and Christopher Vecsey and William Starna, editors, *Iroquois Land Claims* (Syracuse, 1991). Volumes relating to Indian fishing and water rights include Daniel L. Boxberger, *To Fish in Common: The Ethnohistory of Lummi Indian Salmon Fishing* (Lincoln, 1989); Lloyd Burton, *American Indian Water Rights and the Limits of Law* (Lawrence, 1991); Fay G. Cohen, *Treaties on Trial: The*

Continuing Controversy Over Northwest Fishing Rights (Seattle, 1986); Robert Doherty, *Disputed Waters: Native Americans and the Great Lakes Fishery* (Lexington, 1990); and Thomas R. McGuire, et al., editors, *Indian Water in the New West* (Tucson, 1994).

Economy

Several of the volumes cited in the prior section are also related to the subject. In addition, Marjane Ambler, *Breaking the Iron Bonds: Indian Control of Energy Development* (Lawrence, 1990) is an important consideration of the promise and problems of this form of economic growth. Robert H. White, *Tribal Assets: The Rebirth of Native America* offers illuminating contemporary sketches of the Ak-Chin, Choctaw, Passamaquoddy, and Penobscot communities. Stephen Cornell and Joseph P. Kalt have edited an insightful overview of matters being faced by different Indian groups, including gaming, in *What Can Tribes Do? Strategies and Institutions in Indian Economic Development* (Los Angeles, 1992). The question of the development of oil and its impact upon Native groups is explored by Joseph P. Jorgensen, *Oil Age Eskimos* (Berkeley, 1990) and Terry P. Wilson, *The Underground Reservation: Osage Oil* (Lincoln, 1985). Three studies that emphasize earlier decades and that also examine social and cultural change are Peter Iverson, *When Indians Became Cowboys: Native Peoples and Cattle Ranching in the American West* (Norman, 1994); David Rich Lewis, *Neither Wolf Nor Dog: American Indians, Environment, and Agrarian Change* (New York, 1994); and Sam Stanley, editor, *American Indian Economic Development* (The Hague, 1978). James H. Barker furnishes text and photographs to document a traditional economy in *Always Getting Ready Upterrlainarluta: Yup'ik Eskimo Subsistence in Southwest Alaska* (Seattle, 1993).

Education

Studies of Indian education examine efforts to assimilate Indians and Native efforts for self-determination. Margaret Connell Szasz,

Education and the American Indian: The Road Toward Self-Determination pays attention to both themes. K. Tsianina Lomawaima, *They Called It Prairie Light: The Story of Chilocco Indian School* (Lincoln, 1994) and Sally Hyer, *One House, One Voice, One Heart: Native American Education at the Santa Fe Indian School* (Santa Fe, 1990) emphasize Native abilities to influence their overall educational experiences. Devon A. Mihesuah, *Cultivating the Rosebuds: The Education of Women at the Cherokee Female Seminary, 1851–1909* (Urbana, 1993) primarily deals with an earlier period, but, like Lomawaima's book, is noteworthy for its attention to race, class, and gender. Other major analyses of Indian boarding schools include David Wallace Adams, *Education for Extinction: American Indians and the Boarding School Experience, 1875–1928* (Lawrence, 1995); Clyde Ellis, *To Change Them Forever: Indian Education at the Rainy Mountain Boarding School, 1893–1920* (Norman, 1996); and Robert A. Trennert, *The Phoenix Indian School: Forced Assimilation in Arizona, 1891–1935* (Norman, 1988). Additional useful studies on different dimensions of Indian education are Estelle Fuchs and Robert J. Havighurst, *To Live On This Earth: American Indian Education* (2nd ed., Albuquerque, 1983); John Reyhner and Jeanne Eder, *A History of Indian Education* (Billings, 1989); and Wayne J. Stein, *Tribally Controlled Colleges: Making Good Medicine* (New York, 1992).

Health Care, Healing, and Religion

Because the maintenance of one's own mental and physical health is so intertwined with the question of healing and curing, students of Indian health care and students of Native American religions must read overlapping works. Traditional Native healing practices as well as the Native American Church have been vitally important in a great many Indian communities. The attempts to introduce Anglo-American models of medical care have often conflicted with indigenous models. John Adair and Kurt Deuschle provide a thoughtful look at one such attempt in *The People's Health: Medicine and Anthropology in a Navajo Community* (New York, 1970). The standard overview of the Native American Church is Omer

Stewart, *Peyote Religion: A History* (Norman, 1987). David Aberle, *The Peyote Religion Among the Navajo* (Chicago, 1966) analyzes the incorporation of peyote into Navajo life. Fred W. Voget, *The Shoshone-Crow Sun Dance* (Norman, 1984) shows how this important ceremony was brought from one Indian community to another. Joseph G. Jorgensen, *The Sun Dance Religion: Power for the Powerless* (Chicago, 1972) examines its topic in the context of the loss of Ute land and power. Raymond J. DeMallie and Douglas Parks, editors, *Sioux Indian Religion: Tradition and Innovation* (Norman, 1987) presents valuable perspectives on continuity and change. Vine Deloria, Jr., *God is Red: A Native View of Religion* (2nd ed., Golden, Colo., 1994) is a work of great importance. Also significant is James Treat, editor, *Native and Christian: Indigenous Voices on Religious Identity in the United States and Canada* (New York, 1996).

Literature and Fine Arts

Individual Native writers and their work are mentioned in the text. There are also many excellent anthologies that furnish important examples of Native writings. In addition to *Reinventing the Enemy's Language,* other major anthologies include Paula Gunn Allen, editor, *Song of the Turtle: American Indian Literature, 1974–1994* (New York, 1996); Joseph Bruchac, editor, *Songs From This Earth on Turtle's Back: Contemporary American Indian Poetry* (New York, 1983); Geary Hobson, editor, *The Remembered Earth: An Anthology of Contemporary Native American Literature* (Albuquerque, 1981); and Craig Lesley, editor, *Talking Leaves: Contemporary Native American Short Stories* (New York, 1991). For insights into twentieth-century Indian literature, one should consult Kimberley M. Blaeser, *Gerald Vizenor: Writing in the Oral Tradition* (Norman, 1996); Joseph Bruchac, editor, *Survival This Way: Interviews with American Indian Poets* (Tucson, 1987); Louis Owens, *Other Destinies: Understanding the American Indian Novel* (Norman, 1992); and Brian Swann and Arnold Krupat, editors, *I Tell You Now: Autobiographical Essays by Native American Writers* (Lincoln, 1987). Greg Sarris succeeds in "seeing beyond what things seem to be" in his brilliant discussion of Indian oral and written texts, art, and religion, *Keeping Slug Woman Alive: A Holistic Approach to American Indian Texts* (Berkeley, 1993). Lawrence Abbott, editor, *I Stand in the Center of the Good: Interviews with Contemporary Native American Artists* (Lincoln, 1994) and the National Museum of the American Indian's *This Path We Travel: Celebrations of Contemporary Native American Creativity* (Golden, Colo., 1994) present introductions to leading artists. *A Zuni Artist Looks at Frank Hamilton Cushing: Cartoons by Phil Hughte* (Zuni, 1994) and Milford Nahohai and Elisa Phelps, *Dialogues with Zuni Potters* (Zuni, 1995) are two examples of books published by a particular tribe. In *Where There Is No Name For Art: The Art of Tewa Pueblo Children* (Santa Fe, 1996), "art coach" Bruce Hucko offers an appealing look at its subject, graced by the art and voices of children from five Indian communities. Charlotte Heth, editor, *Native American Dance: Ceremonies and Social Traditions* (Washington, D.C., 1992) brings forth vivid images of its subject. Two useful volumes on Native American song are Virginia Giglio, *Southern Cheyenne Women's Songs* (Norman, 1994); and Judith Vander, *Songprints: The Musical Experience of Five Shoshone Women* (Urbana, 1988). Among the many other helpful books on Indian fine arts are Lillian A. Ackerman, editor, *A Song to the Creator: Traditional Arts of Native American Women of the Plateau* (Norman, 1996); Margaret Archuleta and Rennard Strickland, *Shared Visions: Native American Painters and Sculptors in the Twentieth Century* (Phoenix, 1991); Rick Dillingham, *Fourteen Families in Pueblo Pottery* (Albuquerque, 1994); Rick Hill, et al., *Creativity Is Our Tradition: Three Decades of Contemporary Indian Art at the Institute of American Indian Arts* (Santa Fe, 1992); Bill Holm, *Spirit and Ancestor: A Century of Northwest Coast Indian Art at the Burke Museum* (Seattle, 1987); Robert Fay Schrader, *The Indian Arts & Crafts Board: An Aspect of New Deal Indian Policy* (Albuquerque, 1983); and Richard L. Spivey, *Maria* (revised edition, Flagstaff, 1989).

INDEX